The Pfeiffer
Book of Successful
Conflict Management Tools

*The most enduring, effective, and
valuable training activities for
managing workplace conflict*

Pfeiffer
A Wiley Imprint
www.pfeiffer.com

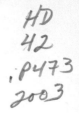

The Pfeiffer
Book of Successful
Conflict Management Tools

*The most enduring, effective, and valuable training
activities for managing workplace conflict*

Edited by Jack Gordon

Pfeiffer
A Wiley Imprint
www.pfeiffer.com

Published by Jossey-Bass/Pfeiffer
A Wiley Imprint
989 Market Street, San Francisco, CA 94103-1741
www.pfeiffer.com

ISBN-13: 978-0-7879-6708-6 (alk.paper)
ISBN-10: 0-7879-6708-4 (alk.paper)
ISBN-13: 978-0-4701-9344-0 (paperback)
ISBN-10: 0-4701-9344-1 (paperback)

Jossey-Bass/Pfeiffer books and products are available through most bookstores. To contact Jossey-Bass/Pfeiffer directly, call our Customer Care Department within the U.S. at 800-274-4434, outside the U.S. at 317-572-3985 or fax 317-572-4002.

Jossey-Bass/Pfeiffer also publishes its books in a variety of electronic formats. Some content that appears in print may not be available in electronic books.

Originally published as *Pfeiffer's Classic Activities for Managing Conflict at Work*.

Printed in the United States of America

Acquiring Editor: Martin Delahoussaye
Director of Development: Kathleen Dolan Davies
Senior Production Editor: Dawn Kilgore
Manufacturing Supervisor: Becky Carreño
Composition: Leigh McLellan Design

HB Printing   10   9   8   7   6   5   4   3

PB Printing   10   9   8   7   6   5   4   3   2   1

How to Use This Resource

This handbook is intended to serve as a working resource for trainers and consultants who seek to help individuals, work teams, and organizations cope constructively with conflict. All of the material in it may be reproduced and used in training sessions and workshops. The presentations, experiential learning activities, and surveys included here are offered as a set of tools to select and employ in a wide range of situations.

It's a top-of-the-line tool kit. This handbook was compiled with an eye toward selecting the very best material on conflict management published in the thirty-year history of the Pfeiffer *Annuals*.

How do you use it? A few examples:

Situation 1

Suppose you're trying to help a work team whose members can't seem to agree on the team's goals or its division of responsibilities, or one where backbiting and insults serve as the standard form of interpersonal "feedback." In the Inventories section of this book you'll find "The Team Effectiveness Critique," a survey that could provide data to isolate particular trouble spots.

After discussing the results with the team, you might lead the members through the experiential learning activity called "What to Look for in Groups: An Observation Guide." It offers not only a quick education in group dynamics but a tool for the team itself to take away and use as an ongoing guide for working together effectively.

To prepare your own remarks for this workshop and to ensure that you sound as if you know what you're talking about, you might want to do some background reading. Turn to the Presentations section, and you'll find a short but very informative article called "Conflict Resolution Strategies."

Situation 2

Suppose your task is to teach managers or workers (or both) how to navigate the eternally shark-infested waters of performance appraisal. Again you might begin with the Inventories section, which offers an instrument called "Communication Audit: A Pairs Analysis." It can measure (among other things) how well individuals communicate with their supervisors. Maybe a good place to start.

As for an experiential exercise, one selection speaks for itself: "Communication Games: Eliminating Unproductive Behavior During Performance Reviews."

What about a handout for managers inclined to dismiss any and all arguments from subordinates as defensiveness or excuse-making? Check out the Presentations section for the article titled "Constructive Conflict in Discussions."

Situation 3

Some kind of organizational-change effort is underway—the company is reorganizing its business units, or redefining some jobs, or slashing some budgets, or merging with another organization—and various groups are at each other's throats. Your task is to help two or more of these groups work together effectively despite conflicting values and aims.

If you don't know this organization well, you might first consider administering the "Conflict Management Climate Index," a survey that gives you a reading on how power is wielded and conflict is handled. Such information about internal politics can keep you from blundering into cultural traps in your efforts to be helpful.

For an experiential exercise with the groups themselves, you might select a role play such as "Budget Cutting: Conflict and Consensus Seeking" or "Piccadilly Manor: Improving Decision Making in a Political Milieu."

To educate yourself and maybe others (that's what photocopiers are for) about the dynamics of conflict and healthy approaches to dealing with it, look in the Presentations section for articles such as "The Art of Creative Fighting" and "Developing Collaboration in Organizations."

USE YOUR JUDGMENT

Those are just a few examples of the kinds of conflict-management challenges this handbook is designed to help you meet. But only you can select the best tools for a given job. There are no "correct" surveys to match with correct exercises and correct presentations in any particular circumstance, and we don't mean to suggest that you will want to use items from all three sections of the book for every training challenge that comes up. Sometimes you'll want only a survey or an experiential exercise—or maybe just some first-rate background reading.

As always, it is up to you, the facilitator, to learn as much as possible about the situation you're trying to address and the people involved in it before you settle on a strategy for setting things right. We offer this handbook as leverage to help you execute the strategy you choose—three decades worth of leverage, provided by some of the cleverest and most talented people who have faced and conquered challenges like yours.

About Jossey-Bass/Pfeiffer

Jossey-Bass/Pfeiffer is actively engaged in publishing insightful human resource development (HRD) materials. The organization has earned an international reputation as the leading source of practical resources that are immediately useful to today's consultants, trainers, facilitators, and managers in a variety of industries. All materials are designed by practicing professionals who are continually experimenting with new techniques. Thus, readers and users benefit from the fresh and thoughtful approach that underlies Jossey-Bass/Pfeiffer's experientially based materials, books, workbooks, instruments, and other learning resources and programs. This broad range of products is designed to help human resource practitioners increase individual, group, and organizational effectiveness and provide a variety of training and intervention technologies, as well as background in the field.

About the Editor

Jack Gordon is the former chief editor of *Training* Magazine. His articles and columns on workplace training have appeared in *The Wall Street Journal, San Diego Chronicle, Minneapolis Star Tribune,* and *Learning & Training Innovations.* He has written on other subjects for numerous publications, including *The Economist, The Journal of Law & Politics,* and *Independent Banker.* He has served as editor of numerous books, including *The Pfeiffer Book of Successful Communication Skill-Building Tools* and *The Pfeiffer Book of Successful Leadership Development Tools.*

Contents

How to Use This Resource   v

About the Editor   ix

Introduction   xv

PART 1: PRESENTATION AND DISCUSSION RESOURCES   1

1. The Art of Creative Fighting   5
   H.B. Karp

2. Conflict-Resolution Strategies   19
   Joan A. Stepsis

3. Win/Lose Situations   25
   Gerry E. Wiley

4. A Taxonomy of Intergroup Conflict-Resolution Strategies   29
   Daniel C. Feldman

5. Developing Collaboration in Organizations   39
   Udai Pareek

6. Constructive Conflict in Discussions:
   Learning to Manage Disagreements Effectively   67
   Julia T. Wood

7. Dealing with Disruptive People in Meetings   75
   John E. Jones

8. Confrontational Communication   81
   Merna L. Skinner

9. A Positive Approach to Resistance   87
   H.B. Karp

10. Breaking Down Boundaries: Breaking Through Resistance 93
    Ron Ashkenas

PART 2: EXPERIENTIAL LEARNING ACTIVITIES 101

Experiential Learning Activities: Conflict and the Team 103

1. What to Look for in Groups: An Observation Guide 105
   Philip G. Hanson

2. Conflict Styles: Organizational Decision Making 113
   Donald T. Simpson

3. Win As Much As You Can: An Intergroup Competition 123
   W. Gellerman

4. Power Poker: What's in It for Me? 129
   Linda Raudenbush and Steve Sugar

5. Trouble in Manufacturing: Managing Interpersonal Conflict 145
   John E. Oliver

6. Dynasell: Hidden Agendas and Trust 155
   William W. Kibler

7. Current Status: A Feedback Activity on Trust 161
   Robert N. Glenn

Experiential Learning Activities: Conflict and the Individual 165

8. Retaliatory Cycle: Introducing the Elements of Conflict 167
   Daniel Dana

9. Alter Ego: Saying What You Mean 173
   Duane C. Tway

10. Conflict Role Play: Resolving Differences 177
    Robert P. Belforti, Lauren A. Hagan, Ben Markens,
    Cheryl A. Monyak, Gary N. Powell, Karen Sykas Sighinolfi

11. Resistance: A Role Play 189
    H.B. Karp

12. Neutral Corner: Deciding on an Issue 197
    Linda Raudenbush and Steve Sugar

13. Communication Games: Eliminating Unproductive 205
    Behavior During Performance Reviews
    Don Morrison

14. The Company Task Force: Dealing with Disruptive Behavior 227
    Suzanne W. Whitcomb

Experiential Learning Activities: Conflict and the Organization   237

15. Budget Cutting: Conflict and Consensus Seeking   239
    Terry L. Maris

16. Winterset High School: An Intergroup-Conflict Simulation   255
    Charles E. List

17. Crime-Fighting Task Force: Understanding Political
    Tactics in Groups   265
    R. Bruce McAfee and Robert A. Herring III

18. Piccadilly Manor: Improving Decision Making in a
    Political Milieu   279
    A. Carol Rusaw

19. Merger Mania: Understanding Intercultural Negotiation   295
    John Chesser

20. Lindell-Billings Corporation: A Confrontational Role Play   313
    Thomas H. Patten, Jr

PART 3: INVENTORIES, QUESTIONNAIRES, AND SURVEYS   319

1. Conflict Management Climate Index   321
   Bob Crosby and John J. Scherer

2. Cornerstones: A Measure of Trust in Work Relationships   335
   Amy M. Birtel, Valerie C. Nellen, and Susan B. Wilkes

3. The Team Effectiveness Critique   347
   Mark Alexander

4. Trust-Orientation Profile   355
   Myron R. Chartier

5. Conflict-Management Style Survey   371
   Marc Robert

6. Communication Audit: A Pairs Analysis   381
   Scott B. Parry

7. Inventory of Anger Communication (IAC)   395
   Millard J. Bienvenu, Sr.

8. The Defensiveness Inventory   405
   Beverly Byrum-Robinson and B.J. Hennig

Introduction

Conflict in the working world takes a thousand forms, and if you want to create a truly sick company, go ahead and try to eliminate it. That way lies folly. This book won't aid the attempt (except in special circumstances) and isn't intended to.

Oh, by all means blow the bugle and charge into battle against the competition. And if you're looking for practical tools that can help service reps cope more effectively with angry customers or team leaders run meetings that don't bog down in endless bickering, you'll find them here.

But most conflict that arises within an organization has to do with divergent ideas and interests. Squelch divergent ideas, and thought dies (along with commitment). Pretend there are no divergent interests among individuals or units in your company, and you stand revealed as a liar or a fool. Try to crush the "resistors" to every new scheme hatched by the powers that be, whether those powers reside in the executive suite or a departmental meeting, and you turn loyal opposition into guerrilla warfare.

Conflict indeed can be destructive. But it must be managed. In some cases it even must be cultivated. It cannot be smiled away. And it must not be smothered.

THIRTY YEARS OF EXPERTISE

This book is a compilation of material chosen from three decades of the Pfeiffer *Annuals* and *Handbooks*. Since 1972, trainers and consultants have found in these volumes a treasure chest of resources for a wide range of training and organization-development needs. They offer not just ideas or educational reading but tools meant to be put to work for training and other purposes.

Like the books that provided its content, this one is organized into three sections: Presentation and Discussion Resources (articles), Experiential Learning Activities, and Inventories, Questionnaires, and Surveys. The selections presented here were picked as the all-time best the *Annuals* and *Handbooks* have to offer on matters pertaining to a specific topic: conflict management.

As the editor who did most of the picking, I have already revealed my primary bias in making selections. That bias shows up most plainly in the opening section, Presentation and Discussion Resources. In choosing articles to lay the conceptual groundwork for a facilitator working with conflict-management issues, I found myself drawn to those that give conflict its due, even when the topic they address is how to resolve it while encouraging its supposed opposite, collaboration.

When conflict comes in the form of a clash of opposing ideas about policies, methods, or objectives most likely to produce successful outcomes, then conflict and collaboration complement each other in organizations and working groups. One is not bad and the other good.

Thinkers who knew this produced a number of excellent articles in the *Annuals* and *Handbooks* of the 1970s and 1980s that stand as timeless statements today. Several are included here. We think you will find them well worth your time. Articles such as "The Art of Creative Fighting," "Developing Collaboration in Organizations," "Constructive Conflict in Discussions," and "A Positive Approach to Resistance" are worth reading as much for the perspective they offer on organizational conflict as for the excellent advice they provide about how to classify and deal with it.

TRUST

If there is a single factor that determines whether the head-butting that occurs in an organization will be healthy or destructive, it is trust. People who trust each other's basic motives can fight the livelong day about methods and work wonderfully together. But let one individual or group distrust the motives of the other (let one team member suspect, for instance, that another has a hidden agenda, or labor believe that management is lining its own pockets at the expense of the company's health), and it matters little whether an observer would detect much overt conflict in the team or the organization. The internecine energies will be devoted mostly to back-stabbing and guarding against the same.

That's why trust is another recurring theme in this book. The word is in the title of two experiential learning activities and a pair of surveys. Other experiential exercises teach participants to recognize the destructive effects of hidden agendas (their own and other people's) and to deal with them. Still others encourage honest, straightforward talk about controversial issues in the organization. Even when trust isn't mentioned by name, it is implicit in much of the material in these pages.

Whether our relationship is manager-to-subordinate or peer-to-peer, the first question is never, Do we disagree? The first question always is, Do I trust the terms of the argument we're having or the feedback I'm getting from you? That is, do I believe this discussion is really about what you say it's about and that your motive is to improve my performance, or the team's, or the organization's? If I think you're a game-player or an outright snake in the grass, then the explicit terms of any conflict we might have are largely meaningless. We aren't going to resolve much of anything until we confront the underlying issues.

That is the raw stuff of working relationships. This book contains instruments to help you measure it (such as the "Trust Orientation Profile" and "Cornerstones: A Measure of Trust in Work Relationships") and experiential activities that let you work with it either close to the bone (as in "Current Status: A Feedback Activity on Trust") or more delicately in the form of role plays (as in "Crime-Fighting Task Force" or "Dynasell: Hidden Agendas and Trust"). Choose wisely how raw you want things to get, based on your experience as a facilitator and your knowledge of the group you're working with.

Tool Kit

Once again, this resource is not intended as a potboiler to be read from cover to cover, but as a collection of working tools. The experiential learning activities and the surveys are complete packages: Duplicate the materials, use them, and adapt them as you see fit for training purposes (indeed, the experiential activities all suggest variations, and you can invent your own). You also may duplicate the articles for use as handouts or background reading.

The exceptions to that liberal copyright policy are that, if noted, reprint permission must be obtained from the primary sources, and that if the materials are to be reproduced in publications for sale or are intended for large-scale distribution (more than one hundred copies in twelve months), prior written permission is required. Please contact Jossey-Bass/Pfeiffer if you have questions.

You hold in your hands thirty years of expertise in the arts and the science of managing conflict. May all of your arguments bear happy fruit. And may this resource help you guide other people's arguments to do the same.

Jack Gordon
Editor

Part 1
Presentation and Discussion Resources

This opening section of the handbook contains recommended background reading intended mostly to provide a conceptual framework for managing conflict in the workplace. You can use the articles for self-education, as the basis for lectures, as handouts in a training session, or as helpful reading to pass along to individuals with particular problems.

In several of the selections you will discern a recurring theme: Managing conflict does not mean eliminating it so that smiling collaboration may reign eternal and supreme. In particular, managing conflict does not mean silencing arguments about the wisdom of initiatives born in the executive suite or even the efficacy of decisions reached by majority rule in a work team. Managing conflict is not about defining all resistance as naysaying and then attempting to crush it.

Which is to say, it's no accident that the first article in the lineup is titled "The Art of Creative Fighting."

Most of the selections come from Pfeiffer *Annuals* published in the 1970s and 1980s. They were chosen as thoughtful, intelligent, and even classic statements of timeless themes, ideas, and strategies. Much has been said and written since about these ideas, but little has been added. When it comes to discussing the interplay of conflict and collaboration, or the basic choices available to us in classifying and deciding how to handle different types of conflict, the "old" articles, paradoxically, have a freshness missing from more recent rehashes of these themes.

All but three of the selections fall into that "conceptual framework" category. Of the three mavericks, two are included with the thought that they might prove useful in specific situations. "Dealing with Disruptive People in Meetings" is an article you might want to copy and keep in a drawer to hand discreetly to a manager or team leader who has tried all of the recommended approaches but now is at wit's end and ready to trade Confucius for Machiavelli. "Confrontational Communication" is offered as a handout or the basis of a lecture about how to deal gracefully with angry people, including angry customers.

The final selection, "Breaking Down Boundaries: Breaking Through Resistance," from the 2000 Pfeiffer *Annual*, puts conflict management into the context of the 21st Century, explaining how several organizations have managed successful change initiatives that probably sound very much like things your organization is trying to do today.

The ten articles in this section include:

- The Art of Creative Fighting: Beware the tendency to view conflict as sin and its absence as a state of grace. But take care to understand what a fight is really about.

- Conflict Resolution Strategies: How to resolve disputes so that they stay resolved.

- Win/Lose Situations: Yes, "win/win" has become a cliché. But thinking like this explains why the phrase caught on in the first place—and why it's still important.

- A Taxonomy of Intergroup Conflict-Resolution Strategies: An overview of strategies and tactics that seek to avoid, defuse, contain, or confront conflicts.

- Developing Collaboration in Organizations: A comprehensive discussion of how to encourage collaboration while giving conflict its due.

- Constructive Conflict in Discussions: The importance of allowing dissenting ideas to be heard.

- Dealing with Disruptive People in Meetings: Then again, not all conflict is constructive. Here's some hard-nosed advice for the meeting leader who has just plain had enough.

- Confrontational Communication: A practical, four-step process for dealing with an angry person, be it a coworker or a customer.

- A Positive Approach to Resistance: Why and how managers must honor the "resisters" to the organization's latest brilliant scheme.

- Breaking Down Boundaries: Breaking Through Resistance: Common change initiatives of today, and how some clever organizations have guided them without running aground.

1

The Art of Creative Fighting

H.B. Karp

Whether the particular setting is the family, the small group, the agency, or the business unit, training individuals to deal effectively with conflict requires a great deal of skill and awareness on the part of the facilitator. When training is unsuccessful in other areas of human resource development, such as communication, problem solving, or motivation, the worst that usually happens is that the situation does not improve with time; in other words, communication remains ineffective, problems are not solved, or productivity fails to increase. In dealing with conflict, however, the situation is quite different. A training error or an inappropriate intervention can make the situation immediately more risky and volatile than it was previously. It also becomes less likely that a positive outcome will emerge.

Several elements contribute to making conflict training such a touchy area:

- The topic itself has a strong tendency to initiate deep feelings on the part of most participants and some facilitators. Most people either do not like conflict or are afraid of it even before they deal with it.

- Training in conflict management is not just a matter of cognitive understanding of relevant theory and technique. Facilitators must be comfortable with conflict and their own unique approaches to dealing with it *before* they can assist others in this regard.

- Despite disclaimers to the contrary, there appears to be a highly preferred, "one-best way" to deal with conflict from the viewpoint of human resource development: collaboration. Facilitators work effectively with people in developing collaborative approaches to conflict issues, but they often ignore or avoid other approaches in the process. This tendency has the effect of limiting alternatives and can lead to an impasse. In fact, such a unidirectional approach may increase rather than lessen the fear of conflict. Although collaboration may be the most preferable method for dealing with conflict, on some occasions a collaborative solution simply is not available.

A pragmatic view of training in the area of conflict indicates that the first essential step is to help people to see the simplest and most basic aspects of conflict, thereby stripping it of its mystic and awesome nature. Conflict certainly demands respect, but it need not generate fear and wonder. The second essential step is to legitimize the process of conflict. The most valuable skill needed in handling a conflict is not the ability to get along well; it is the ability to fight well. The time to get along well is after the fight is over. Indeed, when people are able to fight fully and creatively, it is probable that they will get along better after the resolution than they did before the conflict arose.

THE NATURE OF CONFLICT

Conflict occurs when two or more people attempt to occupy the same space at the same time. This space can be physical, psychological, intimate, political, or any arena in which there is room for only one view, outcome, or individual. Whether cast in the home or the work setting, conflict is absolutely unavoidable as a normal condition of active life. In addition, it is neither good nor bad in itself; it simply is. Whether the outcome of a conflict situation is positive or negative is almost totally determined by the way in which it is managed. When managed effectively, conflict actually becomes a vital asset in that it is a prime source of energy and creativity in a system.

The four major categories of areas in which conflict arises are described as follows, in descending order of the objectivity involved.

1. *Fact.* Conflict over fact is the most frequent variety, the most objective in nature, the least volatile, and by far the easiest to resolve. This type of conflict centers on *what a thing is or is not.* Resolution is usually achieved by comparing the object of the conflict to a standard or by referring to a mutually acceptable authority. For example, if one person believes that a specific object is a hammer and another believes it to be an axe, resolution is simple to achieve: Obtain a picture of each and hold them next to the object in question.

2. *Method.* Conflict over method is a little more subjective and volatile than conflict over fact. Those involved disagree about a procedure and are in conflict over *what is to be done.* Although personal opinion enters into the process, the conflict can be managed objectively for the most part. For example, a conflict about how to conduct a sales campaign can be resolved most easily by achieving mutual agreement on market conditions, advertising capabilities, budget constraints, and so forth.

3. *Objectives.* Conflict over objectives is more subjective and has a greater potential for volatility than the two types previously discussed. It concerns *what is to be accomplished* and is harder fought due to the fact that it incorporates higher degrees of personal commitment and risk, in terms of both personal and organizational variables. For example, "what is best for the company," such as the next project, is often intertwined with "what is best for me," such as the next promotion. Critical to managing this type of conflict is the recognition that the subjective elements involved are as legitimate as the objective elements.

4. *Values.* Conflict over values is almost totally subjective in nature and is, therefore, the most volatile type. It pertains to *what is right or wrong.* Mismanaged conflicts over values can result in divorces and even wars. The basic strategy in dealing with such a conflict is to avoid it if at all possible. If it is unavoidable, the best tactic is to objectify the issue as much as possible, dealing with behaviors or events that arise from the value rather than dealing with the value itself. For example, a heated argument over the morality of capital punishment has a high probability of ending in nothing but rage, self-righteousness, and moral indignation. However, a discussion of capital punishment in terms of its deterrent effects and legal ramifications has a somewhat better chance of resulting in agreement and resolution.

Strategies for Managing Conflict

The three basic strategies that are used to manage conflict are described in the following paragraphs. These strategies concern the way in which the conflict is resolved rather than the way in which it is conducted.

1. *Competition* is known as the "win/lose" approach to conflict; people compete to see who wins, and the winner takes all. The most obvious example of the competitive approach to conflict is an athletic event.

2. *Compromise* is a "lose/lose" approach. All parties agree to sacrifice equal portions of what they want. Subsequently, another mutual cut may be established and another until everyone settles for very little of what he or she originally wanted. An illustration of the result of conflict that is dealt with through compromise is the comparison between the wording of a bill in the House of Representatives prior to its first committee hearing and the final wording when that bill is enacted into law.

3. *Collaboration* is called the "win/win" approach. When this strategy is employed, people agree ahead of time to work with their conflict until they come up with a unique solution that provides each of them with all or almost all of what he or she wants.

There is little question that the collaborative approach to conflict, although it is the most costly in terms of time and energy, has the highest probability of producing the most creative and highest yielding results. However, as mentioned previously, there are times when a collaborative approach is not available and the issues are too important and vital to the individuals involved even to consider compromise. Some conditions that tend to preclude collaboration are harsh time deadlines, poor interpersonal relationships between or among the conflicting parties, severely limited resources, or differing values. Under these circumstances, competition is the only means available for managing the conflict.

Frequently a conflict is first approached competitively due to lack of interest in or unawareness of a collaborative alternative; then, after those involved have competed for a while, they discover a collaborative solution. If the fighting is creative and effective, there is a higher probability that this will occur, given the potential availability of a collaborative solution at the outset.

CREATIVE FIGHTING

It is often the case that people in conflict are unwilling to engage one another powerfully simply because they do not possess the basic skills required for effective fighting. Paradoxically, once an individual has acquired these skills and is comfortable with them, it is much less likely that he or she will have to use them. The newly acquired knowledge and abilities produce a clear confidence that is observable to others, thereby making the individual less subject to unilateral attacks. On the other hand, if a fight becomes unavoidable, he or she can handle it.

The Pfeiffer Book of Successful Conflict Management Tools © 2003 John Wiley & Sons, Inc.

Anger is as appropriate and productive a reaction to events as is any other human response. It is as unavoidably reflexive a response to being frustrated as laughter is to being amused. The issue involved is not whether it is appropriate to feel anger when frustrated, but rather how to deal with anger appropriately when it occurs. People must be made aware that there are techniques of fighting that can be learned and used skillfully. Also, they must be given the opportunity to practice these techniques in a neutral, low-risk setting, such as a training workshop. When all parties involved in a fight have acknowledged the legitimacy of conflict, established the norms for fighting, and are confident in their own abilities and strength, they are likely to approach one another with respect. Under such circumstances, there is little threat to ongoing relationships; in fact, there is a great potential for solidifying and enhancing these relationships.

The following paragraphs describe ten guidelines for the process of preparing people to fight creatively.

Establish the Legitimacy of Fighting

Fighting must be seen as a natural and sometimes appropriate thing to do. Occasionally it is even fun, as long as all parties agree to do it. Above all, fighting must not be viewed as an activity to be avoided at all costs. Whenever two or more people are working or living together, conflicts of interest arise. Sometimes these conflicts can be resolved through peaceful negotiation or willing compliance; sometimes they cannot. When the latter condition exists, fighting is the ultimate and appropriate response, unless one or more of the parties disempower themselves and give in because of fear of confrontation.

As stated previously, when fighting is approached creatively, it has several positive aspects that should be recognized: It is energizing; it honors all of its participants; it frequently produces the best solution under the circumstances; it strengthens, rather than weakens, relationships; and the arena in which it occurs becomes a safer, more "human" place in which to live and work. When fighting is not engaged in creatively, personal relationships deteriorate and become characterized by spite, sniping, silent vows of vengeance, sulking, self-pity, and complaints about being misunderstood.

Deal with One Issue at a Time

In an ongoing relationship, unfinished business frequently coexists with the current source of contention. The temptation when fighting is to bring up unresolved arguments from the past and catch an opponent off guard. When this ploy is successful, the person who initiated it achieves the upper hand and places the opponent on the defensive; the parties involved start a different fight that bears no relevance to the present conflict, and both (or all) of them become vulnerable to attack in this fashion.

Therefore, it is important for those in conflict to maintain a focus on the point of contention. When one person confronts another with an unrelated issue, the individual who is attacked should not respond except to say "That's not what we're dealing with at the moment." Subsequently, the parties may agree to discuss the secondary issue at some time in the future.

Occasionally, during the course of a fight, it becomes obvious that a secondary issue from the past is actually blocking the resolution of the issue at hand. For example, one person might say to another, "The last time you asked me for support and I helped you, you refused to acknowledge my contribution in the final report." When such a situation arises, the current issue should be set aside until closure of the unfinished issue is achieved, at which point the original fight can be continued with greater energy and a higher probability of a successful outcome. The important point is that only one issue should be addressed at a time.

Choose the Arena Carefully

Just because one person is angry with another and wants to fight does not automatically mean that the second party is ready or willing to oblige. Too often, one of the parties is dragged into "the combat zone" when totally unprepared or uninterested, and this situation frequently creates further unnecessary defensiveness, resentment, and personal animosity. To prevent such a development, all parties involved must understand and agree that if one person does not want to fight at a particular moment, no fight takes place at that time. There are three basic responses to consider when a fight is impending.

1. *Engage.* If the timing is right and the point is legitimate, the sooner it is brought into the open and dealt with creatively, the better. The usual outcome of avoiding a fight is that the longer it stays internalized, the higher the probability that it will fester and become more interpersonally volatile.

2. *Accede.* If an issue is important to one party but not to another, the person who feels it to be unimportant may accede to the point. Before engaging in a fight, everyone involved should determine whether the issue

The Pfeiffer Book of Successful Conflict Management Tools © 2003 John Wiley & Sons, Inc.

is worth his or her time and effort. It makes little sense to pursue a goal that is of no personal consequence. One benefit of this response is that it transforms an opponent into an ally. Another positive aspect is that the individual who consciously chooses to accede to another's wishes experiences no loss of power.

3. *Postpone.* If a person is prematurely engaged in a conflict, he or she may choose to acknowledge the issue and then put it aside. This approach involves listening to what the other person says, acknowledging an understanding of the point being made and its importance, and setting a time for assembling everyone involved and dealing with the issue. This response has a tendency not only to defuse the issue for the individual who brought it up, but also to prevent its escalation. In addition, postponing a fight allows time to consider the issue fully and to develop appropriate tactics.

The individual who initiates a confrontation and is met with postponement as a response must remember that an opponent should never be forced to fight before he or she is ready. Agreeing to the postponement can be advantageous in that a fully prepared opponent is less likely to overreact or to wage unwarranted counterattacks than is an opponent who is caught off guard.

Avoid Reacting to Unintentional Remarks

Frequently, in the heat of battle, things are said that are regretted an instant later. This is particularly true if the issue at hand is of deep, personal significance to one or both of the parties; if ego involvement is high; or if the relationship is an important one. A related consideration is the fact that often people do not know precisely what they feel or think until they hear themselves verbalizing these feelings or thoughts.

An important aspect of creative fighting is to establish the norm that when unexpected or unintentional comments are made, none of the parties involved will respond by escalating the fight into a more volatile stage that no one wants. Instead, the preferred tactic should be to stop the conversation when a questionable comment is made and determine whether the comment accurately conveys what the speaker meant. If the speaker disavows the comment, everyone—including the speaker—should ignore it; if he or she confirms it, a deeper point of contention may have arisen. In the latter case, those involved in the fight must then decide which issue to focus on.

Avoid Resolutions That Come Too Soon or Too Easily

Newly married couples are often told, "Never let the sun set on an argument." However, this advice may be too simplistic. When a fight is resolved too quickly or a simple but incomplete resolution is agreed to, there are several negative side effects that are usually more painful and damaging in the long run than the original fight itself.

For example, if a fight ends prematurely, its unfinished elements do not go away; they are temporarily repressed and will almost certainly manifest themselves later. Also, the easiest solution is not always the best one in that it tends to treat symptoms and thereby obscure the real problem. Still another negative effect is that if the solution is complete for one party but not for another, the person who feels unsatisfied is not emotionally free to enter into future fights with total enthusiasm. This last effect, although very subtle, can seriously damage the relationship(s) involved

Each fight has its own, unique level of intensity. Some fights involve simple disagreements and are resolvable "by sundown," whereas those that involve intense feelings, deep-seated values, or complex issues require much more time to be dealt with effectively. With each fight, it is essential that the parties recognize and remain aware of the time element.

There are ways to approach the handling of time. The first is to recognize clearly and specifically the complexity and importance of the issue and then to agree to devote as much time as required to achieve a resolution. The second approach, known as "bracketing," is also quite useful, particularly when complex, interdependent relationships are involved and the issue at hand is complicated. Many times, reality dictates that even though a fight is taking place, everyday life must go on. When this is the case, it is appropriate to fight for the length of time available; "bracket" the fight by setting it aside completely, but on a temporary basis; devote energies to other concerns as necessary; and resume the fight when possible. In many instances, this approach allows adversaries to work together well and energetically in areas that are not affected by the fight; the harmonious functioning is possible because the point of contention, although "on hold," is still actively being honored by the adversaries.

Avoid Name Calling

The function of creative fighting is to manage conflict in such a way that the following outcomes are ensured.

- An effective resolution is found;

- Everyone involved maintains a clear sense of personal dignity throughout; and

- The relationship(s) is (are) in no way damaged.

Nothing blocks these outcomes more effectively than resorting to name calling.

Creative fighting is unlike many other approaches to conflict in which the participants devote their efforts to injuring their opponents as much as possible; instead, when fighting creatively, each participant strives to achieve a specific objective. In most cases these individual objectives are mutually exclusive so that a clear choice must be made as to which will constitute the final outcome. When accomplishing a specific objective is a person's reason for fighting, it is very much in that individual's best interest not to dehumanize the opponent(s).

Name calling usually occurs when logical arguments fail or when one or more of the parties have become frustrated beyond tolerance. In order to avoid name calling, the safest and most productive stance to maintain throughout the fight is to speak strictly for oneself. When everyone invariably speaks only in terms of what he or she wants, feels, or thinks, there is little risk that anyone will be personally offended; consequently, there is little risk that the fight will escalate to a more volatile and unmanageable level.

Avoid Cornering an Opponent

Occasionally, being "right" and devastating one's opponent may be more personally satisfying than achieving the best resolution possible. However, this approach produces only momentary satisfaction and can be very costly. The practice of cornering and devastating an opponent may preclude a solid resolution. Also, the party who is the object of such an attack may eventually retaliate in kind.

One important aspect of conflict is that, regardless of the point of contention, the longer the fight goes on or the greater the intensity, the higher the ego involvement and the greater the need to save face. Everyone involved should keep this in mind and make it as easy as possible to accommodate one another's wishes. Above all, opponents must be allowed to save face. For example, if it is obvious to everyone that an opponent cannot win a particular argument, it is best to let that opponent retire gracefully. The adversary who allows such a retreat not only achieves what he or she wants, but also accords the opponent the respect that is deserved. Thus, this stance usually results in some degree of appreciation on the part of the vanquished opponent, particularly when all parties realize that pain and humiliation could have been inflicted had the party with the upper hand chosen to do so.

Agree to Disagree

Creative fighting demands the generation of alternatives and a conscious choice of one of these alternatives. Although a mutually acceptable resolution is always the desired outcome, sometimes the reality is that such a resolution is not available. In a fight in which the point of contention is basically impersonal, such as an argument over a fact or a method, a mutually acceptable resolution is almost always available. However, in a fight that is waged over a deeper, more personal issue, such as an objective or a value, mutuality is much more difficult and sometimes impossible to achieve. In the latter case, each viewpoint is so innately a part of the individual who holds it that any attempt to minimize its validity will be taken as an attack on the individual personally. Thus, it is almost impossible for someone involved in such a fight to concede a point without feeling personally diminished in the process.

As mentioned previously, the best and most obvious choice in dealing with arguments of a personal nature is to avoid them completely, if at all possible. Sometimes, however, a discussion about one point reveals a more intense point that is really what is at issue. As soon as it becomes evident that the parties involved are diametrically opposed on a deeply personal issue, there is little or no chance that anything can be said to alter the situation. In fact, the longer the confrontation continues, the higher the probability that each party will become more firmly entrenched in his or her position. Thus, the parties should simply agree to disagree and drop the subject for the moment. Once everyone agrees that it is perfectly acceptable to see things differently and that no attempts at conversion will be made, the subject is much safer to discuss in the future should it arise again. In the meantime, all parties can live or work together productively, because the point of difference can be side-stepped.

It is highly improbable that people involved in a long-term work or personal relationship will share all core values. Not to recognize this fact invites unnecessary squabbling. Although there seems to be constant pressure in interdependent relationships to locate common ground, it may be just as important to isolate irreconcilable differences and acknowledge them as being equally natural and "human."

In some rare instances in which a relationship between two people is extremely interdependent and long term, the parties may hold such polarized values that when one pursues his or her value, the pursuance automatically creates pain or severe problems for the other. Some examples of this type of polarization are the need for autonomy versus the need for participation, the need for isolation versus the need for intimacy, and concern with production versus concern for people. When the situation is so extreme that any concession on the part of either person will result in a loss of self-respect, the following procedure should be considered.

1. *Accept the polarity.* The two parties involved must establish the norm that both have a right to their viewpoints, but that neither is required to like the opposite viewpoint.

2. *Establish the importance of the relationship.* The parties should determine all of the positive, productive aspects of the relationship. It is preferable that they complete this task together rather than separately. They must review the basic values that they hold in common as well as their past successes in the relationship. During this process, enjoyable times and instances of mutual support should be recalled, and the potential for similar occurrences in the future should be accepted. In addition, the interdependent nature of the relationship should be acknowledged and defined.

    It is important to note, however, that this step might reveal the possibility that the two parties do not have a solid relationship and that permanent disengagement may be the most realistic, mutually beneficial resolution.

3. *Stay with the fight to the end.* If the parties determine that the relationship is important and worth saving, they must agree to endure the fight. However, neither should acquiesce only to please the other person or to reduce the other's pain; both should be appreciative of attempts to please, but they should not accept concessions that are made strictly for this purpose. If they have evaluated their relationship correctly, they will find ways to continue to work together productively, even though they are both experiencing some degree of pain. Both parties must remember that although they seriously disagree on a specific issue, they do not disagree on all others.

Working or living with someone under these conditions represents an incredibly heavy burden for both parties. Sooner or later, only because of exhaustion, it is probable that they will mutually agree to "let go" of the troublesome issue. More to the point, as the exhaustion increases, so does the importance of other issues, and the originally polarized viewpoints tend to become modified. When this happens, it may be possible to achieve a resolution.

Focus on What Is Wanted Rather Than Why It Is Wanted

Almost all fights, creative or otherwise, arise from the fact that the participants want different things. Also, in many cases compliance from the oppo-
nent(s) is necessary for the attainment of each person's objective. Thus, it is
essential to establish clearly what each party wants and how these objectives
differ. On the other hand, spending time and energy exploring why each
party wants what he or she wants is, at best, a total waste of time and, at worst,
an invitation to a psychological melee.

The point to remember is that people have a right to want what they
want and to want all of it. This point has tremendous impact on creative fighting. When participants answer opponents' inquiries as to why they want specific objectives, they become "defendants" and the opponents become "judges"
who can rule on the worthiness of the reasons supplied. These reasons, once
verbalized, are usually anything but convincing. The reality is that very few people know exactly why they want what they want. In fact, most are not very concerned with their own motivation in this regard; for them, it is simply enough
that they want.

In addition, the answer to the first "why?" usually leads to another "why?"
and still another, and each time the defendant is forced to stray farther from
the original objective in order to provide an answer. Eventually, the issue that
generated the fight becomes obscured. The roles may even be reversed; the defendant may become the judge and counter with questions of his or her own.
Thus, all parties are compelled to defend themselves, and as a result the fight
may escalate.

Therefore, the best strategy is to avoid asking and answering queries
about motivation. Instead, each person should concentrate on accomplishing his or her specific goal.

Maintain a Sense of Humor

Fighting is most often viewed as a grim and serious business. In many cases,
of course, it is quite serious and certainly deserves to be respected. However,
even when the subject of the fight is important and tempers are aroused, it
is important that the participants not lose their perspectives. The best way
to retain one's perspective during a fight is to exercise a sense of humor. For
example, a married couple may be arguing vehemently about finances when
suddenly the husband exclaims, "Not only *that,* but you never really liked my
mother!" At such moments, it is perfectly legitimate to recognize the humor
of the situation and respond accordingly. In fact, the parties involved may

be unable to control their laughter and subsequently may find that the fight has disintegrated. Although the tendency when engaged in a fight is to become more "righteous" as the confrontation progresses, the participants would do well to remember that it is the fight that should be taken seriously—not themselves.

Summary

Training people to deal with conflict in an effective manner requires much of a facilitator. Participants must be taught that conflict is a natural part of life and that dealing with it creatively can actually enhance rather than destroy relationships.

Part of the facilitator's responsibility is to help the participants to see that there are four different sources of conflict—fact, method, objectives, and values—and that each source represents a different level of volatility. In addition, the three basic strategies for handling conflict—competition, compromise, and collaboration—should be presented and explained, and the facilitator should take care not to convey an exclusive prejudice in favor of collaboration.

When all participants are aware of the basic aspects of conflict, they should be allowed to practice fighting creatively in a relatively nonthreatening environment, such as a workshop. As they practice, the facilitator should help them to adhere to the ten guidelines that are detailed in this paper.

Originally published in The 1983 Annual Handbook for Facilitators, Trainers, and Consultants.

2

Conflict-Resolution Strategies

Joan A. Stepsis

Conflict is a daily reality for everyone. Whether at home or at work, an individual's needs and values constantly and invariably come into opposition with those of other people. Some conflicts are relatively minor, easy to handle, or capable of being overlooked. Others of greater magnitude, however, require a strategy for successful resolution if they are not to create constant tension or lasting enmity in home or business.

The ability to resolve conflict successfully is probably one of the most important social skills that an individual can possess. Yet there are few formal opportunities in our society to learn it. Like any other human skill, conflict resolution can be taught; like other skills, it consists of a number of important subskills, each separate and yet interdependent. These skills need to be assimilated at both the cognitive and the behavioral levels (i.e., Do I understand how conflict can be resolved? Can I resolve specific conflicts?).

RESPONSES TO CONFLICT SITUATIONS

Children develop their own personal strategies for dealing with conflict. Even if these preferred approaches do not resolve conflicts successfully, they continue to be used because of a lack of awareness of alternatives.

Conflict-resolution strategies may be classified into three categories—avoidance, diffusion, and confrontation. The accompanying figure illustrates that avoidance is at one extreme and confrontation is at the other.

A Continuum of Responses to Conflict Situations

Avoidance

Some people attempt to avoid conflict situations altogether or to avoid certain types of conflict. These people tend to repress emotional reactions, look the other way, or leave the situation entirely (for example, quit a job, leave school, get divorced). Either they cannot face up to such situations effectively, or they do not have the skills to negotiate them effectively.

Although avoidance strategies do have survival value in those instances where escape is possible, they usually do not provide the individual with a high level of satisfaction. They tend to leave doubts and fears about meeting the same type of situation in the future, and about such valued traits as courage or persistence.

Defusion

This tactic is essentially a delaying action. Defusion strategies try to cool off the situation, at least temporarily, or to keep the issues so unclear that attempts at confrontation are improbable. Resolving minor points while avoiding or delaying discussion of the major problem, postponing a confrontation until a more auspicious time, and avoiding clarification of the salient issues underlying the conflict are examples of defusion. Again, as with avoidance strategies, such tactics work when delay is possible, but they typically result in feelings of dissatisfaction, anxiety about the future, and concerns about oneself.

Confrontation

The third major strategy involves an actual confrontation of conflicting issues or persons. Confrontation can further be subdivided into *power* strategies and *negotiation* strategies. Power strategies include the use of physical force (a punch in the nose, war); bribery (money, favors); and punishment (withholding love, money). Such tactics are often very effective from the point of view of the "successful" party in the conflict: that person wins, the other person loses. Unfortunately, however, for the loser the real conflict may have only just begun. Hostility, anxiety, and actual physical damage are usual by-products of these win/lose power tactics.

With negotiation strategies, unlike power confrontations, both sides can win. The aim of negotiation is to resolve the conflict with a compromise or a solution that is mutually satisfying to all parties involved in the conflict. Negotiation, then, seems to provide the most positive and the least negative byproducts of all conflict-resolution strategies.

NEGOTIATION SKILLS

Successful negotiation, however, requires a set of skills that must be learned and practiced. These skills include (1) the ability to determine the nature of the conflict, (2) effectiveness in initiating confrontations, (3) the ability to hear the other's point of view, and (4) the utilization of problem-solving processes to bring about a consensus decision.

Diagnosis

Diagnosing the nature of a conflict is the starting point in any attempt at resolution through negotiation. The most important issue which must be decided is whether the conflict is an ideological (value) conflict or a "real" (tangible) conflict—or a combination of both. Value conflicts are exceedingly difficult to negotiate. If, for example, I believe that women should be treated as equals in every phase of public and private life, and you believe they should be protected or prohibited in certain areas, it would be very difficult for us to come to a position that would satisfy us both.

A difference of values, however, is really significant only when our opposing views affect us in some real or tangible way. If your stand on women's place in society results in my being denied a job that I want and am qualified to perform, then we have a negotiable conflict. Neither of us needs to change his values for us to come to a mutually acceptable resolution of the "real" problem. For example, I may get the job, but in return agree to accept a lower salary or a different title or not to insist on using the all-male executive dining room. If each of us stands on his principles—maintaining our value conflict—we probably will make little headway. But if, instead, we concentrate on the tangible effects in the conflict, we may be able to devise a realistic solution.

The Israeli-Arab conflict provides a good example of this point. In order to settle the tangible element in the conflict—who gets how much land—ideological differences do not need to be resolved. It is land usage that is the area of the conflict amenable to a negotiated settlement.

It is important to determine whether a conflict is a real or a value conflict. If it is a conflict in values resulting in nontangible effects on either party, then it is best tolerated. If, however, a tangible effect exists, that element of the conflict should be resolved.

Initiation

A second skill necessary to conflict resolution is effectiveness in initiating a confrontation. It is important not to begin by attacking or demeaning the opposite party. A defensive reaction in one or both parties usually blocks a quick resolution of differences. The most effective way to confront the other party is for the individual to state the tangible effects the conflict has on him or her. For example: "I have a problem. Due to your stand on hiring women as executives, I am unable to apply for the supervisory position that I feel I am qualified to handle." This approach is more effective than saying, "You male chauvinist pig—you're discriminating against me!" In other words, confrontation is not synonymous with verbal attack.

Listening

After the confrontation has been initiated, the confronter must be capable of hearing the other's point of view. If the initial statement made by the other person is not what the confronter was hoping to hear, defensive rebuttals, a "hard-line" approach, or explanations often follow. Argument-provoking replies should be avoided. The confronter should not attempt to defend himself or herself, explain his or her position, or make demands or threats. Instead, the confronter must be able to engage in the skill termed reflective or active listening. He or she should listen and reflect and paraphrase or clarify the other person's stand. When the confronter has interpreted the opposition's position to the satisfaction of the other person, he or she should again present his or her own point of view, being careful to avoid value statements and to concentrate on tangible outcomes. Usually, when the confronter listens to the other person, that person lowers his or her defenses and is, in turn, more ready to hear another point of view. Of course, if both people are skilled in active listening, the chances of successful negotiation are much enhanced.

Problem Solving

The final skill necessary to successful negotiation is the use of the problem-solving process to negotiate a consensus decision. The steps in this process are simply stated and easy to apply:

1. *Clarifying the problem.* What is the tangible issue? Where does each party stand on the issue?

2. *Generating and evaluating a number of possible solutions.* Often these two aspects should be done separately. First, all possible solutions should be raised in a brainstorming session. Then each proposed solution should be evaluated.

3. *Deciding together (not voting) on the best solution.* The one solution most acceptable to all parties should be chosen.

4. *Planning the implementation of the solution.* How will the solution be carried out? When?

5. *Finally, planning for an evaluation of the solution after a specified period of time.* This last step is essential. The first solution chosen is not always the best or most workable. If the first solution has flaws, the problem-solving process should be begun again at Step 1.

Since negotiation is the most effective of all conflict-resolution strategies, the skills necessary to achieve meaningful negotiation are extremely important in facing inevitable conflicts.

References

Gordon, T. (1971). *Parent effectiveness training.* New York: Peter H. Wyden, Inc.

Wiley, G.E. (1973). Win/lose situations. In J.E. Jones & J.W. Pfeiffer (Eds.), *The 1973 annual handbook for group facilitators* (pp. 105–107). San Francisco, CA: Pfeiffer.

Originally published in The 1974 Annual Handbook for Group Facilitators.

3

Win/Lose Situations

Gerry E. Wiley

Win/lose situations pervade our culture. In the law courts we use the adversary system. Political parties strive to win elections and to win points in legislatures. Debates are common at schools, universities and in the media. The put-down is generally regarded as wit. Competing with and defeating an opponent is the most widely publicized aspect of a good deal of our sports and recreation.

The language of business, politics, and even education is dotted with win/lose terms. One "wins" a promotion, "beats" the competition, buys a lubricant to obtain "the racer's edge" for his auto. Students strive to "top the class" or "outsmart" the teacher. Although we do recognize cooperative effort and collaboration, it seems that we tend to emphasize "healthy" competition.

In an environment that stresses winning, it is no wonder that competitive behavior persists where it is not appropriate. Imagine a typical committee meeting to decide on a suitable program for a club. Members interrupt one another to introduce their own ideas. Proposals are made that other members do not even acknowledge. Partnerships and power blocs are formed to support one program against proponents of another. When members of such a committee are enabled to analyze the operation of the group, they commonly agree that they were not listening to one another because they were thinking of ways to state a case or to counter the proposal of someone else. They were interrupting to get a point out before the speaker clinched the sale of his idea. In these ways they were acting as competing individuals rather than as a collaborating group. They had started out to reach the best decision regarding a program, but had slipped into a win/lose contest. Very often the original purpose is completely overshadowed by the struggle to win. This failing of committees is common.

Some Potential Win/Lose Situations

Group meetings are not the only sphere in which a win/lose situation can arise. Visualize a consultant discussing a client's problem. For any of a number of reasons, the client may perceive the consultant's helpful suggestions not as they were intended but as criticism of the client. As a result the client might also feel in competition with the consultant. The contest would revolve around whose methods were more effective or who could do the job better. Instead of listening to the recommendations, the client would be trying to shoot them down, while the consultant would be concentrating on defending his or her expertise. When a consultant and client are locked in a win/lose match, the chances are very small that the consultant's advice will be used.

Win/lose contests can also develop in an organization. Individuals may strive for a dominant position. Battles can rage discreetly (and not so discreetly) between departments. For example, a planning department might develop a new assembly procedure. When it is introduced to the assembly department, the workers might resent it and lock horns with planners. It is easy to interpret the situation in win/lose terms. The planners are showing that they know more and can design a procedure better than the men on the job. If the new procedure works well, the planners "win." On the other hand, if the innovation does not improve production, the planners "lose," and, in a sense, the assemblers "win" because their normal operation proved superior. Seen in this light, it should be expected that the assemblers will not be committed to giving the innovation a fair trial. In extreme cases, they may even sabotage it "to show those theoretical snobs in Planning." In fact all efforts to plan for others are plagued by win/lose traps. In some companies and institutions internal win/lose rivalries absorb more effort than the main production or service.

POTENTIAL RESULTS OF WIN/LOSE

Although there are obviously some instances where a win/lose approach can be a positive factor, it is generally destructive. Win/lose is too often poisonous to interpersonal relations and organizational effectiveness. Suppose a husband loses an argument with his wife, and the couple goes dancing instead of to a horse race. He can retaliate by being sullen or obnoxious. He has turned a win/lose situation into an ordeal where both partners are miserable. Often win/lose "victories" become losses for both parties, producing a "lose/lose" result.

The Pfeiffer Book of Successful Conflict Management Tools © 2003 John Wiley & Sons, Inc.

Some of the negative results of win/lose have been shown in the examples already given. The following list identifies fourteen problems that may arise from win/lose confrontations.

1. Divert time and energy from the main issues.
2. Delay decisions.
3. Create deadlocks.
4. Drive unaggressive committee members to the sidelines.
5. Interfere with listening.
6. Obstruct exploration of more alternatives.
7. Decrease or destroy sensitivity.
8. Cause members to drop out or resign from committees.
9. Arouse anger that disrupts a meeting.
10. Interfere with empathy.
11. Leave losers resentful.
12. Incline underdogs to sabotage.
13. Provoke personal abuse.
14. Cause defensiveness.

FROM WIN/LOSE TO WIN/WIN

Since win/lose events will undoubtedly be experienced often in the course of life, it is important to know how to cope with them. If the predominant tendency of win/lose contests is to produce lose/lose outcomes, it becomes a matter of redirecting these toward "win/win" results. In a "win/win" result everyone comes out on top.

It is extremely difficult for one person alone to reorient a win/lose. You are likely to be treated as a third party in the argument, or you may have both adversaries turn on you. Although it would be ideal to have all parties committed to avoiding a win/lose result, the efforts of a significant segment of a group can usually be effective. Even in a one-to-one conflict, one of the parties can often turn off the contest. It takes two to fight. The more people who recognize the dangers in a win/lose struggle and want to adjust the situation, the more likely is a successful outcome.

Some Means of Reorienting to Win/Win

1. Have clear goals, understood and agreed upon. Use the goals to test whether issues are relevant or not.

2. Be on the lookout for win/lose. It can develop subtly. If you feel under attack, or feel yourself lining up support, you are likely in a win/lose contest.

3. Listen empathetically to others. Stop yourself from working on counter arguments while another person is speaking. Take the risk of being persuaded. Try the other person's reasoning on for size.

4. Avoid absolute statements that leave no room for modification. "I think this is the way . . ." is better than "This is THE ONLY way . . ."

5. If you are planning for others, provide some means for their involvement. The doers should feel that they can have influence on decisions that affect them.

6. Try to make decisions by consensus rather than by victory of the majority.

7. Test to see that trade-offs and compromises are truly accepted by all.

8. Draw a continuum line and have members place themselves on it regarding the issue. It often occurs that the different "sides" are not far apart.

9. Be alert to selling or winning strategies in others and avoid using them yourself. "Any intelligent person can see the advantages . . ." would be a danger signal.

This list is not exhaustive, but may provide a beginning toward more productive relationships. The key idea in adjusting a win/lose situation is to strive for what is best for all rather than trying to *get your way*.

Originally published in The 1973 Annual Handbook for Group Facilitators.

4

A Taxonomy of Intergroup Conflict-Resolution Strategies

Daniel C. Feldman

"Intergroup conflict" refers to overt expressions of hostility between groups or their intentional interference with each other's activities. The research on intergroup conflict generally has been in five distinct areas: (1) identifying the causes of intergroup conflict (for example, Lawrence & Lorsch, 1969; Merton, 1940); (2) illustrating the dynamics of intergroup conflict (for example, Blake & Mouton, 1961a; Sherif & Sherif, 1953); (3) analyzing strategies used by groups to gain power (for example, Deutsch, 1949; Pfeffer, 1977); (4) identifying the consequences of intergroup conflict (for example, Dutton & Walton, 1965; Hammond & Goldman, 1961); and (5) examining intergroup conflict-resolution strategies (for example, Pruitt, 1971; Sherif, 1958).

The literature in this last area, intergroup conflict-resolution strategies, consists mainly of field and laboratory experimental studies. Typically, a study examines one conflict-resolution strategy in a pre- and postdesign, analyzing the effectiveness of the strategy in reducing intergroup conflict (affect, perceptions, and/or behavior). Rarely are different strategies compared, either empirically or conceptually. This article presents a taxonomy of intergroup conflict-resolution strategies that frequently are used in organizations and discusses the circumstances in which each strategy is most effective.

The primary dimension along which intergroup conflict-resolution strategies vary is how openly they address the conflict. The chief characteristic of *conflict-avoidance* strategies is that they attempt to keep the conflict from coming into the open. The goal of *conflict-defusion* strategies is to keep the conflict in abeyance and to "cool" the emotions of the parties involved. *Conflict-containment* strategies allow some conflict to surface, but tightly control which issues are discussed and the manner in which they are discussed. *Conflict-confrontation* strategies are designed to uncover all of the issues of the conflict and to try to find a mutually satisfactory solution.

CONFLICT-AVOIDANCE STRATEGIES

Ignoring the Conflict

This strategy is represented by the absence of action. Managers, for example, often avoid dealing with the dysfunctional aspects of conflict. Unfortunately, when they avoid searching for the causes of the conflict, the situation usually continues or becomes worse over time. However, although ignoring the conflict generally is ineffective for resolving important policy issues, there are some circumstances in which it is at least a reasonable way of dealing with problems. One such circumstance is when the conflict issue is trivial. For example, there may be differences of opinion about the wisdom of allowing employees time to attend a one-time training program. This is such a short-run, temporary issue that it does not warrant much attention.

Another circumstance in which ignoring the conflict is a reasonable strategy is when the issue seems to be symptomatic of other, more basic conflicts. For example, two groups may experience conflict over the amount and quality of office space. Such conflicts often reflect more important issues about relative power and status. Resolving the office-space problem would not address the key issues, and attention could be directed more fruitfully to the more basic concerns (Thomas, 1977).

Imposing a Solution

This strategy consists of forcing the conflicting parties to accept a solution devised by a higher-level manager. Imposing a solution does not allow much conflict to surface, nor does it leave room for the participants to air their grievances, so it also generally is an ineffective conflict-resolution strategy. Any peace that it does achieve is likely to be short-lived. Because the underlying issues are not addressed, the conflict reappears in other guises and in other situations.

Forcing a solution can, however, be appropriate when quick, decisive action is needed. For instance, when there is conflict over investment decisions, and delays can be very costly, forcing a solution may be the best strategy available to top management. Likewise, it may be necessary when unpopular decisions must be made and there is very little chance that the parties involved could ever reach agreement (Thomas, 1977). An example of this is when a university must cut back on the funding of academic programs. It is unreasonable to expect that any department would agree to cut its staff and students for the greater good; yet some hard, unpleasant decisions ultimately must be made.

CONFLICT-DEFUSION STRATEGIES

Smoothing

One way that a manager can deal with conflict is to try to "smooth it over" by playing down its extent or importance. The manager might try to persuade the groups that they are not so far apart in their viewpoints as they think they are, point out the similarities in their positions, try to appease group members whose feelings have been hurt, or downplay the importance of the issue. By smoothing the conflict, managers hope to decrease its intensity and avoid escalation or open hostility. Like forcing a solution, smoothing generally is ineffective because it does not address the key points of conflict.

However, smoothing sometimes can serve as a stop-gap measure to let people cool down and regain perspective. In the heat of battle, people may make statements that are likely to escalate the conflict; and smoothing often can bring the disagreement back to a manageable level. Smoothing also may be appropriate when the conflict concerns nonwork-related issues. For instance, as Alderfer (1977) points out, intergroup conflict frequently occurs between older and younger employees because of their different political beliefs and moral values. Smoothing can help to defuse the tension so that the conflict does not spill over into central work issues.

Appealing to Superordinate Goals

Managers can defuse conflict by focusing attention on the higher goals that the groups share or the long-range aims that they have in common. This approach tends to make the current problem seem insignificant beside the more important mutual goals (Sherif, 1958).

Finding superordinate goals that are important to both groups is not easy. Achieving these goals requires cooperation between the groups, so the rewards for achieving the goals must be significant. The most successful and most frequently used superordinate goal is organizational survival: If the subunits do not cooperate sufficiently, the continued existence of the larger organization itself will be severely jeopardized.

CONFLICT-CONTAINMENT STRATEGIES

Using Representatives

One of the strategies that managers use to contain conflict is the use of representatives. In order to decide an issue, they meet with representatives of the opposing groups rather than dealing with the groups in their entirety. The rationale is that the representatives know the problems and can argue the groups' points of view accurately and forcefully (Blake & Mouton, 1961b).

Although this seems to be a logical way of proceeding, the research on the use of representatives as a means of solving intergroup conflict is fairly negative. Representatives are not entirely free to engage in compromise; rather, they must act out of loyalty and are motivated to win (or at least to avoid defeat) even though a solution to the intergroup problem may be sacrificed in the process. A representative who "gives in" is likely to face suspicion or rejection from group members; consequently, if a representative cannot win, he or she will try to deadlock a solution or at least forestall defeat. In one study (Blake & Mouton, 1961b), only two of sixty-two representatives capitulated to the opposition; all other situations with representatives ended in deadlock.

Although individual representatives have difficulty in negotiating an agreement because of their fear of rejection by their groups, two situational factors can increase the effectiveness of this strategy. First, the use of *groups* of representatives from each side can help to overcome individual anxiety about group rejection. The members of each team can provide mutual support when they need to make concessions in order to achieve agreement. Second, groups of negotiators may receive broader support and trust from their respective sides, as each representative may represent a different constituency or bring a different expertise to the negotiations. Most labor negotiations involve several representatives of both management and labor.

Resolving conflict through representatives is more effective before positions become fixed or are made public. After positions become fixed, representatives become even more intransigent; and "giving in" is more likely to be attributed to the personal failure of the representatives than to situational factors.

Structuring the Interaction Between the Groups

Some managers assume that one way to decrease conflict is to increase the *amount* of contact between the groups (if the groups interacted more, they would like each other better and fight less). In reality, increased interaction can merely add fuel to the fire; the two groups spend their time looking for additional reasons to reinforce their negative stereotypes of each other.

However, *structuring* the interaction between the groups can be effective in resolving conflict. Providing constraints on how many issues are discussed and the manner in which they are discussed can facilitate conflict resolution. There are many ways to structure the interaction between groups to deal with conflict; some of the most effective strategies include the following:

- Decreasing the amount of direct interaction between the groups in the early stages of conflict resolution;
- Decreasing the amount of time between problem-solving meetings;
- Decreasing the formality of the presentation of issues;
- Limiting the recitation of historic events and precedents and focusing instead on current issues and goals; and
- Using third-party mediators.

All of these strategies allow some conflict to surface and be addressed, but prevent it from getting out of hand and hardening the groups' positions. Decreasing the amount of direct interaction between the groups early in the conflict helps to prevent the conflict from escalating. Decreasing the amount of time between problem-solving meetings helps to prevent backsliding from tentative agreements. Decreasing the formality of the presentation of issues helps to induce a problem-solving, rather than a win-lose, orientation to the conflict. Limiting how far back historically and how widely precedents can be cited helps to keep the focus on finding a solution to the current conflict. Finally, a mediator can act as a go-between who transmits offers and messages, helps the groups to clarify their positions, presents each group's position more clearly to the other, and suggests some possible solutions that are not obvious to the opposing parties (Wexley & Yukl, 1977).

Structuring the interaction is especially useful in two situations: (1) when previous attempts to discuss conflict issues openly led to conflict escalation rather than to problem solution and (2) when a respected third party is available to provide (and enforce) some structure in the interactions between the groups.

Bargaining

Bargaining is the process of exchanging concessions until a compromise solution is reached.

Bargaining can lead to the resolution of a conflict, but usually without much openness on the part of the groups involved and without much real problem solving. Typically, in bargaining each side begins by demanding more than it really expects to get. Both sides realize that concessions will be necessary in order to reach a solution, but neither side wants to make the first concession because it may be perceived as a sign of weakness. Thus, each party signals a willingness to be flexible in exchanging concessions without actually making an explicit offer; a tacit proposal can be denied later if it fails to elicit a positive response from the other party (Pruitt, 1971). Bargaining continues until a mutually satisfactory agreement is reached between the two groups, although such a solution can be reached without much open discussion of the conflict issues and without much effort to solve the underlying problems. Therefore, bargaining often results in a compromise agreement that fails to deal with the problem in a rational manner and is not in the long-term interests of both groups.

For bargaining to be feasible at all as a conflict-resolution strategy, both parties must be of relatively equal power. Otherwise, one group simply will impose its will on the other, and the weaker group will have no means of obtaining concessions from the stronger one. Bargaining also is more likely to work if there are several acceptable alternatives that both groups are willing to consider. Otherwise, bargaining is likely to end in a deadlock.

CONFLICT-CONFRONTATION STRATEGIES

Problem Solving

Problem solving is an attempt to find a solution that reconciles or integrates the needs of both parties, who work together to define the problem and to identify mutually satisfactory solutions. In problem solving there is open expression of feelings as well as exchange of task-related information. Alderfer (1977) and Wexley and Yukl (1977) summarize the most critical ingredients in successful problem solving:

1. Definition of the problem should be a joint effort based on shared fact finding rather than on the biased perceptions of the individual groups.

2. Problems should be stated in terms of specifics rather than as abstract principles.

3. Points of initial agreement in the goals and beliefs of both groups should be identified along with the differences.

4. Discussions between the groups should consist of specific, nonevaluative comments. Questions should be asked to elicit information, not to belittle the opposition.

5. The groups should work together in developing alternative solutions. If this is not feasible, each group should present a range of acceptable solutions rather than promoting the solution that is best for it while concealing other possibilities.

6. Solutions should be evaluated objectively in terms of quality and acceptability to the two groups. When a solution maximizes joint benefits but favors one party, some way should be found to provide special benefits to the other party to make the solution equitable.

7. All agreements about separate issues should be considered tentative until every issue is dealt with, because issues that are interrelated cannot be settled independently in an optimal manner (Blake & Mouton, 1962, 1964; Walton & McKersie, 1965).

There are two preconditions for successful, integrative problem solving. The first precondition is a minimal level of trust between the two groups. Without trust, each group will fear manipulation and will be unlikely to reveal its true preferences. Second, integrative problem solving takes a lot of time and can succeed only in the absence of pressure for a quick settlement. However, when the organization can benefit from merging the differing perspectives and insights of the two groups in making key decisions, integrative problem solving is especially needed.

Organizational Redesign

Redesigning or restructuring the organization can be an effective, intergroup conflict-resolution strategy. This is especially true when the sources of conflict result from the coordination of work among different departments or divisions. Unlike the other strategies discussed so far, however, organizational redesign can be used either to decrease the conflict or to increase it.

One way of redesigning organizations is to reduce task interdependence between groups and to assign each group clear work responsibilities (that is, create self-contained work groups) to reduce conflict. This is most appropriate when the work can be divided easily into distinct projects. Each group is provided with clear project responsibilities and the resources needed to reach its goals. A potential cost of this strategy is duplication and waste of resources, particularly when one group cannot fully utilize equipment or personnel. Innovation and growth also may be restricted to existing project areas (Duncan, 1979), with no group having the incentive or responsibility to create new ideas.

The other way to deal with conflict through organizational redesign is to develop overlapping or joint work responsibilities (for example, integrator roles). This makes the most use of the different perspectives and abilities of the different departments, but it also tends to create conflict. On the other hand, there may be tasks (for example, developing new products) that do not fall clearly into any one department's responsibilities but require the contributions, expertise, and coordination of several. Assigning new-product development to one department could decrease potential conflict, but at a high cost to the quality of the product. In this case the organization might try to sustain task-based conflict but develop better mechanisms for managing the conflict. For example, providing "integrating teams" can facilitate communication and coordination between the members of interdependent departments (Galbraith, 1974).

SUMMARY

The main dimension along which intergroup conflict-resolution strategies are arrayed is how openly they address the conflict: Conflict-avoidance and conflict-defusion strategies allow little or no conflict into the open; conflict-containment and conflict-confrontation strategies deal with the conflict more openly and thoroughly (see Table 1).

Which strategy is most effective depends on how critical the conflict is to task accomplishment and how quickly the conflict must be resolved. If the conflict arises from a trivial issue and/or must be resolved quickly, a conflict-avoidance or conflict-defusion strategy is most likely to be effective. If the conflict centers around an important work issue and does not need to be solved quickly, a conflict-containment or conflict-confrontation strategy is most likely to be effective.

Originally published in The 1985 Annual: Developing Human Resources.

Table 1. Conflict-Resolution Strategies

Conflict-Resolution Strategy	Goal of Strategy	Appropriate Situations
Ignoring the conflict	Avoidance	• When the issue is trivial • When the issue is symptomatic of more basic, pressing problems
Imposing a solution	Avoidance	• When quick, decisive action is needed • When unpopular decisions must be made, and consensus between the groups appears very unlikely
Smoothing	Defusion	• As a stop-gap measure to let people cool down and regain their perspective • When the conflict is over nonwork issues
Superordinate goals	Defusion	• When there is a mutually important goal that neither group can achieve without the cooperation of the other • When the survival or success of the total organization is in jeopardy
Representatives	Containment	• Before the groups' positions become fixed and made public • When each side is represented by groups of representatives rather than by one spokesman
Structuring the interaction	Containment	• When the previous attempts to openly discuss conflict issues led to conflict escalation rather than to problem solution • When a respected third party is available to provide structure and serve as a mediator
Bargaining	Containment	• When the two groups have relatively equal power • When there are several acceptable, alternative solutions that both parties are willing to consider
Problem solving	Confrontation	• When there is a minimum level of trust between the two groups and no pressure for a quick solution • When the organization can benefit from merging the different perspectives and insights of both groups in making key decisions
Organizational redesign	Confrontation	• When the sources of conflict result from the coordination of work • Self-contained work groups are most appropriate when the work easily can be divided into clear project responsibilities; lateral relationships are more appropriate when activities require much interdepartmental coordination but do not clearly lie within any one department's responsibilities

References

Alderfer, C.P. (1977). Group and intergroup relations. In J.R. Hackman & J.L. Suttle (Eds.), *Improving life at work*. Santa Monica, CA: Goodyear.

Blake, R.R., & Mouton, J.S. (1961a). Comprehension of own and of outgroup positions under intergroup competition. *Journal of Conflict Resolution, 5*, 304–310.

Blake, R.R., & Mouton, J.S. (1961b). Loyalty of representatives to ingroup positions during intergroup competition. *Sociometry, 24*, 177–183.

Blake, R.R., & Mouton, J.S. (1962). The intergroup dynamics of win-lose conflict and problem-solving collaboration in unionmanagement relations. In M. Sherif (Ed.), *Intergroup relations and leadership*. New York: John Wiley.

Blake, R.R., & Mouton, J.S. (1964). *The managerial grid*. Houston, TX: Gulf.

Deutsch, M. (1949). An experimental study of the effects of cooperation and competition upon group process. *Human Relations, 2*, 199–232.

Duncan, R.B. (1977). What is the right organization structure? *Organizational Dynamics, 7*, 59–80.

Dutton, J.M., & Walton, R.E. (1965). Interdepartmental conflict and cooperation: Two contrasting studies. *Human Organization, 25*, 207–220.

Galbraith, J.R. (1974). Organization design: An information processing view. *Interfaces, 4*, 28–36.

Hammond, L.K., & Goldman, M. (1961). Competition and noncompetition and its relationship to individual and group productivity. *Sociometry, 24*, 46–60.

Lawrence, P.R., & Lorsch, J.W. (1969). Organization and environment: *Managing differentiation and integration*. Homewood, IL: Richard D. Irwin.

Merton, R.K. (1940). Bureaucratic structure and personality. *Social Forces, 18*, 560–568.

Pfeffer, J. (1977). Power and resource allocation in organizations. In B. Staw & G. Salancik (Eds.), *New directions in organizational behavior*. Chicago: St. Clair.

Pruitt, D.G. (1971). Indirect communication and the search for agreement in negotiations. *Journal of Applied Social Psychology, 1*, 205–239.

Sherif, M. (1958). Superordinate goals in the reduction of intergroup conflict. *American Journal of Sociology, 63*, 349–358.

Sherif, M., & Sherif, C.W. (1953). *Groups in harmony and tension*. New York: Harper & Row.

Thomas, K.W. (1977). Toward multidimensional values in teaching: The example of conflict behaviors. *Academy of Management Review, 2*, 484–490.

Walton, R.E., & McKersie, R.B. (1965). A behavioral theory of labor negotiations: *An analysis of a social interaction system*. New York: McGraw-Hill.

Wexley, K.N., & Yukl, G.A. (1977). *Organizational behavior and personnel psychology*. Homewood, IL: Richard D. Irwin.

5

Developing Collaboration
in Organizations

Udai Pareek

"Collaboration" can be defined as the efforts of one or more people working with others toward the attainment of a common or agreed-on goal. The literature of experimental research on the subject of collaboration is growing. In such studies collaboration, or cooperation, usually is contrasted with competition. "Competition" can be defined as the efforts of one or more people working against others for the attainment of mutually exclusive goals. The basic difference between collaborative and competitive behavior is the perception of the goal. If the goal is seen as sharable, then collaborative behavior, that is, working with others for the attainment of the goal, generally results. If the goal is seen as unsharable, for example, a situation in which only one person can "win," then rivalry, or competitive behavior, generally results.

FUNCTIONAL AND DYSFUNCTIONAL FORMS
OF COOPERATION AND COMPETITION

Both collaboration (or cooperation) and competition can fall into two categories: one functional (or effective or positive) and the other dysfunctional (or ineffective or negative). We will use the terms Coll (+) and Coll (?) and Comp (+) and Comp (?) to indicate functional and dysfunctional, or positive and negative, collaboration and competition, respectively.

Comp (?) can be defined as a rivalry between two or more people for the attainment of a desired goal. If such competition is used to achieve excellence and to search for or create further challenges for oneself, it is functional or positive competition—Comp (+). Such competition contributes to the development of the sense of self-worth.

When a person focuses on a competitor and how the competitor can be prevented from attaining a goal, the interaction becomes negative—Comp (?). As Likert (1967) has often noted, if competition reduces a person's feeling of self-worth, it is dysfunctional. Likert also gives the example of some salespeople who were motivated by this kind of competition. These salespeople withheld information about better methods of sales, new markets, and new sales strategies from their colleagues.

Similarly, collaboration can be either functional or dysfunctional. Functional collaboration, or Coll (+), can be defined as the tendency to contribute to the joint effort for faster and more effective goal attainment, resulting in mutual trust, respect, and concern. Such collaboration increases self-worth and contributes to the development of other desirable characteristics.

Coll (?) is the tendency to conform to others' demands in order to ingratiate oneself with them or to avoid or escape task stress or task demands. When a person collaborates with another person because the latter is more powerful, or in order to please the latter, such collaboration is also dysfunctional.

Both competition and collaboration are important and can be conceived as complementary qualities. However, they perform different functions. Figure 1 shows these various functions.

Competition Develops	Collaboration Develops
A sense of responsibility	Mutuality
A sense of identity	Alternative ideas and solutions
Internal standards	Mutial support and reinforcement
Excellence	Synergy
Individual creativity	Collective action
Individual autonomy	Supplementary expertise

Figure 1. Functions of Competition and Collaboration

THE ROLE OF COMPETITION

The main function of competition in an organization is to help a person to develop and attain his or her own identity. In this regard, competition serves the following purposes:

Developing a Sense of Identity

In order to be effective, one must develop his or her own identity and function as a person. The development of identity occurs as one realizes his or her own uniqueness, strengths, capabilities, and weaknesses by testing them in the environment with other people.

Developing a Sense of Responsibility

Unless a sense of responsibility is developed, a person's general competence and task involvement will be low. Responsibility includes a realistic assessment of how much one has contributed to a success or has been responsible for a failure. Competition helps to develop a sense of responsibility because it isolates a person to face the consequences of his or her own actions. If the person succeeds in a competitive situation, he or she attributes that success to his or her own efforts and abilities. Similarly, if the person fails, he or she analyzes and takes responsibility for that failure.

Developing Internal Standards of Behavior

When a person takes responsibility for the consequences of his or her actions, that person develops his or her own standards for evaluating what is done well and what needs to be done better. A person who engages in collaboration merely for the sake of conformity will place little value on the outcome, as the decision to cooperate was not based on his or her own values or standards of behavior. Competition, however, helps to develop such internal standards. Successful competitive experiences help one learn to assess what one wants to do, why one wants to do it, and how one views the outcome. This increases one's autonomy in setting goals and taking necessary steps for their attainment.

Developing Excellence

The most important result of competition is the development of a concern for excellence, or what has been called achievement motivation. The success that one achieves in relation to other people produces a desire for even greater success. This occurs not only in relation to the standards set by others but also in relation to one's own standards or past performance. There is a continuous process of self-competition. One who has done very well in the past often wants to excel even more and is, in fact, competing with oneself.

Generally, the word "competition" is used in the context of relations with others. But the sense of competition that a person acquires from "outside" may also be internalized, and it promotes achievement motivation in which competition exists not only in relation to others but also in relation to one's own past behavior. When competition is used properly, it can develop a concern for excellence instead of a desire to pull another person down.

Developing Individual Creativity

Individual identity and a concern for excellence create a desire in a person to find his or her own new and unconventional ways of solving problems, of looking at things, and of acting on decisions. Positive competition often encourages the development of such individual creativity.

Developing Autonomy

Competition helps one to develop one's own ways of looking at problems and finding solutions. It helps one to be original, to think on one's own, and to develop one's own framework and way of doing things. Developing autonomy does not conflict with relating to others or with working for a larger cause. Because autonomy helps to maintain a person's identity, if properly used it can help people to respect one another's identities. Thus, individual autonomy can be maintained in a larger context in which people have to surrender their autonomy on some matters in order to work for a common goal. This leads us to the issue of how competition emerges in collaboration and the role of collaboration.

THE ROLE OF COLLABORATION

Competition by itself is a very important instrument in the development of a person, but it should complement and supplement collaboration. Likewise, collaboration supplements the learnings of competition and allows further personal development.

Building Mutuality

Collaboration helps to build relationships based on mutuality—recognizing the strengths of others and the contributions that other people can make and accepting these contributions. Such a relationship helps the people in an organization to develop respect for one another and to accept one another in a work situation. It also helps them to encourage the strengths of other people, to utilize those strengths, and to contribute to the further development of others.

Generating Ideas and Alternatives

In a collaborative relationship, people stimulate one another in thinking about problems and alternatives and in generating ideas, approaches, and solutions. Because several people may be involved, more ideas are generated than one single person could produce.

Building Mutual Support and Reinforcement

The collaborative relationship plays a significant emotional role by reinforcing members' efforts toward mutual support. In a collaborative situation, people receive immediate feedback from their colleagues, which helps them both to use this feedback as well as to give feedback to the others. In this continual process of feedback and support, successes are reinforced and the team is strengthened.

Developing Synergy

A collaborative relationship produces synergy, the multiplication of talents and resources in the group. Through this process of continual stimulation, the members achieve results beyond the total of all individual resources. This generation of more potent resources in the group has an effect of multiplying resources in an organization.

Developing Collective Action

When people work together in a group or team, their commitment to the goal—their courage to stand by that goal and take necessary action—is likely to be high. The difference in the behavior of a person in isolation and his or her behavior as a member of a team is evident in the case of trade unions, representative committees, and delegations. People act with more of a sense of power when they have several people behind them than they do when they present only their own points of view. This generates courage. The secret of success of a trade union in an organization lies in the strength of collective action that it is able to generate. The higher the level of collaboration, the greater the strength the group will have for collective action.

Supplementing Expertise

The greatest advantage of collaboration is that people go beyond their own limitations, and one person's lack of expertise in a particular area does not keep the group from achieving its goals. The group's pool of strengths and expertise supplements the various individual contributions; as a result the collaborative group is able to generate multidimensional solutions and is not limited by a single person's approach to the problem.

COMPARING COMPETITION AND COLLABORATION

The discussion so far has shown the respective roles that collaboration and competition play in the organization. One is not always "better" than the other because in some instances competition is more functional, while in others collaboration is called for. Much work in an organization is done in groups. These groups may be departments, interdepartmental committees, vertical role groups, or horizontal role groups such as the managers at a particular level. In many cases there may be informal collaborative groups in which two or more people work together on a problem. In most cases, most of the time, people work with other people and, therefore, are continually interacting in either a competitive or collaborative framework. In most such situations the collaborative framework is much more functional than the competitive one because these situations deal with organizations and problems: setting standards, searching for alternatives, and so on. Collaboration is therefore an extremely important dimension in organizational life; if an organization has a low level of collaboration, the possibility of solving multidimensional problems within the organization is rather low.

Many researchers—and those who have worked in the field of management—have reported that on the whole collaboration contributes to better development and has better side effects than competition. Likert (1967), analyzing various studies done with salespeople, reported that the most successful sales managers discovered and demonstrated that when a sense of personal worth and importance was used to create competitive motivational forces, the level of productivity and sales performance was not as high as was expected. It was very high, on the other hand, when motivational forces to cooperate rather than compete were used. The latter results included better performance, lower cost, higher levels of earnings, and much higher employee satisfaction. Likert concluded on this basis that collaboration releases motivational forces that develop people and contribute to the achievement of targets more effectively. Cartwright and Zander (1968), summarizing most of the research done since the famous research by Deutsch (1949) on cooperation and competition, reported that the basic conclusions drawn by Deutsch (that cooperation has a much higher payoff to the organization than does competition) were true in most of the studies surveyed.

Collaboration contributes to better communication, coordination of efforts, an increased climate of friendliness, and pride in one's own group. Cartwright and Sander concluded that these were important qualities for group effectiveness.

Because people increasingly are called to work together to solve multidimensional organizational problems, collaboration becomes very relevant. This study will examine how collaboration takes place and how it can be further developed in the organization. The first question, therefore, is why and how people collaborate. Once this is answered, we can proceed to the next issue: how collaboration should be managed.

BASES OF COLLABORATION

A great deal of research has been done on cooperation and collaboration. Experimental social psychologists have devised ways to study group relationships involving cooperation or collaboration. A frequent vehicle for study is an activity called "Prisoners' Dilemma" (Pfeiffer & Jones, 1974c), in which team members are required to make a move demonstrating either cooperation or competition with another team. If both teams make a cooperative move, they score equally. If one "tricks" the other, it gains points and the other loses points. But if the teams attempt to trick each other, they both lose points. The object is to compare chance scores resulting from competition with the slow but consistent gains resulting from collaboration. A number of studies (Pareek, 1977a) have been done on this structured interaction; some of this research is significant for understanding the bases of collaboration, some of the factors that contribute to collaboration, and the reasons that people collaborate.

Collaborative Motivation

There is a basic need in most human beings, called *extension motivation,* to relate to other people and to be helpful to them. This need is reflected not only in concern for another person but also in concern for larger groups, including the organization to which one belongs and the society at large. Extension motivation is the basis of collaboration. People who have high extension motivation will collaborate more than others. Extension motivation or any other motivation is not innate or inborn. It is a product of many forces, and other factors can contribute to raising or reducing the level of extension motivation. Most of these factors interact with one another; many reinforce others or have implications for others. If extension motivation operates, and if there is reciprocal motivation within the group (if the members of the group have concern for one another and are also concerned about the performance of the total group), the person's motivation is further reinforced. On the other hand, if other members do not demonstrate extension motivation, it will be reduced in individual members.

Group Norms

The norms that prevail in a group have a strong influence on the behavior of the members and can raise or lower motivation. A member with low extension motivation may have a tendency to compete. However, if the collaborative norms in the group are high, this person's extension motivation will also increase in time. Norms are informally evolved; members implicitly agree with them, agree to conform to these standards of behavior, and expect others to conform to them.

Higher Payoff

Generally a person's behavior is dictated by perceived rewards. If one type of behavior is rewarded more (or has higher payoff), the person will repeat that behavior. It is worthwhile, therefore, to examine whether collaborative behavior is rewarded in an organization.

Pareek and Banerjee (1977) have found that competition is not highly correlated with achievement motivation. In the past, achievement motivation (concern for individual excellence and competition) was thought to have a high correlation with competitive behavior. The reason that this has not proved to be true seems to lie in the perceived payoff for competition. People with high achievement motivation are interested in results. If they perceive that by collaborating they can get better results, they are likely to collaborate; if they perceive that the results are better from competition, they are likely to compete. Even those who have a tendency to compete are likely to collaborate if collaborative behavior has a higher payoff. Collaborative behavior, for example, can lead to recognition, a chance to develop one's abilities, increased creativity, increased influence in the system, or perception of one's role as useful or contributing to a cause that is greater than individual interests. Such psychological payoff, in terms of motivation or role efficacy (Pareek, 1980), especially if it supplements a monetary or material payoff, is likely to reinforce collaborative behavior.

Superordinate Goals

Several factors contribute to the development of a superordinate goal. First, the goal should be attractive to the various members; it should be seen as desirable by all concerned.

Second, the goal should be seen as sharable (that is, all people or groups concerned can share it). If the perception is that one party can achieve a goal at the expense of the other party and that the nature of the goal is such that it cannot be achieved jointly by both parties, this situation is called a "zero-sum game," because the sum of the payoff to both parties is zero. All traditional sports are zero-sum games. In a football or hockey match, the goals secured by one team are the positive payoff; the team losing the game has a negative payoff. Adding the payoffs of both teams results in zero. However, within the same team, members play a "nonzero-sum game." The gain by different players within the same team contributes to the higher gain by all members. The sum total of payoff to the different members of the team can be on the plus or the minus side.

Third, if the situation is such that the goal cannot be achieved by a single person or a single group without working with others, the goal is superordinate. In traditional sports, a team that is competing with other teams has the superordinate goal of getting a higher score than the other team. Within the team itself, members play a collaborative game because they perceive the superordinate goal. To all members, the goal of achieving victory is attractive; they see this as sharable and as nonzero-sum, and each member realizes that this cannot be achieved individually—they have to work together to achieve the goal.

When people involved in a situation see a goal as having all three elements described above, the goal is superordinate.

Sherif and Sherif (1953) have described some interesting experiments that demonstrate the value of superordinate goals and have contributed significantly to the understanding of cooperation. Experimental conflict and competition were first created in two groups of adolescents who were taken on a camping trip for several days. Situations were created in which the problems faced by both groups could not be solved by either group alone. It was found that the perception of the superordinate goals by both groups (involved at first in conflict and competition with each other) changed their behavior, and they later engaged in the maximum possible collaboration.

Perceived Power

Another condition that contributes to the development of collaboration in a group is the perception of power. Power can be of two kinds: reward and punishment. Punishment may take the form of depriving another person of reward. Everyone in the system has at least the negative power of depriving another person of something that is desirable to him or her. This may be done by holding back information, by misleading the other person, and so on. Even a person at the lowest level in the organization can use his or her negative power to create annoying situations, delay matters, hold back information, or give information that creates misunderstandings. Every person in the system has some kind of power. If people in the system perceive clearly that they have power that is positive in nature—that they may be able to contribute to and use their influence for the attainment of certain goals—they usually will use their power positively.

Similarly, it is important for people to realize that others who are involved in the situation also have power, both positive and negative. Such power should be not only perceived but also demonstrated. If people do not perceive the power of others, they are likely to use their own power in a competitive or exploitative manner. Pareek (1977a) has reported that unconditional cooperation does not lead to the development of collaboration. Unconditional cooperation by one party may communicate lack of power. If this happens, the other party will find it more and more difficult to enter into a collaborative relationship. For effective collaboration the perception of power of both (equality) is essential. This was dramatically demonstrated in one experiment in which the author was involved with four groups composed of educators from six Asian countries. These groups engaged in a structured activity called "Win As Much As You Can" (Pfeiffer & Jones, 1974c). The activity consisted of ten moves. One of the four groups consistently made cooperative moves and—as was revealed in the later interview and discussion—was fully convinced that, looking at the nature of the game and the implicit rules, only cooperative behavior could help all of the groups to maximize their gains. However, the unconditional cooperation by this group blocked the emergence of cooperation among the other groups, and the first group was exploited by the others. The final result was that the cooperating group stopped communication with the other three groups; and the other groups also refused to negotiate, as they saw themselves in a powerful and advantageous position that could be threatened by negotiation. Other research has shown that cooperation emerges after some competitive moves by the groups concerned; in this process the various parties or individuals demonstrate to one another the power they have and their ability to use power. Research also has shown that a competitive move or a stalemate in a relationship can result in collaboration, particularly in situations in which the parties are competitive by nature. In situations in which the parties are collaborative by nature, a stalemate in negotiation or relationship works against collaboration. The implications of these findings seem to be that when there are highly competitive or noncooperative parties or people, demonstration of their power to one another helps to loosen the situation, and a stalemate may encourage the possibility of collaborating for mutual benefit.

Mutual Trust

Along with the perception of power, it is important that the parties concerned also perceive that the power of the other party will not be used against them. This is trust. Trust is indicative of the high probability that the power of the other party will not be used in a malevolent way. Some degree of mutual trust is likely to lead to cooperation.

As shown in Figure 2, collaboration results from a combination of the perceived power of both parties and a minimal amount of trust in each other. In a no-trust condition, there may be coercion and exploitation if one party is seen by the other party as weak, or submission or compliance if one party is seen by the other as having power. If the perception is that neither has power, there may be indifference to each other; the perception that both have power may lead to either competition or individualistic behavior. A high-trust perception of the partner who has *low* power may lead to nurturance (paternalistic behavior); the perception that the other *has* power may result in dependency; and the perception that *neither* has power may generate mutual sympathy. Collaboration emerges only when trust exists and both parties perceive, as well as clearly demonstrate, that both have power.

Figure 3 shows that collaboration results from three main factors: the perception that the goal is sharable, the perception that both (or all) involved have power, and a minimal level of trust prevailing among those involved in the task. Absence of these may result in low (or the absence of)

	Only 1	Only He/She	Neither	Both
High	Coercion Exploitation	Submission Compliance	Indifference	Competition or Individualistic Task
Low	Nurturance	Dependence	Mutual Sympathy	Cooperation

Trust

Figure 2. Cooperation as a Function of Perceived Power and Trust

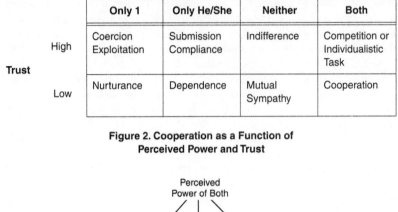

Figure 3. Cooperation as a Function of Sharable Goal, Perceived Power, and Trust

cooperation. We thus see that trust interacts with both power and superordinate goal.

Communication

Another factor contributing to the development of collaboration is communication between the parties involved in the situation. Pareek and Dixit (1977) have reported the results of experiments conducted on adult groups that show the role of communication in the development of collaboration. These and various other experiments have demonstrated that when groups or representatives of groups have an opportunity to communicate with one another, the chances of collaboration increase. Communication also helps the groups to share their perceptions of one another's power and to discover that the power they have can be turned into a positive force for the benefit of all concerned. The experiments showed that communication tends to produce repentant behavior in those who have been exploiting or using power against others. Communication also helps in the development of trust. When groups communicate through representatives, it is important that the groups trust their representatives and that the representatives know their commitments will be honored by the group. Again, experiments have shown that when a group has trust and confidence in its representatives and honors the commitments made by them, collaboration becomes easier.

Fait Accompli

If groups or people live together and share certain norms, they begin to see good points in one another and collaboration begins to emerge. Various experiments aimed at reduction of conflict have employed this technique. People may be prejudiced against one another or have incorrect notions about one another when they do not work together or live together, but through sharing experiences they evolve common norms. When the people work together, it should be in a larger context so that they become members of a larger group. As part of a larger group to which they contribute, they develop new norms that encourage the development of better relationships. When competing groups or people become part of the same group, they slowly lose their identity as individual people or groups in a narrow sense and develop a new identity or sense of belonging to the larger group. This helps in the emergence of collaboration.

Risk Taking

In the final analysis, cooperation results from an initiative taken by one party to cooperate. This is a risk-taking behavior, and it makes that party vulnerable to some degree. In a nonzero-sum game the person or group that makes the cooperative move runs the risk of losing a great deal and of hiding a lower payoff. This risk, the initiative, demonstrating the courage to lose initially for the benefit of all concerned, is the key to the development of cooperation. However, it is only after mutual trust has been achieved and mutual power has been demonstrated that such risk taking is effective. At that point, the fact that one person or group takes the initiative to become vulnerable starts the process of change toward collaboration. The strength that enabled the person or group to make such a move helps to support the collaborative relationship. This is shown in Figure 4.

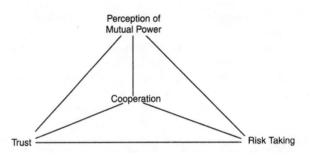

Figure 4. Cooperation as a Function of Individual Risk Taking

INTERVENTIONS TO BUILD COLLABORATION IN ORGANIZATIONS

Several interventions can be used to help raise the level of collaboration in organizations. The interventions discussed here can be classified as *process interventions* and *structural interventions*.

Process interventions focus on the basic processes that contribute to collaboration. They help to demonstrate the effects of collaboration. When people experience some dramatic effects of collaboration in a laboratory situation, they frequently are motivated to collaborate more effectively. Process interventions also help to increase awareness that collaboration is a complex phenomenon and that many conditions and processes promote conditions, so that they may be able to take appropriate actions. Finally, process interventions help people to look at themselves in a self-confrontive manner. If a person analyzes his or her own motivation and realizes that he or she has a tendency either to use collaboration in a minimal way or to use a dysfunctional type of collaboration, that person may be concerned enough to work toward developing collaborative motivation. In this way process interventions provide opportunities for individuals to experiment with new behavior, to explore what methods they can adopt for collaboration, and to see how collaboration helps in a particular situation. Such experiencing and experimenting constitute the basic approach to behavioral change.

While the main role of process intervention is to create motivation and release the process of collaboration, the main role of a structural intervention is to consolidate such change, make it a part of the organizational life, and ensure that the collaborative motivation that has been released is designed into the system and is sustained in the regular life of the organization.

The Pfeiffer Book of Successful Conflict Management Tools © 2003 John Wiley & Sons, Inc.

Structural interventions serve several functions. In the first place, they provide opportunities for people to actually collaborate in real-life situations. When people's motivation for collaboration is high, structural interventions provide them with opportunities to collaborate in order to sustain that motivation. Second, if collaboration is encouraged and rewarded, there will be a greater tendency for people to collaborate, so structural interventions create higher payoffs for collaboration in various forms, continually reinforcing collaborative efforts. In the third place, these interventions legitimize collaboration because they do not leave it to informal arrangements. By formalizing the ways in which people collaborate, the organization recognizes and communicates the value of collaboration; and this process of legitimization helps to make collaboration a regular part of organizational life. Finally, structural interventions help to establish norms of collaboration, making it clear that the organization expects people to collaborate. We have already said that such norms are important determinants of behavior; influencing behavior is an important role of structural interventions.

Figure 5 summarizes the various interventions that will be discussed here.

Motivation-Development Interventions

The development of collaborative motivation is aided by the development of the extension motive, which is characterized by concern for other people and a general feeling that one should be of some use to others. Two interventions can be used to develop extension motivation: a laboratory approach and a simulation activity.

Motivation-Development Laboratory

A laboratory of about one week's duration would be based primarily on the propositions suggested by McClelland and Winter (1969) for building motivation. An extension-motivation lab also can be organized along the lines suggested for a power-motivation lab (McClelland & Burnham, 1976). The design for such a lab would include the following components:

- Helping participants to analyze their levels of extension motivation and whether they are satisfied with them;
- Helping them to analyze various aspects of their jobs and to what extent these jobs provide opportunities to use their extension motivation;

Figure 5. Bases of Collaboration Related Interventions

Bases of Collaboration	Related Interventions
Motivations	Motivation Development Laboratory Simulation Activities
Norms	Norm-Setting Exercises Developing Norms of Sharing Temporary Systems
Reinforcement	The Appraisal System Rewarding Collaboration
Superordinate Goals	Joint Goal Setting Organization Building
Power	Simulation Activities Open Sharing of Feelings Role Negotiation Role Erosion
Trust	Training Groups or Process Groups Nonverbal Exercises Simulation Activities
Communication	Simulation Activities Feedback System
Team Development	Team-Building Laboratories Data Feedback Sharing of Feelings Image Sharing Role Linkage Joint Problem-Solving Groups
Initiative	Process Analysis of Simulation Experiences Recognizing and Rewarding Initiative

- Helping them to diagnose the organizational culture again to see what elements in the culture contribute to or work against extension motivation and collaboration;

- Helping them to analyze the norms prevailing in the organization to determine which norms promote collaboration and which work against it;

- Helping them to share their apprehensions about the consequences of co-operation; and

- Helping them to deal practically with such apprehensions and to see that collaboration can be a strength rather than a means of giving up some powers.

Collaboration eventually should be perceived as, and should in effect contribute to, the development of influence or power in people. Of course, this influence or power is of a particular nature; in the laboratory model, stage 4 of McClelland's (1975) concept of power should be used (Pareek, 1977b; Rao, 1976).

Simulation Activities

Simulations or structured activities also can be used to develop motivation for collaboration. One example is the activity "Win As Much As You Can" (Pfeiffer & Jones, 1974b), described earlier.

Norm-Building Interventions

Interventions can be used to develop norms of collaboration within the organization. Such behavioral standards sustain collaboration in the long run. The following three strategies are suggested in this regard.

Norm-Setting Exercises

De la Porte (1974) has suggested the development of group norms for team building. The interventions that de la Porte has suggested include building new norms by examining old norms, that is, creating understanding and appreciation of the significance of norms; establishing positive norm codes through cooperative normative-change priorities; developing a systematic change strategy by examining and modifying ten crucial areas that relate to norm setting; implementing the change strategy; providing follow-up and maintenance; and providing for continual evaluation of the change strategy.

Developing Norms of Sharing

If people in an organization continually, openly, and jointly share various problems that they face, discuss ideas about solutions, and develop strategies for action, norms for collaboration will develop. Such activities may be conducted both within departments and across departments. Norms cannot develop in an organization unless particular behaviors are established as desirable. Therefore, if collaboration is to result, steps must be taken to establish such norms and to reinforce them.

Temporary Systems

It may be useful to use temporary systems such as task groups, special problem-solving groups, or data-collection groups to solve various organizational problems or to work on specific tasks. Such a group is created for a specific purpose and as soon as that purpose is achieved, the group is dissolved. Usually such groups are composed of people from different departments, sections, or functions. The advantage of an interdisciplinary group is that members share concerns and thereby establish the norm of collaboration on common tasks. The more often such groups are used, the more the norm of collaboration will pervade the organization.

Reinforcing Interventions

Interventions can be used to reinforce collaborative behavior. When behavior is rewarded, it tends to be repeated. Two main interventions are suggested for this purpose.

The Appraisal System

Appraisal of employee performance and potential can be used to strengthen collaboration in an organization. One of the items to be appraised should be the person's contribution to team building and collaboration in the organization. When such an item is pinpointed, the person realizes that value is placed on such behavior and it becomes legitimized. This results in greater effort on the part of individual employees to consciously collaborate and contribute to teamwork. In due course, this helps to develop skills of, and eventually motivation for, collaboration. Similarly, while appraising the potential of a person for higher jobs, the employee's ability to develop a collaborative spirit to contribute to the development of subordinates may also be assessed.

Rewarding Collaboration

Some method of rewarding collaboration in an organization is helpful. The reward may be merely special mention or recognition. For example, if a team consisting of people from several departments or sections has achieved something remarkable, that achievement can be mentioned at board meetings, in the company newsletter, or in a special bulletin issued to describe successful collaborative efforts. Prizes can be given for remarkable work done by teams of workers in relation to specific tasks, when collaboration is a part of such efforts.

Creating Superordinate Goals

As has been discussed, a superordinate goal should be attractive, should be seen as sharable, and should be seen as achievable only through collaborative effort. The following interventions may be used to establish superordinate goals.

Joint Goal Setting

If people from various departments and teams are involved in setting goals, the results are likely to be superordinate goals. In the joint goal-setting process it is important that the goals be defined jointly by the members and seen as worthwhile, attractive, and challenging by all concerned. Resources necessary to attain the goals may also be discussed during such meetings. This frequently occurs in the top levels of organizations; however, at the lower levels the process could be used much more frequently.

Redesigning Work

De (1977) has described this intervention in detail. The intervention essentially consists of redesigning work in which several skilled workers are involved. The redesign is achieved by creating autonomous work teams consisting of members with various skills. They set their own goals, use their own resources, and are responsible for their overall production. In this process they learn one another's skills and replace one another whenever necessary. They take over the task of managing the entire production process in their own group. As De has explained, this approach certainly leads to new problems and dimensions, but more creative ways of managing problems also emerge. For example, as a result of such collaboration, the role of the supervisor must be redesigned. Although there are several repercussions from such work redesign, it is an effective intervention for creating superordinate goals.

Organization Building

Several models of organization building are available. Although these could be called organization development (OD) efforts, they are more elaborate than usual; therefore, the term "organization building" is used. Two major interventions of this nature are those by Blake and Mouton (1964) and Likert (1961, 1967). These two major theories of organization design have been widely used, and the results have been reported from numerous organizations and countries.

Blake and Mouton developed the now-famous "managerial grid," in which several attempts are made to build an organization on the basis of collaborative effort. The major interventions in the grid approach relate to team building. Teams are built in the organizational structure vertically, horizontally, and diagonally. For example, in the vertical slice, teams from various levels within the same department meet to collaborate on problems. In the horizontal slice, people at the same level from different departments come together to work on problems; in the diagonal slice, people from different departments and different levels meet together to build a team. These team-building efforts eventually lead to goal-setting processes and a reshaping of the organization, resulting in a collaborative effort throughout the organization.

Likert proposes a theory of four types of organizations, which he calls type 1, type 2, type 3, and type 4. These types, broadly speaking, can be labeled authoritarian-exploitative, authoritarian-benevolent, consultative, and participative. The main characteristics of the type-4 organization (the participative or ideal organization) relate to collaborative relationships. In a more recent book, Likert and Likert (1976) report new findings confirming that type-4 organizations can be built through emphasis on collaboration and team building. Out of ten items used to measure human organizational variables, six relate directly to collaboration.

Power-Related Interventions

Unless the people or groups involved in the relationship perceive that all concerned in the situation have power, collaboration cannot emerge. Several interventions can be used to create conditions in which people both perceive and increasingly have power in the system.

Simulation Activities

Several simulation activities or structured experiences such as "Win As Much As You Can" (Pfeiffer & Jones, 1974b) or "Broken Squares" (Pfeiffer & Jones, 1974a) involve power, as participants can withhold any help they can provide to the group; even a small piece withheld prevents the group from achieving the task. Such negative power can be converted into positive power for the attainment of a goal. These activities and others used to simulate competitive and collaborative behavior demonstrate the importance of power very dramatically.

Open Sharing of Feelings

One useful intervention to use in connection with a sense of loss of power or of not having enough power in the system is to allow and encourage people to openly share their feelings about being powerless. Sharing such concerns may help people to become aware that they do in fact have some power, and it is important that they recognize the areas in which they do have power. In most cases this perception is very important. Also, the open sharing of concerns and feelings may help to set norms of sharing in the group.

Role Negotiation

Two important interventions relate to roles. Harrison's (1971) intervention called "role negotiation" is very useful. In the role-negotiation intervention, people negotiate their roles on the basis of mutuality. The basic concept of role negotiation is that people have equal power in the system, and they can make demands in exchange for promises of help. Role negotiation effectively utilizes the fact that people have power of different kinds, can use their power positively by helping others, and in turn can demand functional help themselves.

Role Erosion

Another role-related intervention that can be used to increase power within various roles is called "role erosion" (Pareek, 1975, 1976). This activity helps those who feel that they do not have power in the system or that their power has been eroded as a result of reorganization or redesign of roles. The role occupants meet together and prepare maps to indicate in which areas their power has been eroded; they also identify areas of vacuum. After identifying specific areas in which their power seems to be less, they discuss how more power can be built into their roles or how some hidden power that the role occupant is not able to see may exist in the role. This exercise may lead to role negotiation for building more power.

All interventions that deal with power proceed on the basis that power is not a limited quantum. The more power is shared, the more it increases in the organization. It should be regarded as a multiplying entity. The main question is "How much power is needed in what areas by which role in order to be effective?"

Trust-Building Interventions

With the increasing application of the behavioral sciences to organizational matters, trust-building interventions have been more widely used, both with stranger groups and with organizational groups. The basic assumption behind trust-building interventions is that if one is helped to find out why one trusts or does not trust people, one will be able both to learn to trust and to generate trust in others. Three main interventions are worth mentioning in this area.

Training Groups or Process Groups

In the training group—or T-group as it is more widely known—individuals sit without any agenda and explore issues that may be predominant in the group. Through this process they explore their own personal and interpersonal orientations and help one another to look at their personal and interpersonal effectiveness as well as to plan to improve such effectiveness. The T-group explores the various dimensions of trust building and helps members to test how trust can be built in the group. T-groups generally comprise part of a stronger laboratory setting. If the culture of the organization is fairly closed, the use of the T-group may create problems. But T-groups or process groups have been used effectively to create more trust among members and to build norms of trusting behavior within the organization.

Nonverbal Exercises

More recently, nonverbal exercises have been widely used for building trust. One such exercise is what is called a "trust walk." Half of the members of a group are blindfolded, and each blindfolded person forms a pair with one who is not blindfolded. The latter accompanies the former for several hours and in some cases for the whole day. The person without the blindfold leads the blindfolded one around, helping him or her to go for lunch, to attend to various other necessities, and to explore the environment. Sometimes this experience is very dramatic and has a tremendous impact on people in building trust. Some prework on personal relationships and interpersonal dimensions may need to be done before such a nonverbal exercise is used.

Simulation Activities

Several simulation activities have been used for building trust, especially the "Prisoners' Dilemma" (Pfeiffer & Jones, 1974c). This and "Win As Much As You Can" (Pfeiffer & Jones, 1974b) have both been discussed previously.

Communication Interventions

Collaboration increases when communication channels are open. In an emotionally charged situation when there is some kind of stalemate as a result of negative competition, communication can become blocked and the relationship can degenerate into a lose-lose situation. At such a point communication becomes extremely important. Two interventions are useful in establishing helpful communication.

Simulation Activities

Simulation activities dramatically bring out the usefulness of communication, as mentioned earlier.

Feedback System

Another important way to keep communication open is to encourage giving and receiving negative feedback. In a face-to-face situation, if such feedback is allowed and encouraged, communication channels will continue to remain open. This can be done by legitimizing process review and feedback in a collaborative project from time to time. For example, an hour or so per week can be set aside for sharing feelings and other concerns that various group members have in relation to the work being done.

Team-Development Interventions

Team building is most important because it leads directly to collaboration. A variety of structural and process interventions have been used for this purpose.

Team-Building Laboratories

Special programs for team building are often developed for specific organizations. Alban and Pollitt (1973), for example, have developed what they call a "team building group." They contrast the team-building group with the T-group mainly on the basis that team building is done in the organization with members who will work continually with one another and that more structured activities are used. Although the team-building program is more structured in nature, process data are analyzed. Various simulation activities, theoretical inputs, and task work are used in a four-to-five-day program. The authors report effective changes as a result of such team-building activity.

Several team-building laboratories have been reported by other authors. All of these, whether they emphasize process or rely more on structured material, aim at creating teams of people who have respect for one another and who emerge with strengthened collaborative relationships.

Data Feedback

Team building can also be promoted when data collected by an outside consultant from interviews with various organizational members are used as the basis for the team-building activities. This intervention has been found to be especially useful for top-management team building. The consultant interviews each person who will participate in the team-building program and then writes all of the data anonymously on sheets of newsprint. These sheets are posted on the walls before the meeting starts. The feedback from the interviews helps to stimulate discussions about the problems faced by the group and deliberations about how the team building could be attempted.

Sharing of Feelings

Team building is facilitated when people are allowed to share their feelings about what happens in their groups or in the organization. Even when role negotiation has taken place, there may be residual, unexpressed feelings. Legitimizing discussions of the dimensions generated by sharing of such feelings helps in promoting team building and should be practiced regularly whenever special teams are working on projects.

Image Sharing

This intervention was originally suggested by Blake, Shepard, and Mouton (1964) for increasing role effectiveness. Essentially, the members generate images that they have of one another or of other groups and predict what image the other members or groups have of them. These images are shared. The rationale behind this intervention is that the negative images that people have of one another get in the way of working together. So before mutuality can be established and teamwork can be developed, it is necessary that these images be both shared and cleared.

Role Linkage

One very effective team-building intervention is role linkage (Pareek, 1975). Various role occupants come together to determine the amount of linkage existing among their roles. By analyzing such role linkages (an instrument can also be used for this purpose), members become aware of where role linkages are weak and can then work to improve the linkages, leading to team development.

Joint Problem-Solving Groups

Another effective intervention is to set up groups that have joint responsibility for solving certain problems. The organizational problems should be urgent, and most of the members should be concerned about them.

Initiative-Promoting Interventions

As has been discussed, collaboration develops when someone takes the initiative and the risk to cooperate and opens a way to establish a collaborative relationship. This can be promoted in various ways.

Process Analysis of Simulation Experiences

Simulation activities provide data that can lead to understanding why there was a change toward collaboration. For example, it may be that some individuals took the initiative to turn the situation in a positive direction. This kind of process analysis generally can be done with good results.

Recognizing and Rewarding Initiative

It is also important that the initiative taken by a member or a group to establish collaboration is both recognized and rewarded. This will help to set norms of recognizing collaboration as well as to set examples that others can follow.

CONCLUSION

In conclusion, we can say that to build collaboration in organizations it may be useful to treat collaboration and competition as complementary phenomena and to work toward the development of functional (positive) forms of both. Understanding the bases of collaboration (why people collaborate) may help in designing both structural and process interventions in an organization. The interventions suggested here can be applied in a wide range of organizations.

References

Alban, B.T., & Pollitt, L.I. (1973). Team building. In T.H. Patten (Ed.), *OD: Emerging dimensions and concepts*. New York: American Society for Training and Development.

Blake, R.R., & Mouton, J.S. (1964). *The managerial grid*. Houston, TX: Gulf.

Blake, R.R., Shepard, H.A., & Mouton, J.S. (1964). *Managing intergroup conflict in industry*. Houston, TX: Gulf.

Cartwright, D.P., & Zander, A.F. (Eds.). (1968). *Group dynamics: Research and theory*. New York: Harper & Row.

De, N. (1977). *New forms of work organization in India*. New Delhi, India: National Labour Institute.

De la Porte, P.C.A. (1974). Group norms: Key to building a team. *Personnel, 51*(5), 60–67.

Deutsch, M. (1949). A theory of cooperation and competition. *Human Relations, 2*, 129–152.

Harrison, R. (1971). Role negotiation: A tough minded approach to team development. In W.W. Burke & H.A. Hornstein (Eds.), *The social technology of organization development*. San Francisco, CA: Jossey-Bass/Pfeiffer.

Likert, R. (1961). *New patterns of management*. New York: McGraw-Hill.

Likert, R. (1967). *The human organization: Its management and values*. New York: McGraw-Hill.

Likert, R., & Likert, J.G. (1976). *New ways of managing conflict*. New York: McGraw-Hill.

McClelland, D.C. (1975). *Power: The inner experience*. New York: Irvington.

McClelland, D.C., & Burnham, D.H. (1976). Power is the great motivator. *Harvard Business Review, 54*(2), 100–110.

McClelland, D.C., & Winter, D.C. (1969). *Motivating economic achievement*. New York: The Free Press.

Pareek, U. (1975). *Role effectiveness exercises*. New Delhi, India: Learning Systems.

Pareek, U. (1976). Interrole exploration. In J.W. Pfeiffer & J.E. Jones (Eds.), *The 1976 annual handbook for group facilitators*. San Francisco, CA: Jossey-Bass/Pfeiffer.

Pareek, U. (1977a). *Share or fight: Dynamics of cooperative and competitive behavior*. Ahmedabad, India: Indian Institute of Management.

Pareek, U. (1977b). Some new trends in personnel and OD areas. *Administrative*

Change, 5(1), 26–33.

Pareek, U. (1980). Dimensions of role efficacy. In J.W. Pfeiffer & J.E. Jones (Eds.), *The 1980 annual handbook for group facilitators*. San Francisco, CA: Jossey-Bass/Pfeiffer.

Pareek, U., & Banerjee, D. (1976). Achievement motive and competitive behavior. *Manas, 23*(1), 9–15.

Pareek, U., & Dixit, N. (1977). Effect of partner's response and communication on competitive and cooperative game behavior. *Psychologia, 21,* 38–48.

Pfeiffer, J.W., & Jones, J.E. (Eds.). (1974a). *A handbook of structured experiences for human relations training* (Vol. I). San Francisco, CA: Jossey-Bass/Pfeiffer.

Pfeiffer, J.W., & Jones, J.E. (Eds.). (1974b). *A handbook of structured experiences for human relations training* (Vol. II). San Francisco, CA: Jossey-Bass/Pfeiffer.

Pfeiffer, J.W., & Jones, J.E. (Eds.). (1974c). *A handbook of structured experiences for human relations training* (Vol. III). San Francisco, CA: Jossey-Bass/Pfeiffer.

Rao, T.V. (1976). *Stewart maturity scale.* New Delhi, India: Mtnasayan.

Sherif, M., & Sherif, C.W. (1953). *Groups in harmony and tension.* New York: Harper & Row.

_____

Originally published in The 1981 Annual Handbook for Group Facilitators.

6

Constructive Conflict in Discussions: Learning to Manage Disagreements Effectively

Julia T. Wood

Many cases of ineffective decision making on a national level can be cited: the lack of preparation for the attack of Pearl Harbor; the stalemate in the Korean War; the Bay of Pigs invasion; the repeated and unsuccessful escalations in the Vietnam War; the decision to cover up the Watergate break-in. The faulty decisions reached in these instances were a result of an inadequate process of discussion that did not allow members to voice disagreements and to engage in significant conflict of ideas. If conflict is stifled in groups of national policy makers, it is even more likely to be so in lower-level decision-making groups.

To understand why conflict is so often suppressed in problem-solving groups, it is necessary to consider our conceptions of conflict. Webster (1967) defines conflict as "disagreement. . .war, battle, collision, emotional tension. . .the opposition of persons. . . ." Some typical student definitions of conflict concur: "Conflict happens when members of a group are too closed minded to compromise." "It occurs when someone wants his own way in the group." "Hostility among members." "When there is conflict in a group, somebody loses and somebody else wins." These definitions suggest that conflict is regarded as somewhat negative in nature and, perhaps, as something to be avoided. It is unfortunate that such negative connotations have become associated with conflict because, when it is well managed, conflict is highly constructive; in fact, it is essential to effective problem-solving discussions.

There are, of course, both constructive and disruptive methods of dealing with conflict. Its value in a problem-solving discussion is realized or defeated by the participants' skills in managing it. Learning how to disagree productively is a primary consideration for the training of effective discussants.

Conflict As a Positive Force

Reaching consensus on a solution to a shared problem is a major goal of problem-solving discussions. Before a group can achieve consensus, however, the views of different members must be heard, given fair consideration, and critically evaluated. Conflict or disagreement is a natural and essential part of this process. The very idea of discussion, in fact, presupposes the existence of differing viewpoints regarding the "best" method of resolving a common problem or concern.

Although many textbooks have drawn a distinction between argumentation (which is claimed to be appropriate for public speaking) and cooperative, reflective talk (which is associated with problem-solving discussions) (Brilhart, 1967; Wagner & Arnold, 1965), such a separation is misleading. Argumentation in discussion is important, indeed essential. Sound decisions, the goal of problem-solving discussions, depend on an atmosphere that is conducive to the expression of differing opinions, to the rigorous scrutiny of evidence and implications, and to the thorough consideration of all possible alternative courses of action. A group should encourage these activities, which include disagreements, in order to increase its chances of making sound and well-considered decisions. If a group discourages these activities and muffles disagreements, it is more likely to make superficial or unwise decisions.

Most decisions must be made under uncertain conditions. Relevant information may be unavailable and knowledge about future consequences or implications of the problem and its possible solutions may be, at best, speculative. However, it is possible to increase the probability of making sound choices by realizing that good decisions must grow out of the clash and conflict of divergent ideas and out of the serious consideration of differing alternatives.

The traditional dictum for reflective cooperative talk is, of course, useful, but to rule out the argumentative aspects of discussion is to deny the intensity of deliberation that is necessary for sound decision making.

Outgrowths of Conflict

There appear to be at least three noteworthy reasons for encouraging conflict in problem-solving discussions:

1. By entertaining diverse ideas and perspectives, it is possible to gain a broadened understanding of the nature of the problem and its implications.

2. By encouraging the expression of different ideas, a group has potentially more alternatives from which to select a final solution.

3. The excitement that comes from conflicting ideas stimulates healthy interaction and involvement with the group's task.

The first two reasons affect the group product—decisions; the third reason affects the group process.

A Broadened Understanding

In problem-solving discussions the first objective is to agree on the problem, or concern that prompted the meeting of the group. Although many people assume that this is a simple matter, it is a significant phase in the process of decision making. Superficial attention to this first phase often leads to backtracking later or to conclusions that are based on an inaccurate assessment of the problem and that do not address the real problem.

Thus, in the process of determining the problem, conflict should be urged. It allows for differing perceptions and opinions and, thus, results in a broadened perspective on the problem. Walter and Scott (1973) strongly advocate disagreement during the initial stage of problem solving.

> Disagreement is a prerequisite for purposive discussion, and it may often contribute important junctures during discussion from which the participants can build toward better understanding of problems . . . . Disagreements represent various interpretations to weigh and choose; potentially, therefore, they provide profitable inquiries to pursue. (p. 253)

Only when diverse ideas are encouraged can the group hope to achieve the maximally broad understanding of its problem, and this is fundamental to the remainder of the problem-solving process.

Increased Alternatives

A second reason for encouraging conflict in discussions—perhaps the most recognized and accepted rationale—is that through disagreements members can develop more possible solutions from which to make a final selection. Premature commitment to a solution without adequate awareness or consideration of alternative possibilities is all too frequent—it characterized the national fiascos mentioned earlier. A group whose norm precludes disagreement is not likely to have an array of possible solutions from which to select. In this ease, the group's decision or solution is not one that grows out of serious and open-minded deliberation; rather, it is a careless gamble resulting from superficial discussion. Peter Drucker (1973), who has studied decision making in organizations, maintains that one of the most important functions of disagreement is that it alone can provide alternatives to a decision, and alternatives are necessary for anything other than rash decision making. When a group does not have alternatives, it cannot make a reasoned decision; instead, it simply ratifies the only idea that has been allowed to surface. Sound decisions grow out of the consideration—earnest, reflective consideration—of alternatives, and this may occur only when disagreement and conflict are accepted as a constructive part of the discussion process.

Member Interaction and Involvement

The final reason for advocating conflict in discussions is that it serves to stimulate members' interest in the group and the shared problem. Conflict implies vigorous interaction over ideas, and this increases participants' involvement with the task and enhances the process of decision making. A frequently cited value of discussion as a means of making decisions is that it allows for greater creativity in considering and solving problems. This value, however, rests on the assumption that various opinions and values will be invited and seriously considered by all participants so that creative combinations of ideas may occur. Healthy, noncombative disagreements provide a free and open atmosphere for discussion, and, therefore, members' creative energies are loosed for the good of the process. Extensive observation of organizational decision-making groups has led Hoffman, Harburg, and Maier (1962) to conclude that conflict results in more creative thinking, greater member commitment to a decision, and a higher-quality decision. Creativity seems to thrive on constructive conflict.

Thus it should be clear that conflict is not to be avoided in discussions. On the contrary, it seems to be a positive force that can enhance both the process and the products of problem-solving discussion.

MANAGING CONFLICT EFFECTIVELY

Despite the fact that conflict has some significant values for discussion, everyday experience also tells us that conflict can be dangerous—it can destroy a group, lead to stalemates rather than decisions, and cause major interper-

The Pfeiffer Book of Successful Conflict Management Tools © 2003 *John Wiley & Sons, Inc.*

sonal hostilities. Whether conflict enhances or subverts discussion depends on how the conflict is managed. There are both ineffective and effective methods of dealing with it.

Disruptive Conflict

Distributive or disruptive conflict occurs when participants do not understand the value of conflict and do not have or do not use constructive means of channeling it into deliberations. In a distributive situation there is a competitive climate; members perceive the disagreement as a game in which someone will win and others must lose. There is no integration toward a common goal, no sense of team spirit in which all ideas belong to all participants. "Getting my own way" is more important than finding the best understanding of and solution for the group's common problem. In distributive situations members tend to employ such defense mechanisms as aggression, withdrawal, repression, or projection of blame onto others. Members also tend to become locked into their own viewpoints and are unwilling even to consider the possible value of others' ideas. Frequently, in distributive situations, members will resort to personal attacks instead of focusing their disagreement on the issues.

In this type of situation there are naturally some undesirable effects. The group may form cliques or subgroups within itself. Members will be less likely to understand (or even to try to understand) one another's motives and opinions because hostility and distrust are high. When disruptive conflict penetrates discussion it may be impossible to reach any decision because the group becomes deadlocked and no member is willing to shift his or her position. Even if the group does manage to reach a decision, the group members will seldom be satisfied with it. Distributive conflict, then, is negative in its nature and its effects: It is the kind of conflict that should be avoided since it leads to nothing constructive in the process or products of discussion.

Constructive Conflict

By contrast, integrative or constructive conflict develops when members understand the utility of disagreement and when they have acquired methods of managing conflict effectively. In integrative situations there is high team spirit and commitment to group goals. Members assume that their disagreements stem from sincere involvement with the common problem and that by discussing the differing ideas they will eventually come to an agreement that is better than any one individual's initial suggestions. In integrative situations members are cooperative toward one another. They tend to be supportive of others' ideas and open to considering the merits of opinions different from their own. Disagreements are confined to the issues and do not involve personalities.

The effects of integrative conflict are desirable. Group cohesion is usually increased because members have survived some "rough waters" and have emerged with a sound solution; they also have learned that they can trust one another to be fair and open-minded. Through integrative conflict, members usually are able to reach decisions that they are proud of—the cumulative result is a process and a product that satisfies the whole group. Integrative conflict, then, is highly positive in nature because it improves not only the decisions of a group but also the process by which those decisions are made.

SUMMARY

Conflict is a necessary and integral part of realistic and effective problem-solving discussion. It is the essence of sound decision making because disagreement is the best vehicle for broadening perspectives, discovering alternatives, and stimulating creative interaction among members. The effects of disagreement, however, depend on how it is managed by participants. Conflict can be distributive and disruptive or it can be integrative and constructive. When mismanaged, conflict can destroy a group's effectiveness; when handled well, it can greatly increase the quality of a group's work and make members feel proud of their work in the group.

Training in the nature of conflict and the methods of managing it is a pressing need for all people who participate in problem-solving groups. We need to dispel the negative associations of conflict and replace them with more realistic conceptions that make the legitimate distinction between constructive and disruptive conflict. When participants see that conflict can be a positive force in discussion, they are better prepared to adopt effective personal attitudes and behaviors in problem-solving situations. Further, the differences between distributive and integrative conflict can help them learn how their own behavior contributes to the climate of the group to which they belong.

References

Brilhard, J.K. (1967). *Effective group discussion.* Dubuque, IA: William C. Brown.

Drucker, P.F. (1973). *Management: Tasks, responsibilities, practices.* New York: Harper & Row.

Hoffman, L.R., Harburg, E., & Maier, N.R.F. (1962). Differences and disagreements as factors in creative group problem solving. *Journal of Abnormal and Social Psychology, 64,* 212.

Wagner, R.H., & Arnold, C.C. (1965). *Handbook of group discussion* (2nd ed.). Boston: Houghton Mifflin.

Walter, O.M., & Scott, R.L. (1973). *Thinking and speaking.* New York: Macmillan.

Webster's seventh new collegiate dictionary. (1967). Springfield, MA: G. & C. Merriman.

Originally published in The 1977 Annual Handbook for Facilitators.

7

Dealing with Disruptive People in Meetings

John E. Jones

People who conduct meetings often are troubled by the behavior of a person in attendance who is disrupting the proceedings. It is important for leaders to have a repertoire of responses in such situations in order to maintain control and to accomplish the objectives of the meeting. This article enumerates several methods that can be used to prevent, and to respond effectively to, attempts by individual people to dominate meetings at the expense of the leader. The basic theme in this approach is that the leader should take initiatives to minimize disruptions and to maintain control over meetings when dominating behavior occurs.

People can initiate many forms of disruptive behavior in meetings. Some of the more common ones are the following:

- Interrupting, cutting people off while they are talking;
- Making speeches, especially repetitious discourse;
- Sidetracking, jumping to different topics, changing issues, multiplying concerns;
- Polarizing, pushing people to take sides, attempting to win people over to one point of view;
- Emotionalizing issues, expressing fear or anxiety about probable outcomes;
- Challenging the leader and others with regard to data sources, rights, legalities;
- Expressing sarcasm, claiming that a particular idea will wreak havoc or will never win approval;

- Complaining about the system, meeting, leader, agenda;
- Threatening to withhold support, to resign, to deny responsibility, to seek retribution;
- Accusing the leader of being political, impugning motives;
- Pouting, withdrawing from active participation or controversial topics;
- Saying "Yes, but . . ." a lot, discounting the contributions of others;
- Dampening people's enthusiasm by pointing out all possible failures; and
- Personalizing issues and agenda topics, taking all remarks as directed toward people rather than ideas.

Many of these disruptive behaviors constitute attempts to take over or subvert the leadership of the meeting. Whenever possible the leader needs to anticipate these dominating postures and prevent their occurrence. In addition, the leader needs to be able to respond to disruptions when they occur within a meeting, whether they were anticipated or not; and there are some situations in which the leader needs to resort to drastic methods.

It is assumed in this treatment that the leader establishes the agenda, designs the meeting, and facilitates the meeting process. All of these prerogatives are sources of authority and power for the leader, and it is critical for the leader to have a broad power base from which to deal with disruptive behavior. Of course, that includes maintaining high rapport with the majority of those in attendance at the meeting. It is a good rule not to have meetings for which specific goals cannot be articulated and to avoid having meetings that are highly likely to produce negative results. The leader, then, has objectives and needs strategies, tactics, and techniques to ensure that those objectives are not jeopardized by the disruptive behavior of a dominating person.

PREVENTING DISRUPTIONS

A number of political moves can be made prior to the meeting to attempt to preclude a person's domination of the event. These tactics are meant to keep intact the leader's ability to conduct a productive interchange among members. They are "power plays" in the sense that they are designed to erode the other person's base of support and courage and make it possible to carry out leadership functions. These methods are not necessarily nice, but neither is the disruption of an honest meeting. Eight tactics can be considered by the leader in advance of the meeting:

1. Get the dominator's cooperation for this one meeting. Ask the person to agree not to argue from a fixed (and often familiar) position.

2. Give the person a special task or role in the meeting, such as posting the viewpoints of others.

3. Work out your differences before the meeting (possibly with a third-party facilitator) to present a united front to all other members.

4. Structure the meeting to include frequent discussion of the process of the meeting itself.

5. Take all of the dominator's items off the agenda.

6. Set the person up to be concerned about what might be the consequences of disruption. For example, "It has come to my attention that a number of people are angry with you, and I am thinking about opening up their discussion in the meeting."

7. Ask other people to attend the meeting to support you in dealing with the disruptive person's behavior. For example, they can be asked to refuse to argue with the person, give feeling reactions to the dominating behavior, and confront the dysfunctional behavior directly.

8. Make the person's behavior a published agendum.

Obviously, these methods are manipulative in that they involve deliberate attempts to influence the behavior of another person or persons. People who attempt to dominate meetings have energy that can sometimes be channeled productively, and the best outcome of these preventive postures would be that the person who is often disruptive becomes an effective meeting participant. If these methods are not feasible, the leader needs to have options for keeping control during the meeting itself.

DURING THE MEETING

The leader has two major methods for dealing with disruptive individuals during the course of the meeting: (1) to confront the person directly and attempt to change his or her behavior and (2) to use the group of people present to work with the domination. The important consideration is that the leader must maintain control over what is done and must initiate change. Nine tactics can be used in a direct exchange with the disruptive individual:

1. Interview the person, modeling effective listening. The leader may learn something that is significant to the goals of the meeting by developing the dominating person's perspective, and that person may learn how to contribute to the exchange in a productive manner.

2. Turn all of the dominator's questions into statements. This tactic forces the person to take responsibility for expressing a point of view rather than blocking the process through questions.

3. Point out the win-lose character of debates and refuse to argue.

4. Suggest a role reversal. The person can chair the meeting while you attempt to dominate. The person may also be invited to argue the other side of the issue for a time or may be asked to be silent for ten minutes and report the gist of the interchange.

5. Reflect the dominator's feelings and ignore the person's content input. "You seem particularly upset today, especially when I disagree with you. How are you feeling about my interaction with you right now?"

6. Give emotional responses to the dominator. "I feel powerless to accomplish anything here with you, and I get angry when you try to take over by attempting to force your procedural suggestions on the group."

7. Reduce the person's position to absurdity by interviewing the dominator to the logical extremes of the argument.

8. Agree with all of the person's presentation that is not directly germane to the issue. Agree with the person's need to be heard and supported.

9. Draw out the motives of the dominator and respond to these aims rather than to the content of the presentation.

The leader must be careful to remember that the "audience" for such exchanges can be made anxious by these techniques. The leader can inadvertently put the dominator in an "underdog" position, gaining sympathy from other meeting participants. There is a good chance that others in the meeting are just as annoyed as the leader is about the disruptive behavior, and there are ways to use that situation to maintain control. Five interventions can be considered to that end:

1. Have the meeting participants establish ground rules to avoid polarization. For example, the word "issue" can be made illegal; people have to couch their discussions in terms of problem solving rather than right-wrong, either-or dichotomies.

2. Post all points raised on a given topic, without names. This makes the information available to all and can lessen repetition.

3. Post all contributions made by the dominator and set the expectation that everyone has a responsibility to avoid maneuvering to achieve a personal goal.

4. Create small audiences. Give the dominator only one or two people to influence. Instruct subgroups to generate statements by consensus. Pair people with differing points of view, instruct them to interview each other, and have people report to the entire meeting.

5. Structure an agreement between the dominator and a major opponent. Pick the person whose position is most dissimilar to the dominator's (or ask the dominator to do this). Have this pair discuss the topic for three to five minutes and come to an agreement about one piece of the problem. Other participants sit in a circle around the pair, observe their process, and give them feedback afterward.

Leaders can use the "audience" to control disruptive behavior by encouraging others to be open about their responses to the domination. Sometimes, however, these strategies do not succeed completely, and the leader needs more drastic approaches to consider.

When All Else Fails

When the leader feels that the meeting's purposes are being successfully thwarted by the dominator, he or she must be able to intervene in such a way as to protect the objectives. Three options are available:

1. Create a chaotic condition in the meeting, exaggerating if necessary, and show the group a way out. This often-used political ploy capitalizes on people's need for closure and order, and the dominator's position can often be lost in the process.

2. Adjourn the meeting when the dominator takes over.

3. Leave the meeting when the dominator takes over, disavowing responsibility for what is done.

These three methods are, of course, bold; they should not be chosen unless the situation is clearly dangerous for the leader. The final one, sometimes called the "Gromyko Intervention," because of that leader's penchant for walking out of United Nations sessions, requires follow-through in order to maintain the leader's power.

Caveats

All of these methods require that the leader adopt a cool, unruffled posture. Becoming angry means giving away power, and the leader of a meeting needs to focus detached attention on managing the situation in the light of the purposes established for the event. Using many of these techniques in rapid succession can result in "overkill," and the leader needs to make certain that the motive is not to punish a person but to promote functional behavior.

Leaders who use these tactics as a matter of routine style even when they are inappropriate become sources of disruption themselves in that they prevent meeting participants from having the opportunity to influence the discussion. Too-frequent use of these methods can intimidate meeting participants who are less bold than dominators, and the result can be that they contribute less to the meeting out of fear of being confronted.

Disruptive behavior in meetings is almost always a symptom of some defect in the organizational system that the meeting is designed to support. Leaders need to consider that every meeting is, in reality, an organization development session and should be facilitated in ways that isolate problems for remedial action.

Reference

Christie, R. (1978). Mach V attitude inventory. In J.W. Pfeiffer & J.E. Jones (Eds.), *The 1978 annual handbook for group facilitators*. San Francisco, CA: Pfeiffer.

Originally published in The 1980 Annual Handbook for Group Facilitators.

8

Confrontational Communication

Merna L. Skinner

Abstract: Communicating with an angry person should
not be a competition or verbal volley that gathers mo-
mentum until someone "wins." Effective communicators shift the exchange from the emotional to the
rational. A person's power to disarm the emotions of
an antagonist lies in his or her initial ability to understand the nature and causes of anger. The effective
person then connects on a visceral level, as a person,
not as a corporate functionary. Next, effective communicators ask permission to provide information,
which gives the angry person perceived control over
the situation. Finally, by explaining or offering choices,
the effective communicator lays out options and further reduces emotion, replacing it with agreements.

INTRODUCTION

Communicating with an angry person is one of the most difficult business challenges a manager can face. Whether the angry person is a fellow employee, a
client, or an outside third party, being on the receiving end of heightened
emotions is stressful. The challenge of someone pounding a fist, shouting, or

making strong vocal demands forces the recipient to gather all his or her skills in order to respond.

When face-to-face with a hostile person, the natural human response is to respond in kind—to match the level of agitation in order to "stay even." In most professional situations, however, this is not an effective strategy. If you match hostility with hostility, the cycle will only perpetuate itself. The key to breaking this cycle is to establish *mutual understanding*. By finding a common ground of understanding, you can unlock the conflict and begin to build communication step by step.

In most meetings that managers attend, the content and subject matter are usually neutral in nature. Attendees typically establish a conversational rhythm that proceeds in a "give-and-take" pattern. Issues are brought up, discussed, and resolved. But when individuals come to meetings with private grievances or groups of people ban together with lists of grievances, we consider these individuals or groups as "needy." When faced with such a situation, the manager must communicate both an understanding of the grievances and a willingness to collaborate to address them.

The most extreme and challenging situation is when individuals or groups are not only needy, but also highly emotional. These situations call for a show of humanity. You must be willing to hear the other person's concerns. Once an emotionally charged person sees that you are listening and concerned, the anger will likely begin to dissipate. With the anger out of the way, you can shift the discussion to collaboration and a resolution of the issues.

To calm a hostile person and create understanding between divergent thinkers, the following four-step process is useful:

1. Inquire
2. Empathize
3. Ask permission
4. Explain or offer choices

INQUIRE

During the "inquire" phase, employ active listening skills. Focus and fully concentrate on the other person's issues and concerns. Ask open-ended questions, nod, take brief notes, and maintain eye contact as much as possible. The goal during this stage is to let the other person talk. Trying to interrupt

The Pfeiffer Book of Successful Conflict Management Tools © 2003 John Wiley & Sons, Inc.

before the person has gotten it all out is counterproductive and will only delay a resolution of the conflict.

If you are in a larger group, be sure to solicit representative opinions from as many others as possible. Although there is no way you can always poll everyone, being attuned to different points of view will build your credibility as someone committed to knowing the full extent of the issues.

EMPATHIZE

To "empathize" means to connect with someone on his or her emotional level. Empathy is not typically shown in our day-to-day business conversations; however, empathy is essential to success in an emotionally charged situation. It can best be communicated by employing a two-step process:

1. "I" to "You": This first step toward empathy simply communicates that "I" relate to how "you" feel. To do this effectively, name the emotion the person is feeling. For example:

Relate to the Person	Name of the Emotion
I appreciate	your frustration
I understand	your doubt
I share	your concern

2. "I, Too": The second step is empathizing with the person to let him or her know that you, too, feel or have in the past felt the same way. Key phrases that accomplish this are:

   - "I also felt the way you do."
   - "I, too, have felt that way."
   - "I, too, would want to know the same thing if I were in your position."

Managing the other person's emotions at this point is about continuing to let the person calm down. Respond to high pitched or loud remarks quietly and calmly. The contrast in volume and tone will dissipate the intensity and emotionality of the situation. In the same way, if the angry person is gesturing wildly or pacing up and down, remain still and composed. Consistently applied calm responses are a powerful means of calming an antagonist down.

It may take some time to establish empathy with an angry person. He or she may at first reject what you say as "lip service." Only when you have sincerely communicated that you really see how he or she feels can you move to the next step.

ASK PERMISSION

The natural inclination when someone has verbally attacked you is to retaliate with a quick and self-protective response. Resist this "knee jerk" reaction; instead, ask whether or not the other person would like to hear some information. By specifically requesting permission, you are putting the angry person in control—hence decreasing his or her tension. Here are some examples of appropriate language to use:

- "Would it be helpful for you to know what we have done in this area thus far?"
- "What information can I provide you?"
- "Would it be helpful to you if we . . . ?"

If your listener says "no" to all of these questions, you can then ask: "What, then, would be helpful?" All of these permission questions communicate that you are a reasonable person doing your best to reach a common ground of understanding. Once your listener says "yes," you can proceed to the final step.

EXPLAIN OR OFFER CHOICES

When you have permission to explain something, keep the explanation short and simple. You may also ask other questions to confirm your understanding. If an explanation of some sort is not appropriate, you may want to offer the angry person choices. For example:

- "Do you want to see our analysis of the situation next Tuesday or next Thursday?"
- "Would seeing the plans or the actual figures help you?"

The Pfeiffer Book of Successful Conflict Management Tools © 2003 John Wiley & Sons, Inc.

The more choices you give the other person, the greater his or her sense of control will be. Knowing that there really are ways to resolve the issue will lessen the angry person's hostility. When he or she is in a more neutral and rational state, you can start to solve the problem together.

Note that this model for defusing anger does not always move in a simple and linear fashion. You may find yourself in a situation in which some residual anger surfaces just when you thought the problem had been solved. You may have to cycle through the model again or spend a longer time on an individual step. It is likely, for example, that the angry person may take quite a long time to vent his or her initial anger. Remembering that anger is essentially fear turned inside out, you must let the other person express the anger before you can move forward. In the same way, you may succeed in laying out options—but none will be acceptable. The other person's frustration may mount again, so be prepared to let him or her talk about it before attempting to lay out other options.

CONCLUSION

Remember that your success in dealing with an angry person lies in your ability to communicate with sincerity, consistency, and flexibility. He or she should know that what you are saying and how you say it are coming from the heart, not the head. Establishing a consistent pattern of responses—clear, focused, and simple—will give the angry person more security. Remember that being flexible means not being so structured or verbally disciplined that you are not prepared to address new issues that come up.

Originally published in The 2001 Annual, Vol. 2, Consulting.

9

A Positive Approach to Resistance

H.B. Karp

In most modern organizations there is a strong value system that stresses the need for collaboration, cooperation, and trust. Although this viewpoint certainly has much to recommend it, a problem has arisen in that this emphasis on "positive" reactions leads to a tendency to discount "negative" reactions such as competition, anger, and resistance. The reality is that there are no inherently negative reactions.

Given the proper circumstances, every human reaction has the potential to be expressed in an appropriate and effective manner. To discount any reaction when human interaction is concerned is to limit resources and to reduce the range of alternatives that are available. Such limitation is hardly a prescription for individual or organizational growth and effectiveness. There is a time to listen and a time not to listen, a time for contemplation and a time for action, and a time to grow and a time to stand firm. It is always the situation that determines what is appropriate, what is effective, and sometimes even what is ethical.

The reaction that probably is most under fire today is resistance. If cooperation is seen as a universally good reaction, then resistance as its opposite is usually seen as bad or negative. Everyone has heard admonitions such as "Don't be defensive," "You've got to learn to compromise," or "You're thinking of your own welfare." Employees need to know when to express resistance, how to express it appropriately so that the results are positive for all of those concerned, and how to deal with another person's resistance.

The ability to resist can be seen as a personal asset in that it keeps one from being hurt and from overloading oneself. It also allows one to make clearer choices about what is good for oneself, and it helps in blocking out unimportant distractions that would hinder the achievement of one's goals. Resistance also can be seen as an organizational asset in that it allows systems to differentiate talent, provides new information about what might not work well, and produces a lot of needed energy.

Because resistance has traditionally been disparaged, most managers tend to use one or more of the following low-yield strategies to deal with it:

1. *Breaking it down.* The attempt to break down resistance is usually carried out by threatening, coercing, selling, or reasoning.

2. *Avoiding it.* This strategy is pursued through deflection, "not hearing," or attempting to induce guilt.

3. *Discounting it.* This approach involves dismissing the resistance as unimportant, promoting tradition as the alternative to the resistance, or appealing to the resister's need to conform.

Although the low-yield strategies may work to some degree in that they may evoke positive responses from resisters for the moment, they rarely provide lasting solutions and are often quite costly. In some cases, such as with threats and attempts to induce guilt, they may even produce more and deeper resistance at a later time.

DEALING POSITIVELY WITH RESISTANCE

Two basic assumptions underlie a positive approach to dealing creatively with resistance:

1. *Resistance is.* People will always resist, knowingly or not, those things that they perceive as not in their best interests.

2. *Resistance needs to be honored.* It must be dealt with in a respectful manner.

If resistance is handled from a perspective that incorporates these two assumptions, it becomes an organizational asset and can enhance rather than injure a relationship between any two employees, be they supervisor and subordinate, peers, or line and staff. Another condition must exist in order for the positive approach to work: The demander—the individual who confronts the resister—must be absolutely clear about what he or she wants from the resister and must be as specific as possible in relating this information to the resister. When the demand is stated in terms of time frames, specific outcomes, potential benefits, concrete behaviors that are needed, and so forth, the probability that the demander will achieve compliance from the resister is great. Even if compliance is not possible, the resistance will become more workable.

The positive approach consists of four separate steps: (1) surfacing, (2) honoring, (3) exploring, and (4) rechecking. Each step should be completed before moving to the next step.

Surfacing the Resistance

After the demander has clearly stated what he or she wants from the other party, the first—and probably most difficult—step is to get the resistance out in the open. Many people intentionally withhold their resistance for a number of reasons: experience with a past heavy emphasis on the low-yield strategies, mistrust, a poor interpersonal relationship, or a lack of awareness of their own resistance. The surfacing of resistance can be approached easily and effectively by keeping two guidelines in mind:

1. *Make the expression of resistance as "safe" as possible.* The demander should state clearly—and publicly, if possible—that he or she wants to hear the resistance. It is a good idea to include an explanation of why the resistance is important and to be straightforward. Once the resister is aware that he or she is not going to be attacked, punished, or "sold" on what the demander wants, the demander has a much greater chance of exposing the real source of the resistance.

2. *Ask for all of it.* Listening to a resister's statement of what he or she does not like about the very thing that the demander wants is rarely a pleasant experience. Nevertheless, it is the best approach to resistance. When the resistance exists, it is much better to hear all of it than to try to work through the situation in partial ignorance.

Honoring the Resistance

Honoring involves the following process:

1. *Listen.* When a person states resistance openly, he or she provides the demander with a vital source of information about what the demander wants and the potential pitfalls in achieving what is wanted. In addition, the resister is making a personal statement about who he or she is. Any attempt to discount the information not only stops the information but also carries a clear message to the resister that his or her opinion does not matter; the resister will interpret this to mean that he or she does not

matter. It is of critical importance at this stage that the demander make no attempt to reinforce his or her original position, to sell, to reason, or in any way to imply that the resister should not feel as he or she does. The correct approach is simply to listen.

2. *Acknowledge the resistance.* The act of acknowledgment does not imply that the demander agrees with the point of resistance. It is a simple affirmation of the resister's right to resist. Statements such as "I see how that could be a problem for you" or "You certainly have a right to be concerned" allow the demander to respond to the resister's concern without relinquishing anything. The demander should acknowledge the resistance, but not agree with it.

3. *Reinforce the notion that it is permissible to resist.* The demander should keep in mind that openly resisting in a safe environment may be a new experience for the resister. Periodically reinforcing that the resistance is valuable and that the resister is safe and appreciated for stating his or her resistance creates a positive atmosphere. Statements such as "It's really all right that you don't like all of this" or "I can see why you are angry" maintain the demander's control of the situation while making the environment continually safe for the resister.

Exploring the Resistance

Exploring involves the following tasks:

1. *Distinguish authentic resistance from pseudo resistance.* Authentic resistance is directed toward the specific demand that has been made; pseudo resistance is real but has nothing to do with the demand. Pseudo resistance usually originates in feelings such as resentment of authority, old grudges, the need for attention, and lack of clarity about one's desires. The demander's task is to uncover the authentic resistance. If the demander is having difficulty determining which kind of resistance is manifesting itself, he or she can simply ask the resister, "What is your objection?" The resister either will or will not be able to state clearly what the specific objection is. It is best to address the cause of the pseudo resistance later rather than at the moment unless it is blocking progress.

2. *Probe the resistance.* Once the resistance has been surfaced, honored, and judged authentic and the resister has realized that he or she is safe, the demander can help the resister to assume a proactive stance by simply asking, "What would you prefer?" In responding to this question, the resister works with the demander *toward* the objective rather than against it. The

resister will suggest alternative approaches to meeting the demand in ways that provide the demander with what is wanted and permit the resister to obtain something for himself or herself at the same time. At this point it is a good idea to encourage negotiation and to keep in mind that something must change positively for the resister in order for the resistance to be permanently reduced. The end point of probing should be the development of some kind of agreement about the action to be taken.

Rechecking

Before the meeting is over, the last step is to recheck the status of the current resistance and the agreements that have been made. This step is essential because it provides closure to the issue and ensures that no agreement will be forgotten. If there is to be a second meeting, rechecking provides a basis on which to start the next meeting so that the entire process of dealing with the resistance does not have to be repeated.

CONCLUSION

The demander should always keep the following points in mind when confronted with a resister:

1. The objective is not to eliminate *all* resistance because it is not possible to do so. Instead, the objective is to work with and reduce the *needless* resistance. The reduction is usually enough to allow proceeding with the demand effectively.

2. Always keep paper and pencil handy to make notes during the process. When the problem is recorded, the resister's objection is honored and there is less chance that important points will be forgotten. Making notes also facilitates the last step, rechecking.

3. Once the resistance is at a workable level, thank the resister and move on. It is important not to try to persuade the resister to *like* the demand. It is enough that the resister is willing to agree to it.

This approach has universal application. It can be used in any situation in which resistance is an issue, such as in managing conflict, scheduling work, or raising teenagers.

Originally published in The 1988 Annual: Developing Human Resources.

10

Breaking Down Boundaries: Breaking Through Resistance

Ron Ashkenas

Abstract: As the 21st Century dawns, the new drivers of competitive success are speed, flexibility, integration, and innovation. Gaining ground in any of these areas almost always requires making organizational boundaries more permeable. Boundaryless organizations are those which have loosened up the vertical boundaries between levels of the hierarchy, horizontal walls between functional areas, external barriers between members of the value chain, and geographic boundaries between home and abroad.

Boundaryless behavior is the art of the fluid. Consultants, external and internal, are challenged to help their clients break away from rigid thinking, old categories, and habitual patterns of behavior. To meet this challenge, they must break out of their own boxes and design learning experiences that are innovative and responsive to changing needs.

For much of the 20th Century, the success of organizations has been a function of their ability to grow in size, achieve role clarity, specialization, and control. Sears, IBM, General Motors, Digital Equipment Corporation, Eastman Kodak, and other respected companies have prospered. However, as the century draws to a close, the advent of the microprocessor, the dizzying speed of information processing and communications, and the arrival of the global economy have conspired to shift the basis of competitive success radically. Faced with a rate of change that in many cases has exceeded their ability to respond, these organizations have faltered and their profitability has suffered. But other companies, included Wal-Mart, GE Capital, and Microsoft, have been able to capitalize on these forces of change. Instead of relying on size, role clarity, specialization, and control to ensure their success, these companies offered a superior level of speed, flexibility, integration and innovation.

These four factors have emerged as the new success drivers that organizations must master to survive. The key to developing these capabilities is the extent to which businesses can ensure that ideas, resources, expertise, talent, and technical advances flow to where they are needed rapidly and easily.

The effectiveness of this resource flow is in turn determined by the presence or absence of organizational boundaries. Vertical boundaries divide one level in an organizational hierarchy from other levels and impede the communication from one to another. Horizontal boundaries trap information and ideas in functional silos. External boundaries separate one organization from another, preventing partners in a value chain from cooperating to solve problems or make better use of resources. Geographic boundaries created by distance and cultural difference make it difficult to transfer resources and learning from one place to another. But companies that have mastered the new drivers of success have been able to lower these boundaries, work across them, make them more permeable.

These companies can be termed "boundaryless." Tearing down the walls has not happened quickly or easily, but iteratively and cumulatively. The learning and confidence gained from taking the first steps have been the foundation for taking bigger and bolder steps.

Boundary breaking feels scary because boundaries have traditionally defined organizations. Rearranging the lines of demarcation—between managers and employees, between departments, between the company and its customers, between home and abroad—hits people where they live. They no longer have the safety of knowing who's who and what's what, and often a kind of organizational immune response kicks in. Resistance, both overt and covert, emerges.

Some years ago, a senior manager at a manufacturing company decided that the workers in a newly acquired machine-building plant should be reshaped into a "high performance" workforce. He brought in a new plant manager who believed in empowerment and set out immediately to make it happen. The plant manager removed all time cards from the factory and put the employees on salary. This was meant to be a gesture of goodwill, but the employees did not see it that way. They strenuously objected to having the time cards removed, seeing the gesture as a ploy to keep them from earning overtime pay.

This story has an unhappy ending. A union campaign was launched. Within months the plant manager was gone. The employees were deeply mistrustful of management. The dream of a model, high-performance plant went down in flames. The immune system did its work, and the boundaries, instead of becoming permeable, were more fortified than before.

Success at boundary busting does not often come from abstract concepts like "empowerment" or grand designs for creating "high performance work forces." Rather, the process is driven by concrete business needs. Something has to be done soon, and it can't be done using the old structures and processes. To achieve a measurable result, something has to give, and that something is often a traditional boundary.

Those of us in consulting, training, and developmental roles are often in a position to cut through the resistance, get the ball rolling, and jump in with the particular learning experiences that enable people to work in fast and integrated ways. We, too, must be flexible and innovative in our designs for developing the competencies that our organizations need to be competitive now. We need to be both creative and responsive in deciding when and where some specific skills training, a "stretch" challenge, a retreat, or boot camp experience will make a meaningful, measurable difference. Here we offer many examples of steps that companies have taken to become more boundaryless.

In our experience, it is unwise, even impossible, to tackle vertical, horizontal, external, and geographic barriers all at once. Boundaryless behavior tends to spread because success breeds success, so the best place to start is wherever will make the most positive difference in the bottom line.

TOWARD A HEALTHY HIERARCHY

Everyone knows the downside of traditional command-and-control hierarchies. It takes too long to make decisions, respond to customer requests and complaints, and adapt to changing market conditions. Progress is difficult because so much is invested in the way things have always been done. Creative people are viewed as subversive, and new ideas rarely see the light of day. Employees often feel unappreciated and unrewarded and don't put forth the effort and loyalty they are capable of. Ultimately, customers don't like dealing with the organization either.

Although everyone knows that the military hierarchical model is no longer in any company's best interests, changing it is a slow and difficult process. By now it has become clear that lopping out layers doesn't automatically create a healthy organization, nor does sharing information, decisions, and rewards necessarily mean that employees are happy and productive. Many companies have also learned through experience that not all employees want to be "empowered" and that not all middle managers resist spreading the authority and control around.

It has always been evident that training is essential for changing people's attitudes. If people at all the levels below the executive suite are going to have more responsibility and more authority, they need a much better understanding of the company's overall direction and strategy, and they need to acquire and develop new skills. But training alone cannot dispel the old patterns of top-down decision making and central control.

Chase Manhattan Bank, for example, spent enormous amounts of money training corporate lending professionals in the mid-1980s around a shift from standard commercial products, such as loans, to sophisticated investment banking products, such as advisory services and financial engineering. Chase Manhattan then had a group of relationship managers who knew all about investment banking products. Unfortunately, they had no information system to support the new products, and they were still measured and rewarded on the basis of corporate loans and still subject to a decision-making process that required deals to be evaluated on the same credit-risk parameters they had always used.

When employees are trained and competent to act in new ways, but not allowed to act on that competence, frustration flares up, but walls don't come down.

Training is necessary *but not sufficient* for rewiring hierarchies. It's also necessary to have a two-way flow of information, authority to act close to where decisions need to be made, and rewards that reinforce performance. The St. Louis branch of Farm Credit Bank mustered all those elements when it hit a rough spot. At one point, Farm Credit's loan portfolio was greater than the value of the farm land on which the loans were based. Instead of blaming the loan agents, the bank gave them what they needed to work in the best interests of both the bank and the customers. The loan agents were provided with detailed information about the status of each farmer's loan, so they could work with the farmers to meet their obligations. They were given special training in how to work with customers in a cooperative way during a crisis. They were given the authority to devise individual plans to help each farmer work his or her way out of financial trouble, and they had the authority to foreclose, if that was the only option. The loan agents were rewarded not only on how quickly they resolved loan issues, but also on the quality of their relationships with the farmers. The upshot was that farmer morale around St. Louis was much higher than in the bank's other branches; the branch solidified its relationship with its customers and paved the way to future business.

GOING BEYOND TURF AND TERRITORY

Horizontal boundaries are almost as ingrained in our minds as vertical boundaries. Specialties and subspecialties have been proliferating in organizations for decades and, to a point, dividing up tasks this way promotes efficiency and prevents redundancy. Functional groupings also appeal to the natural tendency of people to want to congregate and bond with their own kind and make it easier for employees of large organizations to feel a sense of belonging.

But when horizontal boundaries are too rigid, the process of handing a project from one department to the next, all down the line, takes too long. Employees become caught up in protecting and defending their own turf. Organizational goals become subordinated to departmental goals. And when a company has many divisions and products, a customer may wind up dealing with a dozen different representatives and receiving conflicting advice and information.

When horizontal boundaries are this haywire, the biggest obstacle to change is usually employee mind-set. Words such as "not my department" and "those guys" linger on, even when cross-functional teams and task forces are established.

A good first step for overcoming resistance to horizontal change is to create new mental models to replace the old. For example, executives at World Bank, as part of a major change effort in 1994, recognized that the human resource function had to be aligned better with operations. Human resources was going to have to be much more flexible and able to pull together a variety of disciplines and tools to meet changing needs of operations managers and staff. Because the basic HR approach had been in place for years, this idea was met with skepticism and confusion. The HR people could not visualize what the management group had in mind. To create a new mental model, groups of HR professionals and their internal clients at the bank visited Chase Manhattan Bank, Northern Telecom, Hewlett-Packard, and other organizations that were already using flexible HR teams in the ways envisioned by World

Bank's management. These site visits, and subsequent discussions about them, helped management refine its thinking and generated enough support to move the new structure along.

It is vitally important to teach teamwork, to set up measures of shared success, to reward people for sharing resources, and to restructure smoothly across functions, but conceptual learning is a good first step. Most people need a new vision before they can drive out old, reflexive ideas and habits.

Toward Partnership with Customers and Suppliers

The idea of cozying up to suppliers and customers is new and, to many people, strange. Every-company-for-itself is the time-honored attitude, and the weight of legal tradition supports this, as each piece of the value chain looks out for itself and tries to maximize its own profits, even at the expense of suppliers and customers.

This attitude in untenable in the fast-paced modern world. As product life cycles shrink, global competition heats up, the cost of product development shoots up, customers demand more, and everything moves faster, companies see that they can no longer work alone. They need to join forces to drive new technologies, expand distribution, enter new markets, ensure sources of supply, and match end-user expectations.

Obviously, sharing information with potential partners—who may well be your competitors in other arenas—is not easy. Partnerships are increasingly necessary, but they are also fraught with peril; horror stories abound. But when companies coordinate their operational planning and accounting and measurement systems, when they solve common problems together, and when they can share resources, enormous gains in speed, flexibility, integration, and innovation can be made.

At the individual employee's level, the main obstacle to this kind of co-operation is simply ignorance. Most employees don't get out much. Suppliers and customers are, at best, voices on the phone. Strengthening the value chain begins with getting acquainted with those outside the company.

A very easy first step is to bring in speakers from the companies in the value chain. Ask a supplier or customer representative to organize a talk around these questions:

- How does my business work?
- Who are our customers and competitors?
- What are our goals?

- What do we need to do differently?

- What changes in the market are we losing sleep over? What are the risks and problems?

- How can we do business together in more effective ways?

- If we were one company instead of two, what would we do differently?

- What could we do to reduce transaction costs, eliminate paperwork, or speed up cycle time?

Another way to begin the process is to take employees to visit some of the other companies. Allied Chemical Fibers (now AlliedSignal Fibers) took this approach in connection with a plant-wide quality effort. Two bus loads of hourly and middle-management people from the company's plant in Columbia, South Carolina, went to visit a customer's carpet mill. The mill workers showed them how certain fiber quality defects shut down their knitting machines. Until then the Allied employees had not thought about how their work affected other people. Once they got back, they immediately went to work on reducing defects, without a lot of prodding from management. Everyone pitched in with suggestions, and defect levels began dropping in a matter of weeks. Over the next year, the company visited other customers and reduced costs by eliminating several recurring quality problems—also boosting customer satisfaction.

When employees hear from the customers themselves and actually see the impact of their work, the value chain becomes real to them. Whether or not members of the chain become formal or strategic partners, "getting to know you" experiences like this pay off powerfully.

Toward the Global Corporation

Global reach has quickly become a new business standard. For many companies, "going global" is a matter of competitive survival. Newer technologies such as videoconferencing and e-mail have made this kind of expansion easier and more compelling. The challenges for breaking through global boundaries include establishing a workable global structure, hiring global supermanagers, designing unifying mechanisms to create a global mind-set, and overcoming a whole new level of complexity.

It is crucial to lay the groundwork, beginning with HR practices, the most basic of which is to sensitize people to the world beyond their doors. Foreign language training is also necessary, although English is the international language of business. Employees who will be working with people in other countries need at least enough proficiency in the language of the country to get along in social situations.

A second basic requirement is cultural awareness. Attitudes and values, business practices, etiquette, and social customs vary greatly from one part of the world to another. Violating the rules and rituals of another country, however unknowingly, can have disastrous repercussions.

Travel is usually the next step, usually fact-finding missions and discussions, and living abroad. Consider what Samsung, South Korea's largest company, did. The company sent about four hundred of its brightest young employees to "goof off" in other countries for a year. Those who came to the United States were encouraged to hang out at malls, watch television, observe consumer behavior, and travel around the country.

SUMMARY

Many innovative individuals and companies are moving a step at a time to overcome boundaries and to increase the flow of ideas, resources, and expertise within organizations. Each example presented here has demonstrated an openness to new ideas and the courage to challenge long-held assumptions about what success is, who can learn from whom, and how change occurs. Each has shown willingness to give up some control and certainty for the sake of achieving a faster, more flexible, more innovative organization.

All of us who are instrumental in moving our clients toward boundaryless behavior must confront our own walls and boxes. To lead the journey we need not only to overcome the natural resistance in our organizations, but also to overcome our own needs for control, clarity, and certainty.

Originally published in The 2000 Annual, Vol. 2, Consulting.

Part 2
Experiential Learning Activities

Experiential learning activities are exercises in which people learn by doing something as opposed to just listening to a lecture or watching a demonstration. Since to date no substitute has been found for practicing the skill you're trying to learn, or for witnessing, directly, the truth of a lesson someone is trying to impart, experiential activities have special power as a training method.[1]

Chosen from thirty years of the Pfeiffer *Annuals* as the best activities pertaining to conflict management, the learning experiences in this section of the handbook are designed as complete packages. Each includes full instructions for the facilitator and participants, as well as all necessary handouts. Each includes suggested variations the facilitator might find useful (you also are welcome to create your own variations). And each includes questions to be asked and discussed in order to ensure that learning took place.

The recommended group size and time required for each activity are listed, as are the learning goals each one was designed to meet. (Note: You

---

[1]The special power of experiential learning activities is a double-edged sword; they also have special dangers. This is not the place for a discussion of caveats, but trainers who lack experience in the use of such activities are strongly urged to read the "Introduction" to the *Reference Guide to Handbooks and Annuals* (1999 Edition). It presents the theory behind the experiential-learning cycle and explains the need to complete each phase of the cycle to allow effective learning to occur.

are better positioned than any exercise's creator to determine whether it will suit the needs of your particular group.)

The activities adopt several different formats and processes. Some are games, some are problem-solving exercises, some are role plays, and some delve directly into actual conflicts, taking their material from real issues facing real individuals in the training room.

Conflict management is always about people, in the plural, but to aid the reader in sorting through the twenty activities we have organized them into three sections: Conflict and the Team, Conflict and the Individual, and Conflict and the Organization. The categories are somewhat arbitrary and the boundaries admittedly get blurry, but here's what we have in mind:

- Section 1, Conflict and the Team, includes activities we believe you most likely will use with an intact work team (or a group of people who work closely together). The learning goals have to do mainly with conflict and collaboration within a working group.

- Section 2, Conflict and the Individual, includes activities that focus on building broad-based conflict-management skills in individual participants or on specific situations such as meetings and performance reviews.

- Section 3, Conflict and the Organization, includes activities designed for two or more different work groups and those that teach lessons about coping with the politics of conflict outside one's own team.

The Pfeiffer Book of Successful Conflict Management Tools © 2003 John Wiley & Sons, Inc.

Conflict and
the Team

Some of the experiential learning activities in this section focus directly on the dynamics of conflict, collaboration, and trust in an intact team or working group. Others address organizational conflict in ways we suspect many facilitators will find particularly well-suited to intact groups.

Please do not misunderstand. Only two of these exercises, "What to Look for in Groups" and "Current Status," are designed *exclusively* for intact teams. Also, if you're hunting for an activity to serve the needs of a particular team, don't limit your search to this section. The work team is ground zero for conflict-management issues in modern organizations, and many exercises in the following two sections are perfectly appropriate for intact teams. We suggest simply that for many common team needs, you might want to examine some of these seven exercises first.

- What to Look for in Groups: An Observation Guide—Provides a structured way for a team to monitor its ongoing health along several dimensions.

- Conflict Styles: Organizational Decision Making—Participants experience different approaches to conflict management, and discuss which ones are appropriate in different situations.

- Win As Much As You Can: An Intergroup Competition—A game in which participants slowly discover that you win more by collaborating than by competing.

- Power Poker: What's in It for Me?—A more elaborate game leading to the discovery that collaboration beats competition—and that collaboration requires trust.

- Trouble in Manufacturing: Managing Interpersonal Conflict—Role players experience the results of unproductive behaviors in situations where consensus is needed.

- Dynasell: Hidden Agendas and Trust—Role players experience the effects of distrust on their group's effort to complete a task.

- Current Status: A Feedback Activity on Trust—Members of an intact work team confront and explore the degree to which they trust one another.

1

What to Look for in Groups:
An Observation Guide

Philip G. Hanson

Goal

- To assist group members in understanding and being more perceptive about group process.

Group Size

Two subgroups of at least ten members each.

Time Required

Three hours.

Materials

- A copy of the What to Look for in Groups handout for each participant.
- Paper and pencil for each member.

Physical Setting

A large room with movable chairs.

Process

1. The facilitator distributes the handout and leads a thirty-minute theory session on group process based on the material in the handout.

2. The facilitator asks the group members to number off, one through ten (and begin with one again if there are more than ten members in a single subgroup). He or she assigns the "ones" the section in the handout entitled "Participation," "twos" the section entitled "Influence," etc.

3. The facilitator then divides the participants into two subgroups (A and B), ensuring that all ten sections are represented in each subgroup. He or she explains that each subgroup will complete some appropriate task that will provide the subgroups with "group process" to observe, each member observing in terms of his or her assigned section of the handout.

4. Group A completes an assigned task while Group B observes. This phase of the experience should take no more than thirty minutes.

5. The facilitator asks Group B to give feedback to Group A based on the handout. (Approximately fifteen minutes.)

6. Group A is given ten minutes in which to respond to the feedback from Group B.

7. The facilitator asks everyone to take a fifteen-minute break.

8. The experience resumes with Group A observing Group B completing an assigned task, Group A giving feedback to Group B, and Group B responding to the feedback with the same time indications as above.

Each subgroup processes the feedback from the entire experience separately. The facilitator may move between subgroups to observe and assist in the processing of feedback.

Originally published in The 1972 Annual Handbook for Group Facilitators.

What To Look For In Groups

In all human interactions there are two major ingredients—content and process. The first deals with the subject matter or the task on which the group is working. In most interactions, the focus of attention of all persons is on the content. The second ingredient, process, is concerned with what is happening between and to group members while the group is working.

Group process, or dynamics, deals with such items as morale, feeling tone, atmosphere, influence, participation, styles of influence, leadership struggles, conflict, competition, cooperation, etc. In most interactions, very little attention is paid to process, even when it is the major cause of ineffective group action. Sensitivity to group process will better enable one to diagnose group problems early and deal with them more effectively. Because these processes are present in all groups, awareness of them will enhance a person's worth to a group and enable him or her to be a more effective group participant.

Following are some observation guidelines to help one analyze group process behavior.

1. Participation

One indication of involvement is verbal participation. Look for differences in the amount of participation among members.

- Who are the high participators?
- Who are the low participators?
- Do you see any shift in participation, e.g., highs become quiet; lows suddenly become talkative. Do you see any possible reason for this in the group's interaction?
- How are the silent people treated? How is their silence interpreted? Consent? Disagreement? Lack of interest? Fear? etc.
- Who talks to whom? Do you see any reason for this communication pattern in the group's interactions?
- Who keeps the ball rolling? Why? Do you see any reason for this in the group's interactions?

2. Influence

Influence and participation are not the same. Some people may speak very little, yet they capture the attention of the whole group. Others may talk a lot but are generally not listened to by other members.

- Which members are high in influence (that is, when they talk others seem to listen)?
- Which members are low in influence? Others do not listen to or follow them. Is there any shifting in influence? Who shifts?
- Do you see any rivalry in the group? Is there a struggle for leadership? What effect does it have on other group members?

3. Styles of Influence

Influence can take many forms. It can be positive or negative; it can enlist the support or cooperation of others or alienate them. How a person attempts to influence another may be the crucial factor in determining how open or closed the other will be toward being influenced. The following items are suggestive of four styles that frequently emerge in groups.

- *Autocratic:* Does anyone attempt to impose his or her will or values on other group members or try to push them to support his or her decisions? Who evaluates or passes judgment on other group members? Do any members block action when it is not moving in the direction they desire? Who pushes to "get the group organized"?
- *Peacemaker:* Who eagerly supports other group members' decisions? Does anyone consistently try to avoid conflict or unpleasant feelings from being expressed by "pouring oil on the troubled waters"? Is any member typically deferential toward other group members—gives them power? Do any members appear to avoid giving negative feedback, i.e., being honest only when they have positive feedback to give?
- *Laissez faire:* Are any group members getting attention by their apparent lack of involvement in the group? Does any group member go along with group decisions without seeming to commit himself or herself one way or the other? Who seems to be withdrawn and uninvolved; who does not initiate activity, participates mechanically and only in response to another member's question?

- *Democratic:* Does anyone try to include everyone in a group decision or discussion? Who expresses his or her feelings and opinions openly and directly without evaluating or judging others? Who appears to be open to feedback and criticisms from others? When feelings run high and tension mounts, which members attempt to deal with the conflict in a problem-solving way?

4. Decision-Making Procedures

Many kinds of decisions are made in groups without considering the effects of these decisions on other members. Some people try to impose their own decisions on the group, while others want all members to participate or share in the decisions that are made.

- Does anyone make a decision and carry it out without checking with other group members (self-authorized)? For example, the group member decides on the topic to be discussed and immediately begins to talk about it. What effect does this have on other group members?

- Does the group drift from topic to topic? Who topic-jumps? Do you see any reason for this in the group's interactions?

- Who supports other members' suggestions or decisions? Does this support result in the two members deciding the topic or activity for the group (handclasp)? How does this affect other group members?

- Is there any evidence of a majority pushing a decision through over other members' objections? Do they call for a vote (majority support)?

- Is there any attempt to get all members participating in a decision (consensus)? What effect does this seem to have on the group?

- Does anyone make any contributions that do not receive any kind of response or recognition (plop)? What effect does this have on the member making the contribution?

5. Task Functions

These functions illustrate behaviors that are concerned with getting the job done, or accomplishing the task that the group has before it.

- Does anyone ask for or make suggestions as to the best way to proceed or to tackle a problem?

- Does anyone attempt to summarize what has been covered or what has been going on in the group?

- Is there any giving or asking for facts, ideas, opinions, feelings, feedback, or searching for alternatives?

- Who keeps the group on target? Who prevents topic-jumping or going off on tangents?

6. Maintenance Functions

These functions are important to the morale of the group. They maintain good and harmonious working relationships among the members and create a group atmosphere, which enables each member to contribute maximally. They ensure smooth and effective teamwork within the group.

- Who helps others get into the discussion (gate openers)?

- Who cuts off others or interrupts them (gate closers)?

- How well are members getting their ideas across? Are some members preoccupied and not listening? Are there any attempts by group members to help others clarify their ideas?

- How are ideas rejected? How do members react when their ideas are not accepted? Do members attempt to support others when they reject their ideas?

7. Group Atmosphere

Something about the way a group works creates an atmosphere which in turn is revealed in a general impression. In addition, people may differ in the kind of atmosphere they like in a group. Insight can be gained into the atmosphere characteristic of a group by finding words that describe the general impressions held by group members.

- Who seems to prefer a friendly congenial atmosphere? Is there any attempt to suppress conflict or unpleasant feelings?

- Who seems to prefer an atmosphere of conflict and disagreement? Do any members provoke or annoy others?

- Do people seem involved and interested? Is the atmosphere one of work, play, satisfaction, taking flight, sluggishness, etc.?

8. Membership

A major concern for group members is the degree of acceptance or inclusion in the group. Different patterns of interaction may develop in the group that give clues to the degree and kind of membership.

- Is there any subgrouping? Sometimes two or three members may consistently agree and support one another or consistently disagree and oppose one another.
- Do some people seem to be "outside" the group? Do some members seem to be "in"? How are those "outside" treated?
- Do some members move in and out of the group, e.g., lean forward or backward in their chairs or move their chairs in and out? Under what conditions do they come in or move out?

9. Feelings

During any group discussion, feelings are frequently generated by the interactions among members. These feelings, however, are seldom talked about. Observers may have to make guesses based on tone of voice, facial expressions, gestures, and many other forms of nonverbal cues.

- What signs of feelings do you observe in group members: anger, irritation, frustration, warmth, affection, excitement, boredom, defensiveness, competitiveness, etc.?
- Do you see any attempts by group members to block the expression of feelings, particularly negative feelings? How is this done? Does anyone do this consistently?

10. Norms

Standards or ground rules may develop in a group, which control the behavior of its members. Norms usually express the beliefs or desires of the majority of the group members as to what behaviors should or should not take place in the group. These norms may be clear to all members (explicit), known or sensed by only a few (implicit), or operating completely below the level of awareness of any group members. Some norms facilitate group progress and some hinder it.

- Are certain areas avoided in the group (e.g., sex, religion, talk about present feelings in group, discussing the leader's behavior, etc.)? Who seems to reinforce this avoidance? How do they do it?

- Are group members overly nice or polite to each other? Are only positive feelings expressed? Do members agree with each other too readily? What happens when members disagree?

- Do you see norms operating about participation or the kinds of questions that are allowed (e.g., "If I talk, you must talk"; "If I tell my problems you have to tell your problems")? Do members feel free to probe one another about their feelings? Do questions tend to be restricted to intellectual topics or events outside of the group?

Conflict Styles:
Organizational Decision Making

Donald T. Simpson

Goals

- To identify ways of dealing with organizational or group conflict.
- To discuss when and why different methods of resolving conflict are appropriate to different situations.
- To provide an experience in group decision making.

Group Size

An unlimited number of subgroups of five to seven participants each.

Time Required

Approximately one and one-half hours.

Materials

- A Conflict Styles Work Sheet for each participant and an extra copy for each team.
- A pencil for each participant.

- A copy of the Conflict Styles Theory Sheet for the facilitator.
- Newsprint and a felt-tipped marker.

Physical Setting

A room large enough to accommodate all participants, with adequate tables and chairs available for each team.

Process

1. The facilitator introduces the experience by commenting on the inevitability of conflict in groups and how conflict can be used as a constructive force.

2. The facilitator then gives the participants copies of the Conflict Styles Work Sheet and instructs them to complete the work sheet in fifteen minutes.

3. At the end of this time, the facilitator divides the participants into subgroups of five to seven members each and appoints one observer for each subgroup. Observers are briefed on what to look for.[1]

4. A copy of the Conflict Styles Work Sheet is given to each subgroup, and the subgroups are instructed to complete the work sheet as subgroups. They are advised to avoid conflict-reducing techniques such as the use of majority power (voting), minority power (persuasion based on pressure), or compromise (giving in to keep the peace). The facilitator also urges them to view differences of opinion as constructive and to make their ranking decisions as a subgroup, based on logic as well as mutual understanding. They are told that they will have forty-five minutes in which to complete the work sheet.

5. The observers report to their respective subgroups, explaining how the subgroup handled the ranking task and any conflict that arose. Specific incidents are described to provide the group members with pertinent feedback.

6. When the observers have made their reports to the subgroups, the total group is reassembled, and each subgroup's decision is posted on newsprint. If any subgroups' decisions differ widely (a "1" and a "5" choice for the same problem), the facilitator may focus on intergroup conflict by having each of the subgroups explain the rationale for each of its responses.

---

[1] A useful guide for what to look for in groups can be found on pp. 156–160 of this volume.

7. The five styles of handling organizational conflict are discussed, based on the Conflict Styles Theory Sheet. The facilitator provides an example of each style, when appropriate, and so on. Participants may be urged to discuss these styles in terms of what they have just experienced. The participants then identify by style the ways of dealing with conflict listed for each case on the Conflict Styles Work Sheet. (Usually they are able to identify the responses correctly.)

8. The facilitator processes the activity with the group by considering the learnings gained from the experience and their application to real-life situations. Major points are listed on newsprint.

Variations

- The facilitator can increase the pressure on the subgroups by reducing the time allotted for the ranking task to thirty minutes.

- The situations described on the Conflict Styles Work Sheet can be rewritten to reflect the interests or needs of the participants or groups involved (supervisors, sales personnel, governmental or clerical staffs, educators, etc.).

Originally published in The 1977 Annual Handbook for Group Facilitators..

CONFLICT STYLES SOLUTION

Case One

A. Compromise

B. Power

C. Integration

D. Denial

E. Suppression

Case Two

A. Power

B. Denial

C. Suppression

D. Integration

E. Compromise

Case Three

A. Integration

B. Compromise

C. Denial

D. Power

E. Suppression

Case Four

A. Denial

B. Suppression

C. Compromise

D. Integration

E. Power

The Pfeiffer Book of Successful Conflict Management Tools © 2003 John Wiley & Sons, Inc.

CONFLICT STYLES WORK SHEET

Instructions: Your task is to rank the five alternative courses of action under each of the four cases below, from the most desirable or appropriate way of dealing with the conflict situation to the least desirable. Rank the most desirable course of action "1," the next most desirable "2," and so on, ranking the least desirable or least appropriate action "5." Enter your rank for each item in the space next to each choice.

Case One

Chris is lead operator of a production molding machine. Recently Chris has noticed that one of the workers from another machine has been coming over to Chris's machine and talking to one of the operators (not on break time). The efficiency of Chris's operator seems to be falling off, and there have been some rejects due to this operator's inattention. Chris detects some resentment among the rest of the crew. If you were Chris, you would:

_____ A. Tell your operator to limit conversations during on-the-job time.

_____ B. Ask the supervisor to tell the lead operator of the other machine to keep the operators in line.

_____ C. Confront both workers the next time you see them together (as well as the other lead operator, if necessary), find out what they are up to, and tell them what you expect of your operators.

_____ D. Say nothing now; it would be silly to make something big out of something so insignificant.

_____ E. Try to put the rest of the crew at ease; it is important that they all work well together.

Case Two

Pat is the senior quality-control (Q-C) inspector and has been appointed group leader of the Q-C crew. On separate occasions, two of the crew have come to Pat with different suggestions for reporting test results to the machine operators. Gayle wants to send the test results to the supervisor and then to the machine, because the supervisor is the person ultimately responsible for production output. Sam thinks the results should go directly to the lead operator on the machine in question, because it is the lead operator who must take corrective action as soon as possible. Both ideas seem good, and Pat can find no ironclad procedures in the department on how to route the reports. If you were Pat you would:

_____ A. Decide who is right and ask the other person to go along with the decision (perhaps establish it as a written procedure).

_____ B. Wait and see; the best solution will become apparent.

_____ C. Tell both Gayle and Sam not to get anxious about their disagreement; it is not that important.

_____ D. Get Gayle and Sam together and examine both of their ideas closely.

_____ E. Send the report to the supervisor, with a copy to the lead operator (even though it might mean a little more copy work for Q-C).

Case Three

Terry is a module leader; the module consists of four very complex and expensive machines and a crew of five. The work is exacting, and inattention or improper procedures could cause a costly mistake or serious injury. Terry suspects that one of the crew is taking drugs on the job or at least is showing up for work under the influence of drugs. Terry feels that are some strong indications, but knows they are not enough to have a "case." If you were Terry you would:

_____ A. Confront the worker outright, explaining what you suspect and why and that you are concerned for the worker and for the safety of the rest of the crew.

_____ B. Ask that the suspected offender keep this drug habit off the job; what is done on the job is part of your business.

_____ C. Not confront the individual right now; it might upset or drive the worker underground.

_____ D. Give the worker the "facts of life"; explain that it is illegal and unsafe and that if the worker gets caught, you will do everything you can to see that the individual is fired.

_____ E. Keep a close eye on the worker to see that the individual is not endangering others.

The Pfeiffer Book of Successful Conflict Management Tools © 2003 John Wiley & Sons, Inc.

Case Four

Robin is a supervisor of a production crew. From time to time in the past, the Product Development section has "tapped" the production crews for operators to augment their own operator personnel to run test products on special machines. This has put very little strain on the production crews, because the demands have been small, temporary, and infrequent. Lately, however, there seems to have been an almost constant demand for four production operators. The rest of the production crew must fill in for these missing people, usually by working harder and taking shorter breaks. If you were Robin, you would:

_____ A. Let it go for now; the "crisis" will probably be over soon.

_____ B. Try to smooth things over with your own crew and with the development supervisor; we all have jobs to do and cannot afford a conflict.

_____ C. Let development have two of the four operators they requested.

_____ D. Go to the development supervisor or the manager and talk about how these demands for additional operators could best be met without placing production in a bind.

_____ E. Ask the supervisor of production (Robin's boss) to "call off" the development people.

CONFLICT STYLES THEORY SHEET

In any group, conflict is inevitable because different people have different viewpoints. In a work group or organization, particularly, group members see the needs of the organization differently because of their different job orientations.

A sales representative and a manufacturing manager, for example, have different jobs: The sales rep wants to promise speedy delivery (a key point in making a sale), which means large inventories in many field locations. The manufacturing manager, on the other hand, wants to keep inventories low since they tie up materials, storage space, and production schedules. A natural conflict exists between the marketing and manufacturing divisions, and management must find a way to handle these differences productively.

In another example, some members of a church congregation may want the church to concentrate on aiding the poor, while other members think the church should focus on the spiritual needs of the congregation. The minister is caught in the middle of these factions and must resolve the conflict.

Even in marriage—the "group" that, logically, should be most intimately concerned with mutual help and love for its members—there are disagreements and differences. Few married people will testify that their marriage is free from conflict.

Healthy Conflict

Because much conflict is natural, the goal of a group is not to eliminate conflict, but to view it as essentially healthy. It can be healthy if it is handled and resolved constructively. The group or organization is enhanced by exploring differences; new ideas and new learnings result. Usually when conflict arises and is dealt with openly, people are stimulated to creativity, alternatives are considered, better ideas come forth, and a better course of action results.

Ways of Dealing with Organizational Conflict

There are five common ways of dealing with organizational conflict. Any one method of dealing with conflict will not apply to all situations or all personalities. The leader in a group must consider when to employ what style, and with whom. If a leader has used one method successfully, he or she may use it to excess. Learning about the alternative means of handling conflict gives a wider choice of actions to employ in any given situation and makes it possible to tailor the response to the situation.

The Pfeiffer Book of Successful Conflict Management Tools © 2003 John Wiley & Sons, Inc.

Denial or Withdrawal

With this approach, a person attempts to "get rid of" conflict by denying that it exists or refusing to acknowledge it. Usually, however, the conflict does not "go away"; it grows to the point where it becomes all but unmanageable. When the issue or the timing is not critical, denial may be the most productive way of dealing with conflict.

Suppression or Smoothing Over

"We run a happy ship here." "Nice people don't fight." A person using suppression plays down differences and does not recognize the positive aspects of handling the conflict openly. Again, the source of the conflict rarely goes away. Suppression may, however, be employed when it is more important to preserve a relationship than to deal with an insignificant issue through conflict.

Power or Dominance

Power is often used to settle differences. The source of the power may be vested in one's authority or position (including referral to "the system," higher supervision, and so on). Power may take the form of a majority (as in voting) or a persuasive minority. Power strategies, however, result in winners and losers, and the losers do not support a final decision in the same way that winners do. Future meetings of a group may be marred by the conscious or unconscious renewal of the struggle previously "settled" by the use of power. In some instances, especially where other forms of handling conflict are clearly inappropriate, power is effective. Voting is used in national elections, for example, and "the law" applies equally to all.

Compromise or Negotiation

Although often regarded as a virtue, compromise ("You give a little, I'll give a little, and we'll meet each other halfway") has some serious drawbacks. Bargaining often causes both sides to assume an inflated position, because they are aware that they are going to have to "give a little" and want to buffer the loss. The compromise solution may be watered down or weakened to the point where it will not be effective. There is often little real commitment by any of the parties. Yet there are times when compromise makes sense, such as when resources are limited or it is necessary to forestall a win-lose situation.

Integration or Collaboration

This approach requires that all parties to the conflict recognize the abilities and expertise of the others. Each individual's position is well prepared, but the emphasis of the group is on trying to solve the problem at hand, rather than on defending particular positions or factions. Everyone fully expects to modify his or her original views as the group's work progresses. Ultimately, the best of the group's thinking will emerge. The assumption is that the whole of the group effort exceeds the sum of the individual members' contributions. If this approach is allowed to become an either/or settlement, or if the conflict is resolved—due to lack of time, money, or understanding— by a form of power, the final decision will suffer accordingly.

Conclusion

Knowing some of the different methods of dealing with conflict is extremely useful to anyone working with groups or organizations. If a group leader is aware of these methods and their advantages and disadvantages, he or she will be more effective in handling conflict.

3

Win As Much As You Can: An Intergroup Competition[1]

W. Gellerman

Goal

- To acquaint the members of two teams with the merits of competition and collaboration in both intragroup and intergroup relations.

Group Size

This activity is designed for two teams of eight members each. Teams of more than eight members can be accommodated easily by having the participants play the game in trios instead of pairs and/or assigning some participants to be process observers. If either team has fewer than eight members, single participants may work by themselves (instead of in pairs) or the facilitator may alter the game on which the activity is based.

Time Required

Approximately one hour.

---

[1]This activity is based on the classic "Prisoner's Dilemma" problem as adapted by W. Gellermann.

Materials

- A copy of the Win as Much as You Can Tally Sheet for each pair.
- A pencil for each pair.

Physical Setting

A large room with movable chairs for all members of both teams. The teams are seated well apart from each other. Each team is divided into four pairs; the pairs are seated far enough away from one another so that they can discuss strategy privately, yet close enough so that all team members can interact when asked to do so. Figure 1 is a suggested configuration for one team.

Process

1. The members of each team are instructed to form four pairs and to arrange themselves into a configuration such as that shown in Figure 1. Each pair is given a copy of the tally sheet and a pencil; the members of each pair are instructed to spend a few minutes studying this sheet and discussing their understanding of the game.

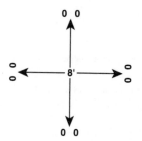

Figure 1. Suggested Seating Configuration

2. The facilitator elicits and answers questions about the game and then reads the following directions aloud:

   - "The title of this activity is 'Win As Much As You Can.' Be sure to keep that goal in mind throughout the experience.

- "There are three rules:

  a. "You are not to confer with other members of your team, except your own partner, unless you are given specific permission to do so. This rule applies to nonverbal as well as verbal communication.

  b. "Each pair must agree on a single choice for each round.

  c. "You are to ensure that the other members of your team do not know your pair's choice until you are instructed to reveal it.

- "There are ten rounds to this activity. During each round you and your partner will have one minute to mark your choice for the round. Remember the rules. You may now take one minute to mark your choice for round one." *[The facilitator pauses for one minute.]*

  a. "If you have not marked your choice, please raise your hand." *[The facilitator makes sure that each pair has completed the task before proceeding, but also keeps the activity moving.]*

  b. "Share your decision with all of the other members of your team." *[The facilitator pauses for two minutes while the team members confer.]*

  c. "Mark your score card on the tally sheet for round 1 according to the payoff schedule."

  d. "Are there any questions about the scoring?" *[The response to all questions concerning the purpose of the activity should be "The name of the game is 'Win As Much As You Can.'"]*

- "You have one minute to mark your decision for round 2." *[The facilitator pauses for one minute.]*

  a. "Has any pair not finished?" *[The facilitator encourages the pairs to make their decisions quickly.]*

  b. "Now share your decision with the rest of your team." *[The facilitator pauses for two minutes while the team members confer.]*

  c. "Mark your score card for round 2."

- *[The facilitator conducts rounds 3 and 4 in the same fashion as Rounds 1 and 2.]*

- "Round 5 is a bonus round. You will note that the tally sheet indicates that all amounts won or lost during this round will be multiplied by three. Before I ask you to mark your choice for this round, I'm going to let you discuss this phase of the activity with the other members of your team. After the team discussion, you and your partner will have one minute to discuss your decision, as before. You may now have three minutes for team discussion." *[The facilitator pauses for three minutes.]*

a. "You and your partner now have one minute to mark your decision for round 5. Remember that the rules are now in effect." *[The facilitator pauses for one minute.]*

b. "Has any pair not finished?" *[The facilitator encourages the pairs to make quick decisions.]*

c. "Now share your decision with the other members of your team." *[The facilitator pauses for two minutes.]*

d. "Mark your score card for round 5."

■ *[The facilitator conducts rounds 6 and 7 in the same fashion as Rounds 1 through 4.]*

■ *[Round 8 is conducted in the same fashion as round 5, with the bonus value increased from three to five times par.]*

■ *[Round 9 is conducted in the same fashion as rounds 1 through 4 and rounds 6 and 7.]*

■ *[Round 10 is conducted in the same fashion as rounds 5 and 8, with the bonus value increased to ten times par.]*

3. The facilitator asks each team to compute its net score from the pair scores. (Example: +18, –21, +6, and +2 = +5. It is possible for a team to score a maximum of +100—+25, +25, +25, and +25—if all four pairs choose Y, the collaboration option, in each round.)

4. The facilitator opens the discussion of the process and its implications. The following questions should be addressed:

■ Does the "you" in "Win As Much As You Can" mean you as a pair or you as a team? How was your perspective on this issue revealed in your behavior during the activity?

■ What were the effects of competition in this game? What were the effects of collaboration?

■ How does your team's net score compare to the possible net score of 100?

■ How does this activity relate to your previous experiences with your fellow team members? How does it relate to your previous experiences with members of the other team?

- How can you use what you have learned in future interactions with your fellow team members and in interactions with members of the other team?

Variations

- The activity may be carried out using money instead of points.
- If the teams are large (each consisting of several more than eight members), they may send representatives to the meetings on bonus rounds.
- In round 10 each pair may be asked to predict the choices of the team's other three pairs. These predictions may be posted before announcing the actual choices, as shown in Figure 2. (Actual choices are recorded in the circles after the predictions are announced.)

Predicting Partnership	Predicted Choices			
	Partnership A	Partnership B	Partnership C	Partnership D
A	◯			
B		◯		
C			◯	
D				◯

Figure 2. Prediction Chart

Originally published in The 1972 Annual Handbook for Group Facilitators.

Win As Much As You Can Tally Sheet

Instructions: For ten successive rounds you and your partner will choose either an X or a Y, and each of the other pairs will make the same choice. Each round's payoff depends on the pattern of choices made in your team.

Payoff Schedule

4 X's:	Lose $1.00 each
3 X's:	Win $1.00 each
1 Y:	Lose $3.00
2 X's:	Win $2.00 each
2 Y's:	Lose $2.00 each
1 X:	Win $3.00
4 Y's:	Lose $1.00 each
4 Y's:	Win $1.00 each

You are to confer with your partner in each round and make a joint decision. In rounds 5, 8, and 10, you and your partner may first confer with the other pairs in your team before making your joint decision, as before.

	Round	Your Choice (circle)	Cluster's Pattern of Choices	Payoff	Balance
	1	X Y	___ X ___ Y		
	2	X Y	___ X ___ Y		
	3	X Y	___ X ___ Y		
	4	X Y	___ X ___ Y		
Bonus Round → Payoff x 3	5	X Y	___ X ___ Y		
	6	X Y	___ X ___ Y		
	7	X Y	___ X ___ Y		
Bonus Round → Payoff x 5	8	X Y	___ X ___ Y		
	9	X Y	___ X ___ Y		
Bonus Round → Payoff x 10	10	X Y	___ X ___ Y		

4

Power Poker
What's in It for Me?

Linda Raudenbush and Steve Sugar

Goals

- To demonstrate the dynamics of negotiating, competition, and power.
- To explore issues involved in comparing individual values to group values.
- To discuss issues of hidden and open agendas.
- To explore issues of group member status.
- To demonstrate issues of trust.

Group Size

Up to thirty-six, preferably a number divisible by six.

Time Required

Forty-five to ninety minutes to play a minimum of two rounds and discuss all the issues. If time is limited, select only the most pertinent discussion questions.

Materials

- One copy of the Power Poker Facilitator Notes for the facilitator.
- One Power Poker Sample Play Sheet for the facilitator
- One Poker Power Swap Sheet per player per round.
- One Power Poker Ranking/Scoring Chart handout per participant.
- One deck of fifty-two playing cards per subgroup.
- Three index cards per player.
- Pens or pencils for participants.
- A flip chart and felt-tipped markers.
- (Optional) Colorful markers or crayons.

Physical Setting

Tables, preferably round, with five or six seats per table.

Process

1. Prior to the workshop, read through the Power Poker Facilitator Notes and Power Poker Sample Play Sheet so that you understand the process thoroughly.

2. First, discuss the goals of the activity in general terms. Then divide the participants into subgroups of five or six players each. Have additional participants act as observers. Seat each subgroup at its own table.

3. Distribute one deck of playing cards to each group. Distribute one Power Poker Swap Sheet, one Power Poker Ranking/Scoring Chart, three index cards, and a pen or pencil to each player. Go over the Power Poker Ranking/Scoring Chart to demonstrate the points awarded for each type of poker hand. (Ten minutes.)

4. Have each subgroup select one player to act as dealer. The dealer also plays the game after dealing the cards. Explain that the deal will rotate clockwise on each new round of play and that the game play and ranking of hands is based on the standard rules for poker.

5. Go over the following rules for Round 1 with the group:

   Round 1: Distributing the Cards: The dealer distributes five cards to each player. Each player records his or her original five cards on the Power

Poker Swap Sheet. Each player places one card face down (hole card) and the other four cards face up. (*Note:* Experience has shown that players prefer to place the cards they wish to trade in the face-up position.)

Round 1: Preparing the Index Card: Each player represents the value and suit of the hole card on the index card, using the colored markers and crayons if desired, and then places the index card in a place that can be seen by all other players. The dealer then selects one card from the deck—the "power" card—and places it face up on the table. All players may use this card to help form their hand.

Round 1: Trading Period: Players have five minutes to trade cards with any other player in their subgroup. Rules of the trade:

- Players may trade only the cards that are face up.

- Players may trade only one card at a time.

- All trades are voluntary; no one is required to trade any of their cards during the trading period.

- All players must record each of their trades on their Power Poker Swap Sheets.

When the trading is complete, give the players two minutes to verify their Power Poker Swap Sheets.

After all trades are completed and recorded, tell players they may trade in one to three cards for new cards from the deck. Say that before receiving the replacement card(s), the player must turn over his or her hole card and place it next to the index card. Players receive all replacement cards face down. (Fifteen minutes for the first round, less time for subsequent rounds.)

6. Now tell players that they may wager pennies or chips on their final hand if they wish to do so. When everyone is ready, have all players reveal all of their cards to the rest of their subgroup. Tell them to score points for their hands based on the Power Poker Ranking/Scoring Chart. Remind them that the winning hand receives a twenty-point bonus. (Five minutes.)

7. Post the points for each player in the subgroup and then tally the total of each subgroup as one score. Record each subgroup's score on the flip chart. (Five minutes.)

8. Allow each subgroup to meet for five minutes and then continue with the next round. All rounds are played in the same way. (At least two rounds should be played, but you may allow five or six rounds if desired.) Declare the team with the most points the winner. (Ten minutes.)

9. Help people reflect on their experiences and find meaningful learning around any or all of the following ten issues.

Group Dynamics: Individual and Group Efforts

- How did you begin playing the game? Did you see it as an individual or group effort?

- Did you want to improve your hand at the cost of all others? Some others? One other?

- When (if you did) did you begin to see that it was a group effort? Why?

- What did you do to help others?

- How are issues of individual and group efforts played out in your workplace?

Group Dynamics: Hidden and Open Agendas

- What did you write on the index card? Were you open or closed with how much you revealed?

- What did the index card represent for you?

- Did the index card represent how you wanted to be seen?

- How are issues of hidden and open agendas relevant to your workplace?

Group Dynamics: Honest and Open Communication

- What did you write on the index card? Were you honest about the card you held?

- What did the index card represent for you?

- Did the index card represent how you wanted to be seen?

- What would you think/do if a player's index card did not match his or her hole card? How would that affect your future dealings with that player? If this happened, could you leave it in the training room?

- How are issues of hidden and open agendas relevant to your workplace?

Group Dynamics: Cooperation and Competition

- How did you see yourself and others as you played the game? As collaborators? As competitors? Explain.

- Were you never/sometimes/always actively participating?

 The Pfeiffer Book of Successful Conflict Management Tools © 2003 John Wiley & Sons, Inc.

- Did you experience conflicting self-talk?

- Were you able to listen carefully to others? Stay focused? Stay on track?

- How are issues of cooperation, collaboration, and competition relevant to your workplace?

Group Dynamics: Loyalty and Factionalism

- Was your subgroup marked by individualism? Factionalism? Loyalty to the whole? Loyalty to the individual?

- How are issues of individuality, group loyalty, and factionalism relevant to your workplace?

Group Dynamics: Individual and Group Goals

- What was your individual goal during Round 1? Round 2? Round 3? Etc.

- What were the goals of others in your group for each round?

- Did individual and group goals coalesce? How did this happen?

- In your workplace, how important is it for individual goals to coincide with group goals to accomplish your organization's mission?

- What can be done to merge individual and group goals?

Group Dynamics: Incentive and the Role of Money in Motivation

- How did you recognize and then celebrate success? Describe individual/group success recognition and celebration.

- How did you/others reinforce success?

- During the poker game, what were your incentives?

- At work, what are some effective incentives for you?

- Many play poker for money. How did you/others react when you found out you were playing for points instead of cash?

- If you used the "penny option," how did the use of real money affect the play of the game? Did it carry over into the next round(s)?

- At work, is money a low/medium/high motivator for you/for others?

- How are issues of recognition/celebration of success relevant to your workplace?

Group Dynamics: Group Member Status

- Was there a hierarchy in your poker group? If so, how was the ranking established?

- How would an observer recognize high/low status individuals in your group?

- At work, what are the individual/group/organizational effects of status? Are the effects mostly positive or negative?

- At work, how can the positive effects of status be promoted and the negative effects be reduced?

- What can/should be done to close the status gap in your workplace?

Group Dynamics: Urgency/Faster Work Completion

- Was your subgroup eager to complete each round quickly?

- Did the timed segments help/not help/hinder play?

- Were some individuals faster paced than others?

- How did the subgroup, as a whole, feel in terms of urgency?

- Was urgency achieved by strategic thinking/planning? Effective communications?

- How can a sense of urgency in the workplace contribute to better customer service? More effective competition?

- What roles do leaders/workers play in creating a sense of urgency for faster product/service delivery?

Group Dynamics: Trusting the Group Process to Succeed

- When confronted by a challenge or problem in playing poker, how did you proceed as an individual? As a subgroup?

- How did you solve the problem? Individually, or as a subgroup?

- Once successful at a problem solution, did you/your subgroup use the same process for the next play/round?

- How is this problem-solving process similar/different from work? Do you solve problems individually or as a group?

- Do you individually or with others develop successful processes to meet challenges/solve problems?

- To what extent do you trust this individual/group problem-solving process? (*Note:* Research shows that, with additional time, most group/

participative problem-solving processes result in solutions of higher quality than those achieved by individuals working alone.)

- How can you and others trust the group process to succeed when confronted with challenges and problems in the workplace?

(Twenty minutes.)

Originally published in The 2002 Annual, Vol. 1, Training.

POWER POKER FACILITATOR NOTES

Here are some thoughts you may wish to consider before conducting your first session of the game:

Poker Deficient? If you wish to be more familiar with the rules of poker, refer to the rules in a reference, such as the *Encyclopedia of Card Games*. You may also want to play a few rounds to learn the basics of the game.

Observers. You might consider using one player-observer for each subgroup. The observer should be briefed or given a "behavior checklist." The observer could also track the cards traded between players.

Swap Sheet Option. The Swap Sheets act as the group memory, documenting the trades between the players. If you feel that the Swap Sheet may slow down or impede game play, then eliminate its use during play. This duty could be assigned to the observer.

Hole Card. Placing one card face down—the hole card—represents the personal agenda we all bring to the game. An entire discussion could be based on sharing and openness—what we know about ourselves and what we are willing to share with others. As the players create the index:

- Do they hesitate or write down the value immediately?
- Do they look around to "size up" the rest of the group?
- Do they write down the true value?

Reality Check. If you feel that the "reality check" (when the hole card is turned face up and does not match the index card) presents too much of a risk of a player losing face with the rest of the group, then remove this element of the game. For example, in the Power Poker Sample Play Sheet, when Player 2 shows his hole card, surprise is expressed by the other players because the hole card does not match the index card. This disclosure can be a very powerful discussion item, with special relevance to the workplace.

Secret Role. You can assign the task of misrepresenting the hole card to one of the players. This would protect the "role player," while allowing the dynamic of deceit and disclosure to be part of the game play.

Confidentiality. The issues of trust and openness explored in this game may require reminders to the players that the behaviors shown in each subgroup are part of the game play and must remain confidential to this game session.

Continuing Behavior. The first round involves negotiation, collaboration, strategizing, and communicating as players try to improve their own hand—hence: "What's in It for Me?" Some players and groups might continue this behavior into the second round. By the third round, all players and groups should realize that working together to maximize the group score is to everyone's advantage. After Round 1 and/or Round 2, watch for the players to experience this "aha!" awareness.

The Penny Option. Add an economic challenge to the first round of play by distributing pennies to all of the players and then allowing them to wager on their final poker hands. Determine whether this first round dynamic imprints the competition-cooperation issue in the following rounds.

POWER POKER SAMPLE PLAY SHEET

The participants form a subgroup of four players (for simplicity of the example, only four players). The subgroup is seated at a table equipped with one deck of playing cards. Each player receives a Power Poker Swap Sheet and three index cards. The subgroup selects a dealer.

Round 1

Card Distribution and Set-Up*

- The dealer distributes five cards, face down, to each of the players, including herself. Player 1 is dealt 2c, 2h, 4d, 8d, and 9s. Player 2 is dealt Ad, Ac, Ah, 3h, and Qs. Player 3 is dealt 3c, 5d, 7d, 8s, and Js. The dealer, or Player 4, is dealt 3d, 4h, 6d, Kc, and Kd. Each player records his or her original hand on the Swap Sheet. Each player reviews his or her hand and then shows the following cards face up: Player 1 shows 2h, 4d, 8d, and 9s—the 2c is the hole card. (Rationale: Player 1 wants to build on his pair of twos.)

- Player 2 shows Ad, Ah, 3h, and Qs. The Ac is the hole card. (*Rationale:* Player 2 wants to collect four aces or a full house.)

- Player 3 shows 3c, 7d, 8s, and Js. The 5d is the hole card. (*Rationale:* Player 3 is hoping to collect a straight.)

- Player 4 shows 3d, 4h, 6d, and Kd. The Kc is the hole card. (*Rationale:* Player 4 wants to build on her pair of kings.)

- Each player then depicts his or her hole card on an index card and places it face up in front of his or her hand.

  - Player 1's index card represents the 2c as the hole card.

  - Player 2's index card represents the 5c** as the hole card.

  - Player 3's index card represents the 5d as the hole card.

  - Player 4's index card represents the Kc as the hole card.

- The dealer draws the "power" card*** from the deck and places it in the middle of the table. The power card = 4s.

Note: c = clubs; h = hearts; d = diamonds; s = spades; A = ace; K = king; Q = queen; J = jack.
**Note:* The facilitator asked Player 2 to misrepresent his hole card.
***Note:* Any player can use this card to help form a hand.

The Pfeiffer Book of Successful Conflict Management Tools © 2003 John Wiley & Sons, Inc.

The Trading Period

- Player 2 needs a pair to create a full house. Player 2 offers to trade the Qs to Player 3 for the 3c. Player 3 agrees and the trade is made. Both players record the trade on their Swap Sheets.

- Player 2 holds a full house: Ad, Ah, 3h, 3c, and Ac (hole card). Player 3 now holds 7d, 8s, Js, Qs, and 5d (hole card).

- Player 3 needs another spade card to create a flush. Player 3 offers to trade the 7d to Player 4 for the Ks. Player 4 refuses, wanting to keep the pair of kings.

- Player 3 offers to trade the 7d to Player 1 for the 9s. Player 1 agrees and the trade is made. Both players record the trade on their Swap Sheets.

- Player 3 now holds a flush: 8s, 9s, Js, Qs, and 4s (power card**). Player 1 now holds 2h, 4d, 7d, 9d, and 2c (hole card). This ends the trading period.

Replacement Cards

- Player 1 holds 2h, 4d, 7d, 8d, and the 2c (hole card). Player 1 decides to keep the two pairs (2h, 2c, and 4d, 4s—power card). Player 1 turns over the hole card and turns in the 7d and 8d for replacement cards. Player 1 receives the 2d and 10s. Player 1 holds a full house: 2c, 2d, 2h, and 4d, 4s (power card***).

- Player 2 holds a full house: Ad, Ah, 3h, 3c, and Ac (hole card). Player 2 does not want to replace any cards.

- Player 3 holds a flush: 8s, 9s, Js, Qs, and 4s (power card***). Player 3 does not want any replacement cards.

- Player 4 holds 3d, 4h, 6d, Ks, and Kc (hole card). Player 4 turns over the hole card and turns in the 3d, 4h, and 6d for replacement cards. Player 4 receives the 3s, Qh, and Kh. Player 4 holds three of a kind: Kc, Kh, and Ks.

Show and Score

- Player 1 has a full house: 3 twos and 2 fours. Player 1 receives 25 points from the Ranking and Scoring Chart.

- Player 2 has a full house: 3 aces and 2 threes. Player 2 receives 25 points from the Ranking and Scoring Chart. Player 2 has the winning hand and receives a 20-point bonus. (When comparing two full houses, the three-of-a-kind cards are compared to each other. In this case, the aces are ranked higher than the twos.)

- Player 3 has a flush: 4, 8, 9, J, Q of spades. Player 3 receives 20 points from the Ranking and Scoring Chart.

- Player 4 has three of a kind: three kings. Player 4 receives 10 points from the Ranking and Scoring Chart.

Final Tally

- The facilitator tallies the final scores.

  Player 1 = 25 points

  Player 2 = 25 + 20 = 45 points

  Player 3 = 20 points

  Player 4 = 10 points

  Subgroup Total = 100 points

Power Poker Swap Sheet

Original Hand

Hole Card _____

Trade 1

Hole Card _____

Trade 2

Hole Card _____

Trade 3

Hole Card _____

Power Poker Ranking/Scoring Chart

Scores

Straight Flush = 45 points

Four of a Kind = 30 points

Full House = 25 points

Flush = 20 points

Straight = 5 points

Three of a Kind = 10 points

Two pairs = 7 points

Two of a Kind = 5 points

Winning Hand = 20-point bonus

Definitions

Straight Flush. Any five cards of the
same suit in numerical sequence,
such as the ten, nine, eight, seven,
and six of any one suit.

Four of a Kind. Any four cards of the
same denomination, such as 4 tens.

Full House. Three cards of one denomination and two of another, such
as 3 jacks and 2 tens.

The Pfeiffer Book of Successful Conflict Management Tools © *2003 John Wiley & Sons, Inc.*

Flush. Any five cards of the same suit, but not in sequence, such as the jack, nine, eight, six, and two of any one suit.

Straight. Any five cards in numerical sequence, such as the ten, nine, eight, seven, and six of any suit.

Three of a Kind. Any three cards of the same denomination, such as 3 tens.

Two Pairs. Two different pairs of cards, such as 2 tens and 2 jacks.

Two of a Kind. Any two cards of the same denomination, such as 2 kings.

Trouble in Manufacturing: Managing Interpersonal Conflict

John E. Oliver

Goals

- To examine ways of managing interpersonal conflict in an organizational setting.

- To provide the participants with an opportunity to practice conflict management.

Group Size

Three subgroups of five or six participants each.

Time Required

Approximately one and one-half hours.

Materials

- A copy of the Trouble in Manufacturing Primer on Conflict for each participant.

- A copy of the Trouble in Manufacturing Case-History Sheet for each participant.

- A set of role sheets for each subgroup. Each set consists of one copy each of Trouble in Manufacturing Role Sheets 1 through 4.

- A copy of the Trouble in Manufacturing Observer Sheet for each observer.

- A pencil for each observer.

Physical Setting

A room with a table and chairs for each subgroup. The three tables should be positioned in such a way that the subgroups do not disturb one another while they work.

Process

1. The facilitator announces the goals of the activity.

2. Each participant is given a copy of the Trouble in Manufacturing Primer on Conflict and is asked to read this handout. (Five minutes.)

3. The facilitator elicits questions about the handout, explaining the various methods of conflict management as necessary. (Ten minutes.)

4. The participants are assembled into three subgroups of five or six members each. The facilitator distributes copies of the Trouble in Manufacturing Case-History Sheet and asks the participants to read the sheet. (Ten minutes.)

5. After eliciting and answering questions to ensure that the participants understand the task, the facilitator distributes role sheets and observer sheets; within each subgroup four of the members receive different role sheets, and the remaining member or members receive observer sheets. The facilitator does not answer questions about the roles and does not provide any further information. (Ten minutes.)

6. The facilitator reminds the subgroups of their time limit and instructs them to begin the activity.

7. At the end of the twenty-minute period, the facilitator stops the role plays and reassembles the total group.

8. The facilitator debriefs the activity, asking the observers to report their observations and allowing the participants to realize that no subgroup achieved a consensus. To illuminate the situation further, role descriptions are shared. (Fifteen minutes.)

9. The experience concludes with a discussion of the following questions:

- How did you feel as the discussion progressed?

- How would you evaluate your behavior during the activity?

- What steps were taken to manage the conflicts that arose among the members of your subgroup?

- How does what happened reflect the information provided in the primer on conflict?

- During this activity what measures could have been taken to manage conflict more effectively?

- How can you apply these measures in your back-home environment?

Variations

- In step 2 the facilitator may deliver a lecturette on conflict. In this case the primer on conflict may be eliminated as a handout.

- The case-history sheet may be altered so that it focuses on interpersonal conflicts between the supervisor and one or both subordinates (that is, between Pat and Lee and/or Pat and Chris).

- The facilitator may wish to emphasize inner conflict (individual stress) and intergroup conflict and competition as well as interpersonal conflict. If this is the case, the changes on the following page should be made.

- A separate room should be provided for each subgroup.

- The Trouble in Manufacturing Primer on Conflict should be altered to include information about inner conflict and intergroup conflict and competition.

- The subgroups should be told that they are in competition with one another during the activity and that the subgroup whose course of action is judged to be the "best" will be the winner. A system should be developed for judging the results, rewarding the winner (if any), and processing the feelings generated by the competition.

- The following steps should be added between steps 6 and 7:

  - After five minutes the facilitator visits each subgroup and says that the other subgroups are progressing so well that the time limit is being cut to a total of fifteen minutes.

- After five more minutes, each subgroup is again visited and told that the other subgroups have completed the task and are waiting and that only five more minutes can be allowed.

- Subsequently, in step 7, the participants should be asked to return to the main assembly room.

- Appropriate questions should be added to step 9.

Originally published in The 1984 Annual: Developing Human Resources.

TROUBLE IN MANUFACTURING PRIMER ON CONFLICT

Much organizational activity creates interpersonal conflict. Because such conflict can be either destructive or useful, the organizational climate must be managed to ensure that destructive conflict is resolved and that useful and creative conflict is encouraged.

Interpersonal conflict occurs between or among individuals and is usually the result of differing goals, competition for resources or rewards, or personal differences. There are several ways to react to interpersonal conflict. With *avoidance*, a conflict can be ignored or smoothed over, but it usually resurfaces at a later date. Another tactic is *defusion*, which consists of postponing dealing with the conflict, primarily to alleviate the anger or frustration of those involved. As is the case with avoidance, defusion rarely results in a satisfactory resolution of the problem. Still another approach is to handle the situation through formal *power* or an *appeal* to people who are higher in the organizational hierarchy than those involved in the conflict. Although this short-term solution may allow those involved to work around the issue for a short period of time, the conflict still exists and continues to affect other transactions in the relationship.

The more effective methods for dealing with conflict usually involve some sort of *confrontation* between the parties involved so that both (or all) sides can express their feelings, perceptions, and frustrations. This allows *collaboration* to take place, which results in negotiation and compromise. If appropriate methods of managing conflict are used, it is possible to achieve a "win-win" situation in which everyone receives at least part of what he or she wants. This outcome is the opposite of the traditional "win-lose" situation in which one of the parties achieves personal goals at the expense of the others who are involved.

TROUBLE IN MANUFACTURING CASE-HISTORY SHEET

Background

Pat, the manager of a small garment-manufacturing plant, has identified a problem: Two employees, Lee and Chris, have an interpersonal conflict that hampers their work. Lee, the plant superintendent, is fifty-one years old and has been with the company for thirty-four years, having quit high school to start working at the plant as a maintenance helper. For a number of years, Lee has scheduled production through the plant using a method based on sophisticated guessing. During the last three years, however, this method has not worked well, largely because the volume of production and the variety of products being manufactured in the plant have increased.

In an effort to address the scheduling difficulties, Pat recently hired Chris, who is twenty-five years old and just received a Master of Science degree in industrial engineering from an Ivy League college. Pat met with Lee and Chris to explain that Chris was to assume full responsibility for scheduling. Since then, Chris has impressed Pat by setting up a computerized system for scheduling production and controlling inventory. Because of this system, Pat has saved money for the company by carrying less inventory, purchasing in larger lots, and reducing setup time for plant equipment by increasing the length of production runs. The warehouse has reported fewer instances of stock depletion, and Pat has been able to give the company superiors more accurate information regarding dates when out-of-stock items will be available. For the first time in the history of the plant, there is a three-month production schedule that is not only fairly accurate, but also flexible enough that it can be updated as necessary.

Pat's satisfaction with these improvements is marred by the fact that Lee and Chris just cannot get along. They fight about almost everything concerning the scheduling system and its benefits to the plant. At first Pat tried to ignore this problem, hoping that it would go away, and then tried to act as a go-between in order to keep Lee and Chris from sniping at each other. Now no decisions are being made unless Pat assumes the responsibility for them. In addition, Sandy, one of the plant foremen, has come to Pat and complained about being in the middle of a disagreement between Lee and Chris.

It is obvious that both Lee and Chris could do a better job if each would cooperate with the other. For instance, Chris needs feedback on how the production schedule is working in order to make adjustments, and Lee could gain some valuable insight into more efficient plant operation by learning the theory behind Chris's plans. Pat wants to learn why the conflict is occurring so that an effective method for dealing with it can be selected.

Instructions

The task assigned to your subgroup is to *decide what Pat should do* to resolve the conflict between Lee and Chris. The subgroup members must be in *total agreement* about the course of action that Pat should take. You have twenty minutes in which to complete this task.

Do not begin working until you are instructed to do so.

Trouble in Manufacturing Role Sheet 1

Your primary goal in completing this task is to help the members to reach total agreement about what Pat should do. This goal takes precedence over any other concerns that you may have during the course of the activity, such as promoting a course of action that you personally prefer.

Do not share this information with anyone until you are instructed to do so.

Trouble in Manufacturing Role Sheet 2

During this activity you are to function as a "devil's advocate." No matter what ideas are proposed, you are to think of every possible disadvantage of these ideas and voice them to your fellow members. If, after thorough discussion, you decide that a particular course of action is worthy of your support, you may agree to it.

Do not share this information with anyone until you are instructed to do so.

Trouble in Manufacturing Role Sheet 3

Your objective during this activity is to block consensus. You may participate actively in the discussion, but do not agree to any particular course of action under any circumstances.

Do not share this information with anyone until you are instructed to do so.

Trouble in Manufacturing Role Sheet 4

During this activity you are to generate as many ideas as possible about what Pat should do. Encourage the other members to join you in a discussion of each idea. When the time comes to choose one course of action, use your best judgment.

Do not share this information with anyone until you are instructed to do so.

TROUBLE IN MANUFACTURING OBSERVER SHEET

During this activity you are to observe your subgroup as the members attempt to reach agreement regarding what Pat should do. Be sure to make notes about answers to the following questions; later you will be asked to share these answers with the total group.

1. What occurred in the subgroup? Were the members able to complete their task?

2. Which of the following approaches to conflict were used? In each case how effective were they?

   ■ Avoidance

   ■ Defusion

   ■ Collaboration

   ■ Confrontation

   ■ Power

6

Dynasell: Hidden Agendas and Trust

William W. Kibler

Goals

- To demonstrate the impact of distrust on collaboration in a task group.
- To heighten awareness of one's personal responses when the motives of others are in question.

Group Size

Several subgroups of five to seven members each.

Time Required

One and one-half to two hours.

Materials

- A copy of the Dynasell Instruction Sheet for each participant.
- A copy of the Dynasell Special Instruction Sheet for each participant.
- A set of children's building blocks, five sheets of blank paper, a felt-tipped marker, a roll of cellophane tape, and a pair of scissors for each subgroup.

Physical Setting

A room with enough space to provide a work area for each subgroup.

Process

1. The facilitator introduces the activity but does not emphasize the element of distrust. The facilitator then divides the participants into subgroups of five to seven members each.

2. The facilitator distributes one copy of the Dynasell Instruction Sheet and one copy of the Dynasell Special Instruction Sheet to each participant, directing each person to follow the special instructions *only* if the appropriate block at the bottom of the page is checked. (In reality, none of the participants is assigned this role and the alternate block is checked on all sheets.) The facilitator cautions the participants not to discuss their assigned roles.

3. The facilitator directs the subgroups to separate locations and informs each subgroup that it has thirty minutes in which to complete the task and that the facilitator will represent the Dynasell company in determining which city will be awarded the contract.

4. The facilitator gives each subgroup a set of building blocks, five sheets of blank paper, a felt-tipped marker, a roll of tape, and a pair of scissors and tells the members that they may use any or all of the materials to construct their model, but may not write on the blocks.

5. The facilitator states that if a participant is voted out of a subgroup during the work time, he or she is to leave the work area for the remainder of the task activity. If any workers are voted out of subgroups, they are joined by the facilitator and are instructed to reflect on the behaviors that triggered this response.

6. At the end of thirty minutes, the facilitator calls time and reassembles the total group. The winning model is selected, and the basis for the choice is stated. The facilitator then informs the participants that *no one* was assigned the role of the self-seeking person.

7. All group members, including any members who were voted out, reconvene in their subgroups to discuss their reactions to the activity. The following points may serve to guide this discussion:

   - The impact of distrust on subgroup members' attitudes and/or behaviors,

The Pfeiffer Book of Successful Conflict Management Tools © 2003 John Wiley & Sons, Inc.

- How distrust affected the subgroup's *concern* for the task,
- How distrust affected the *quality* of the task accomplished,
- Whether some ideas, suggestions, or modifications were ignored because of subgroup members' concern for suggested motives,
- The feelings of those participants who may have been voted out of a subgroup.

(Thirty minutes.)

8. Subgroup members are directed to discuss their learnings in terms of the effects of mistrust on their task behavior and their feelings toward the subgroup. (Fifteen minutes.)

9. The facilitator instructs each subgroup to formulate a short list of things members could say or do to prevent the build-up of mistrust and the hindrance of progress in a task group. (Fifteen minutes.)

10. The large group reconvenes, and subgroups report their lists of strategies. (Ten minutes.)

11. The facilitator instructs individual participants to spend a few minutes writing notes to themselves on the implications of these learnings in terms of their back-home work groups. (Five minutes.)

Originally published in The 1981 Annual Handbook for Group Facilitators.

DYNASELL INSTRUCTION SHEET

Background: Dynasell is a young company that has grown rapidly in recent years. Dynasell manufactures and sells canned foods on a retail basis. The company is interested in building a new headquarters for its executive and clerical staff. It has narrowed its selection site to one of several cities: yours or one of the neighboring cities represented here today.

Instructions: You are a member of the planning and development committee for your city. The committee is composed of five members. Together you are to construct a scale model of the proposed new building. Dynasell will study your model and the neighboring cities' models. The site selected will depend on the attractiveness of the scale model of the building submitted by each of the planning and development groups. Your committee is most anxious to have the new headquarters located in your city in order to increase job opportunities, tax revenue, and so on.

You are concerned about the motives of the other members of your committee. A reliable source has given you reason to suspect that one member of your group is not committed to this project. You believe that this individual stands to benefit personally if the new Dynasell building were to be constructed in a neighboring city that is also competing for the site selection. You suspect that this person will hinder the development of the model if possible.

During the building of your model, if you have reason to suspect the identity of the saboteur based on the effects that someone's behavior is having on the work of your committee, you can attempt to have that person removed by a unanimous vote of the remaining members.

You will be instructed when to begin working on your model. Your group will have thirty minutes to complete the task.

The Pfeiffer Book of Successful Conflict Management Tools © 2003 John Wiley & Sons, Inc.

Dynasell Special Instruction Sheet

If the block below designates you as the individual with the personal motive for sabotaging the project, follow this script:

For personal reasons, you are opposed to having Dynasell construct its new headquarters in your city. You have a friend in a neighboring city (which is also competing for the site selection) who has agreed to pay you $250,000 in cash if your committee's model is not selected.

Your objective is to hinder your committee if you can. You can do this in many ways, e.g., making improper design suggestions, delaying decisions. Make every effort to be subtle. If the other committee members become suspicious of your motives, they can vote for your dismissal from the committee, causing you great personal embarrassment and a possible loss of $250,000.

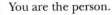 You are the person.

 You are not the person.

7

Current Status:
A Feedback Activity on Trust

Robert N. Glenn

Goals

- To examine unexpressed feelings of trust or distrust within an ongoing group and to clarify the reasons for these feelings.
- To increase feelings of trust within the group.
- To promote self-disclosure and risk taking.
- To provide a basis for subsequent assessment of group trust.

Group Size

Eight to twelve members.

Time Required

Approximately one and one-half hours.

Materials

- A Current Status Inventory and a pencil for each participant.
- A clipboard or other portable writing surface for each participant.

Physical Setting

A room large enough for participants to work privately.

Process

1. After approximately one-half hour of group interaction, the facilitator introduces the activity. He or she distributes copies of the Current Status Inventory and pencils and explains that the inventory allows participants to examine their current feelings toward other group members.

2. The facilitator leads the group in establishing a working definition of the word "trust."

3. The participants are told that they will have ten minutes to complete the inventory.

4. After all members have completed their inventories, the facilitator records the average trust score from each member (question 12). The range of scores is examined and discussed.

5. Each member is encouraged to share at least one answer with the other group members. Participants are free to share as many answers as they wish, and others may comment on the answers.

6. The facilitator builds an experiential lecture from the comments of the group members. He or she may list ways to increase feelings of trust in the group or encourage the group members to revise their working definition of trust or to create a theory showing the relationship between trust, risk taking, and self-disclosure. Each member should specify at least one behavior he or she will attempt to change in subsequent sessions.

7. The facilitator tells members that they will complete the inventory again at a later date to review changes in their feelings.

Variation

- Group members may begin by answering questions 3, 4, 8, and 9 to identify behaviors that contribute to feelings of trust. Questions 5, 6, 10, 11, and 13 may be examined subsequently to identify behaviors associated with distrust.

Originally published in The 1977 Annual Handbook for Group Facilitators.

The Pfeiffer Book of Successful Conflict Management Tools © 2003 John Wiley & Sons, Inc.

CURRENT STATUS INVENTORY

Name _____ Date _____

Directions: Complete all the following questions. Your answers are confidential; however, you are free to share any of your answers after completing this inventory.

1. How did you feel as the group began?

2. How do you feel right now?

3. Which person in this group do you feel the most positive about right now?

4. Describe what makes you feel good about that person.

5. Toward whom in this group do you react most negatively right now?

6. Describe what that person does that produces this negative feeling.

7. What prevents you from being more open and honest in this group?

8. Which person in this group do you perceive as feeling the most positive toward you right now?

9. Why do you feel that this person feels positive about you?

10. Which person in this group do you perceive as feeling the most negative about you right now?

11. Why do you feel that this person experiences negative feelings toward you?

12. Rate each of the group members on a 5-point scale according to how much trust you feel toward him or her. Use "1" to indicate "very little" and "5" to indicate "very much."

Name	Rating
1. _____	_____
2. _____	_____
3. _____	_____
4. _____	_____
5. _____	_____
6. _____	_____
7. _____	_____
8. _____	_____
9. _____	_____
10. _____	_____
11. _____	_____
12. _____	_____

Total Score _____

Average Score (Total Score ÷ N) _____

13. For those individuals to whom you have given low trust ratings, list several ways in which:

■ You can change your behavior to increase your feelings of trust toward them.

■ They might behave to allow you to feel more trust toward them.

The Pfeiffer Book of Successful Conflict Management Tools © 2003 John Wiley & Sons, Inc.

Conflict and
the Individual

The seven exercises in this section all could be used effectively with groups of people who do not work together, as well as with people who do. Only one, "Alter Ego," requires that they work for the same organization. These are activities that seek to increase awareness or build skills having to do with handling conflict in general or with greasing the gears in particular kinds of interactions—such as boss-subordinate relations, performance appraisals, and meetings.

- Retaliatory Cycle: Introducing the Elements of Conflict—Illustrates the building blocks of conflict—five sequential elements that are always present.
- Alter Ego: Saying What You Mean—Practicing honest talk about actual controversial issues in the participants' organization.
- Conflict Role Play: Resolving Differences—How to handle interpersonal conflicts in which one player has more power than the other.
- Resistance: A Role Play—Illustrates and examines the effects of two different approaches to handling resistance.
- Neutral Corner: Deciding on an Issue—Exploring the reasons why other people see things differently than you do.
- Communication Games: Eliminating Unproductive Behavior During Performance Reviews—Conflict management as applied to performance appraisal.
- The Company Task Force: Dealing with Disruptive Behavior—An exercise directed specifically at how to handle unproductive conflict in meetings.

8

Retaliatory Cycle:
Introducing the Elements of Conflict

Daniel Dana

Goals

- To identify the five sequential elements that are present in every interpersonal conflict.

- To understand how conflict escalates (spirals up) and how it causes relationships to wither (spiral down.)

- To illustrate that conflict is always a reciprocal process.

Group Size

Eight to twenty.

Time Required

Forty minutes.

Materials

- One overhead transparency of the Retaliatory Cycle Model.

- One copy of the Retaliatory Cycle Handout for each participant.
- Overhead projector and screen.

Physical Setting

Any comfortable setting with a writing surface for participants.

Process

1. Introduce the activity by stating the objectives, pointing out that the retaliatory cycle describes the relationships among the cogitative (thinking), emotional (feeling), and behavioral (acting) components that are present in all interpersonal conflicts.

2. Display the overhead transparency of the Retaliatory Cycle Model, briefly explaining each step in the cycle. Use an actual example from your personal experience to illustrate each step. (Five minutes.)

3. Ask learners to form discussion pairs and give each person a copy of the Retaliatory Cycle Handout. Refer learners to their handouts as you read aloud each of the five questions.

4. Ask participants to form discussion pairs. Explain that each discussion partner will have about five minutes to describe a conflict in his or her personal experience (in terms of the model) to his or her partner. Explain that you will give a signal in five minutes to indicate that it is time to switch roles. Urge participants to use any extra time to answer the additional questions at the end of their handouts. (Fifteen minutes.)

5. After ten minutes have passed, draw out two or three examples from the group. Ask the participant whose example is being used to try to describe the cycle from the other person's point of view—that is, what was the trigger, perceived threat, and acting out, as experienced by the other person? Make the point that it is likely that the triggering event for the other person was the self-protective acting out behavior used by the first person. This discussion helps learners to appreciate the reciprocal nature of the retaliatory cycle and to recognize that the other's behavior makes sense in the context of how the situation was perceived. (Twenty minutes.)

Originally published in The 2000 Annual, Vol. 2, Consulting.

RETALIATORY CYCLE MODEL

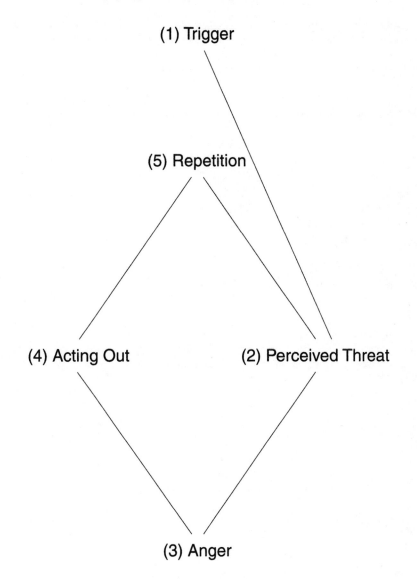

(1) Trigger

(5) Repetition

(4) Acting Out   (2) Perceived Threat

(3) Anger

Retaliatory Cycle Handout

Instructions: Think of a conflict that you have experienced with another person. Take turns with your discussion partner, and respond to the following questions. The facilitator will tell you when to change roles. Jot notes in the spaces provided to use during the group discussion to follow.

1. *Triggering Event.* What was said or done by the other person that triggered the conflict episode?

2. *Perceived Threat to Your Self-Interest.* This could arise from actual hostile intent or simply from carelessness by the other person. What did you assume was behind the other person's triggering action (cognition/thinking)?

3. *Anger.* Defensive anger is the natural emotional response to perceived threat, and it is necessary for mobilizing energy for self-protection. Describe your feeling of anger (emotion/feeling):

4. *Acting Out.* What did you do with your anger? How did you respond? Was your anger expressed through "noncommunication" (spiraling down) or "power play" (spiraling up) behavior or acting?

The Pfeiffer Book of Successful Conflict Management Tools © 2003 John Wiley & Sons, Inc.

5. *Repetition.* How did the other person react to your acting out? What do you assume he or she perceived to be your intentions? What did the other person do to retaliate? Describe the next round of the retaliatory cycle from the point of view of the other person.

Additional Questions

■ Were you able to break out of the retaliatory cycle?

■ If yes, what did you or the other person do to end the conflict?

■ Whether yes or no, was your relationship harmed by the conflict? In what way?

Alter Ego:
Saying What You Mean

Duane C. Tway

Goals

- To encourage open, honest communication.

- To offer participants an opportunity to practice honest communication and receive feedback on their communication.

- To promote the idea that open, honest communication leads to more effective problem identification and solution.

Group Size

Six to thirty participants, all from the same organization, department, or unit. The participants work in pairs for the majority of the activity. If there is an uneven number of participants, the facilitator may participate.

Time Required

Thirty-five to fifty minutes.

Materials

- A flip-chart poster with a controversial issue (for example, job sharing, periodic drug testing, affirmative action, sexual-harassment policies, diversity programs, total-quality management) written on it. The issue should be one that is relevant to the participant group.

- A flip-chart poster with the procedure for the activity written on it (see Process, step 2).

- Masking tape for posting newsprint.

Physical Setting

A large room with plenty of space separating the pairs so that they can converse without disturbing other pairs. Movable chairs should be provided.

Process

1. The facilitator explains the goals of the activity and makes the following statement:

   "During conversations about organizational problems, people often find it difficult to say what is really on their minds. They hesitate for many reasons, such as concern about embarrassing themselves or others and fear of retribution. Consequently, they remain silent or couch their language in diplomatic terms that make their meaning hard to understand. But when people hold back part or all of the truth as they see it, they make the task of identifying a problem and solving it more difficult."

2. The facilitator instructs the participants to assemble into pairs and states that each pair needs only one chair. The facilitator displays the flip-chart poster with the issue written on it and the one with the procedure written on it and explains the procedure:

   - One partner sits in the chair and the other stands behind the chair.

   - The seated partner discusses his or her viewpoint about the posted issue.

   - Whenever the listening partner hears a comment that sounds like "diplomatic talk," he or she touches the seated partner's shoulder and then suggests what the seated partner might have meant but did not really say. *The listening partner is careful to be helpful rather than judgmental.*

- *If the suggested rephrasing was accurate,* the seated partner raises his or her right hand to indicate the degree of accuracy: straight up to indicate "completely right," about halfway up to indicate "partially right."

- *If the seated partner believes that the original comment was accurate,* he or she does not raise a hand.

- *If the seated partner believes that neither the original comment nor the rephrasing was quite accurate,* he or she raises the left hand, indicating a desire for further help in rephrasing.

- The pair continues this procedure, with the seated partner trying to increase the openness and honesty of his or her comments, until the facilitator calls time.

After explaining the procedure, the facilitator asks the pairs to begin. (Ten minutes.)

3. After five minutes the facilitator determines how the pairs are proceeding and decides whether more time should be allotted. If more time is needed, the facilitator gives the pairs an extra five minutes. (Five to ten minutes.)

4. After the facilitator calls time, the partners are instructed to trade places and complete steps 2 and 3 again. (Five to ten minutes.)

5. At the conclusion of the second round, the facilitator reconvenes the total group for a concluding discussion based on these questions:

- How did you feel when your partner signaled that you might not be saying what you really meant?

- How did you feel when your partner rephrased your comments? How accurate was that rephrasing?

- When the rephrasing was accurate, how did you feel when you heard or said what you really meant? What had stopped you from saying what you really meant the first time?

- What does this experience tell you about the way you typically voice your opinion on controversial organizational issues?

- What might need to happen in your organization for you to speak your mind freely?

- How can you use what you have learned in future discussions about controversial issues and organizational problems? How can you assist your organization in supporting openness and honesty?

(Fifteen to twenty minutes.)

Variations

- This activity may be used as part of a team-building intervention.

- This activity may be used with scenarios about things that are difficult to say to another person at work.

- The procedure may be changed so that the listening partner asks after every comment, "Is that what you really mean? Could you say it more honestly?" If this option is chosen, the facilitator should emphasize that these questions must be asked in a helpful rather than judgmental way.

Originally published in The 1998 Annual, Vol. 1, Training.

10

Conflict Role Play: Resolving Differences

Robert P. Belforti, Lauren A. Hagan, Ben Markens,
Cheryl A. Monyak, Gary N. Powell, and Karen Sykas Sighinolfi

Goals

- To examine individuals' reactions to situations in which a "double standard" of behavior operates.

- To allow participants to explore their emotional responses to conflict.

- To examine the problem-solving behavior of participants in conflict situations in which a power difference exists.

Group Size

Two or more subgroups of three members each.

Time Required

Approximately two hours.

Materials

- Two copies of one of the three sets of Conflict Role Play Sheets for each subgroup (the sheets are cut to separate the manager and subordinate roles).

- A sheet of blank paper and a pencil for the observer in each subgroup.

- Newsprint and a felt-tipped marker.
- Masking tape.

Physical Setting

A room that is large enough for each subgroup to meet without disturbing the other subgroups.

Process

1. The facilitator introduces the activity as one that will examine problem-solving behavior in situations that involve conflict. No mention is made of the "double standard" aspect of the role play.

2. The facilitator separates the participants into subgroups of three members each and instructs the members of each subgroup to assume the roles of manager, subordinate, and observer. The manager and subordinate in each subgroup receive only their own role descriptions from the Conflict Role Play Sheet; the observer in each subgroup receives the complete Conflict Role Play Sheet (both role descriptions), a sheet of blank paper, and a pencil. If there are only two or three subgroups, each subgroup receives a different Conflict Role Play Sheet. (Five minutes.)

3. The facilitator directs the members of each subgroup to study their role descriptions in preparation for a meeting between the manager and the subordinate. (Five minutes.)

4. The facilitator directs each subgroup to a separate area and tells the managers and subordinates that they will have fifteen minutes in which to conduct their meetings while the observers watch. The observers are told that they may take notes during the role plays if they wish. The role plays begin. (Fifteen minutes.)

5. The facilitator calls time and reassembles the complete subgroup.

6. The facilitator solicits the participants' reactions to the experience, including:
   - Reactions of the subordinates to the situations involving double standards.

- How the managers felt about presenting situations that involve double standards.

- Comments from the observers regarding whether the issue of double standards was raised in each of their role plays and how that issue was dealt with.

(Five minutes.)

7. The discussion then is focused on the problem-solving behaviors (or lack of them) that emerged during each role play. The participants' various attempts to solve their problems are discussed, and the observers offer their comments. (Fifteen minutes.)

8. The facilitator divides the participants into three subgroups: one of managers, one of subordinates, and one of observers. The subgroup members are directed to discuss their responses (both feeling and behavioral) to the role-play conflicts in which there was unequal power and to compare these with their typical responses to conflict. (Fifteen minutes.)

9. The total group is reassembled, and the facilitator asks for reports from the discussion subgroups on the members' typical modes of response to situations involving conflict. These may be listed on newsprint. (Ten minutes.)

10. The facilitator then introduces a discussion of the problem-solving behaviors that worked and why these were effective. The facilitator then summarizes the most effective modes of response to conflict and solicits additional ideas and comments from the participants. Key points are noted on newsprint and posted. (Fifteen minutes.)

11. The participants are directed to form discussion subgroups of four or five members each and to discuss ways in which they can apply their learnings from the experience to real-life situations. (Fifteen minutes.)

Variations

- The role plays can be used to focus primarily on double standards across sexes.

- The same role play can be conducted with two subgroups in which the sexes of the manager and subordinate are reversed across subgroups for comparison.

- The facilitator can provide each participant in a subgroup the opportunity to be the manager, subordinate, and observer by conducting all three role plays with each subgroup and rotating the roles.

- The facilitator can provide each participant the opportunity to be the manager and the subordinate by eliminating the role of observer and conducting two of the role plays with each subgroup.

- If there are only four to six participants, role plays can be conducted consecutively by two persons, with the non-role players serving as observers.

Originally published in The 1983 Annual Handbook for Facilitators, Trainers, and Consultants.

Conflict Role Play Sheet

Role Play 1:

Manager's Role

You are Kenneth Potter, regional sales manager for the APEX Corporation, a manufacturer of heavy industrial equipment. You have worked as a sales representative and instructor in the company for twenty-three years and have been in your present position for five years. You have sixteen sales representatives working for you; of these, only Janet Wilson and two males qualified for the prestigious "100% Club" this year. The hard work exhibited by Janet and the two men has resulted in their being invited to the annual 100% Club awards convention, to be held in a city that is known for its exotic entertainment. The convention consists of meetings and expositions during the day, and the various award winners go their separate ways at night. Ninety percent of the convention attendees are male. In addition to the daytime activities, many informal parties have been planned for the evenings. However, Perry Smith, the general sales manager, has reminded you that these are not the types of parties that "nice women" attend and he has suggested that you discourage Janet from attending. You realize that Janet's attendance at these parties could have detrimental effects on her future with the company as well as on your own career. You have decided to approach Janet on the subject.

CONFLICT ROLE PLAY SHEET

Role Play 1:

Subordinate's Role

You are Janet Wilson, a twenty-four-year-old sales representative for the APEX Corporation, a manufacturer of heavy industrial equipment. You have been with the company for eighteen months and have made your full quota in your first year. As a result, you have been invited to the annual "100% Club" awards convention, to be held in a popular resort city. The convention consists of meetings and expositions during the day, and it seems to you that the various award winners go their own ways at night. About ninety percent of the convention goers are male. You are looking forward to attending the awards ceremony on the last night of the convention and to the informal parties that follow. You have been told that it is a "super time" and that many valuable business contacts are established at these events. You have just seen your boss, Kenneth Potter, approaching, and you have decided to tell him how glad you are to be attending the convention.

CONFLICT ROLE PLAY SHEET

Role Play 2:

Manager's Role

You are Pat Miller, the manager of an accounting unit within the Great Northwest Insurance Company, where you have worked for the past ten years. At a recent company cocktail party, you became engaged in a stimulating conversation with Lee, the very attractive spouse of one of your subordinates, Chris Rogers. As the conversation progressed, you had the distinct impression that Lee, the spouse, had more than a casual interest in you. Deciding that there was no harm in taking advantage of the situation, you felt compelled to "make a move."

Now you have the feeling that Lee has told Chris about your behavior, and the relationship between you and Chris has become strained. You are willing to let bygones be bygones, but Chris seems to be holding a grudge.

There is a meeting scheduled for today between you and Chris to discuss Chris's possible promotion, which would depend in large part on a good recommendation from you. You are wondering just what tone the meeting will take.

CONFLICT ROLE PLAY SHEET

Role Play 2:

Subordinate's Role

You are Chris Rogers, a young accountant. You have been in the same position for seven years. Finally, you are a candidate for a higher position in your company.

You were recently invited to a cocktail party that was also attended by the corporate vice presidents and all of your supervisors. You realized the importance of your attendance and the possible implications for your career. Because it was a "couples" gathering, you brought your spouse, Lee, who is very attractive. Soon after you arrived, Lee came and asked to speak with you privately. Obviously disturbed, Lee then told you that your boss, Pat Miller, had made obvious advances. You know that Lee is not one to exaggerate and you wonder if you should confront Pat or ignore the issue.

You are upset about what has happened. The relationship between you and Pat has become strained, and the open-door policy between the two of you has ceased to exist. Communication now usually is through written correspondence.

You realize that you need your supervisor's recommendation for the promotion. A meeting has been scheduled for today between you and Pat to discuss the promotion.

The Pfeiffer Book of Successful Conflict Management Tools © 2003 John Wiley & Sons, Inc.

CONFLICT ROLE PLAY SHEET

Role Play 3:

Manager's Role (if the subordinate is male)

You are Lynn Baxter, the head architect and building designer for Pyramid Ltd., a large and growing firm in the Sun Belt. Several months ago, you hired Seth Malloy, a promising young architect. When you interviewed Seth, you had some misgivings about his effeminate manner, but you had to admit that he was the top candidate for the job.

Your entire staff was invited to Ace Construction's open-house cocktail party, to celebrate the opening of its latest facility. Because you wanted to maintain a good relationship with such a potentially good client, you urged each of your staff members to come and to bring a guest. Because you never had heard Seth mention a female friend, you expected to see him alone at the party.

However, Seth has just arrived at the party with a "friend," whose name is Virgil. It is obvious that they are more than just friends. Mr. Chambers, the vice president of Ace Construction, has just pulled you aside and stated that this is a largely conservative gathering and that he does not approve of such a couple being present. He strongly suggested that you take steps to remedy the situation immediately.

CONFLICT ROLE PLAY SHEET

Role Play 3:

Manager's Role (if the subordinate is female)

You are Lynn Baxter, the head architect and building designer for Pyramid Ltd., a large and growing firm in the Sun Belt. Several months ago, you hired Karen Malloy, a promising young architect. When you interviewed Karen, you had some misgivings about her masculine manner, but you had to admit that she was the top candidate for the job.

Your entire staff was invited to Ace Construction's open-house cocktail party, to celebrate the opening of its latest facility. Because you wanted to maintain a good relationship with such a potentially good client, you urged each of your staff members to come and to bring a guest. Because you never had heard Karen mention a male friend, you expected to see her alone at the party.

However, Karen has just arrived at the party with a "friend," whose name is Jill. Obviously they are more than just friends. Mr. Chambers, the vice president of Ace Construction, has just pulled you aside and stated that this is a largely conservative gathering and that he does not approve of such a couple being present. He strongly suggested that you take steps to remedy the situation immediately.

 The Pfeiffer Book of Successful Conflict Management Tools © *2003 John Wiley & Sons, Inc.*

Conflict Role Play Sheet

Role Play 3:

Subordinate's Role (for Seth or Karen Malloy)

You are a promising young architect and you are determined to become a star in your field. You graduated from an established school and now hold a good position with Pyramid Ltd., a large and growing firm in the Sun Belt.

At a recent staff meeting, it was announced that Ace Construction, a potentially lucrative client, would be holding a cocktail party at which staff members and their guests would be welcome. You decide to attend with a date, who is of the same sex as yourself. You feel justified in bringing your companion, because everyone else has his or her own choice of guest.

You and your guest enjoy each other's company, and you like the looks of this party. Your guest is very affectionate, which is a quality that you admire, but you recognize the inappropriateness of such a display at a public gathering.

You notice that people seem to be avoiding the two of you. Just now, you have spotted your immediate supervisor, Lynn Baxter, approaching the two of you. Lynn has a great deal of influence over any promotion that you might receive, and you are anxious to engage Lynn in conversation to see if you can learn anything about your prospective future with the firm.

11

Resistance: A Role Play

H.B. Karp

Goals

- To provide an opportunity to experience the effects of two different approaches.[1]
- To increase awareness of typical responses to attempts to break down resistance.
- To develop strategies for coping with resistance from others.

Group Size

Subgroups of five to seven members each.

Time Required

Two to two and one-half hours.

---

[1]This activity is based on the Gestalt theory of resistance presented by Edwin C. Nevis at the Gestalt Institute of Cleveland. to dealing with resistance.

Materials

- A copy of the Resistance Team Member Role Sheet for each team member.
- Two copies of the Resistance Rating Sheet for each team member (excluding the two vice presidents) in each subgroup.
- A copy of the Resistance Role Sheet: Vice President A for the member from each subgroup who will play vice president A.
- A copy of the Resistance Role Sheet: Vice President B for the member from each subgroup who will play vice president B.
- A Resistance Data Analysis Chart (prepared on newsprint by the facilitator).
- Newsprint and a felt-tipped marker.

Physical Setting

A room large enough for subgroups to listen to their vice presidents' presentations without being disturbed by other subgroups, or a separate room for each subgroup.

Process

1. The facilitator discusses the goals of the experience.

2. The facilitator divides the participants into subgroups of five to seven members each and directs each subgroup to select a member to play vice president A and one to play vice president B.

3. The facilitator distributes Resistance Team Member Role Sheets and two copies of the Rating Sheet to all team members but not to the two persons who will role play the vice presidents in each subgroup. The facilitator gives a copy of the Resistance Role Sheet: Vice President A to each member playing vice president A and a copy of the Resistance Role Sheet: Vice President B to each member playing vice president B.

4. Subgroup members read over the materials. (Ten minutes.)

5. The facilitator takes the vice presidents aside for a few minutes to coach them on their roles and to clarify any questions they may have. (Five minutes.)

6. The vice presidents rejoin their subgroups, and the subgroups are directed to separate locations.

   The Pfeiffer Book of Successful Conflict Management Tools © 2003 John Wiley & Sons, Inc.

7. The facilitator directs each vice president A to try to convince his or her team of his or her position for fifteen minutes.

8. The facilitator calls time and directs all team members to fill out one copy of the Resistance Rating Sheet, designating A as vice president. (Five minutes.)

9. Each vice president B then attempts to convince his or her team to accept his or her position. (Fifteen minutes.)

10. Each team member fills out the second Resistance Rating Sheet regarding vice president B. (Five minutes.)

11. Team members debrief the activity, and the members playing the roles of the vice presidents comment on their experiences. (Fifteen minutes.)

12. Each team then calculates the average score for each question on both rating sheets. The results are entered on the Resistance Data Analysis Chart (prepared on newsprint by the facilitator), and the chart is posted. (Ten minutes.)

13. The facilitator leads the total group in discussing and comparing members' reactions to the experience, using the information from the rating sheets as the basis of comparison. The group discusses differences on the Resistance Data Analysis Chart for vice presidents A and B. Consistent differences across subgroups are identified and the implications of these differences are discussed. (Twenty to twenty-five minutes.)

14. Subgroup members reconvene to discuss ways in which they can use their learnings from the experience in back-home situations involving resistance. (Fifteen minutes.)

Variations

■ With large groups, the activity can be conducted by a "presenting group" with other participants serving as observers. Observers focus on identifying the impact of the vice presidents' behavior in attempting to cope with team members' resistance.

■ To shorten the time required for the activity, both vice presidents can attempt to cope with team members simultaneously, thus heightening the differences in their coping styles. Team members then record their reactions to the experience in total.

Originally published in A Handbook of Structured Experiences for Human Relations Training, Volume VIII *(1981).*

RESISTANCE TEAM MEMBER ROLE SHEET

You are an experienced manager and have been a department head in this company for four years. You take pride in your ability to get things done in your own way, and the company has recognized this with the rapid promotions and pay increases that you have received.

Recently you have been aware of increasing unrest on the part of the younger workers and supervisors in the organization. In your opinion, if other department heads acted more directly and independently with their subordinates, this kind of problem would be minimized.

About ten days ago, you received an enthusiastic memo from the executive vice president, to whom you report, regarding a recent seminar on team building. The vice president has decided that the top level of management should be reorganized and trained to begin functioning as a management team. The memo identified the managers included in this reorganization, and you are one of them.

You are not happy about this designation because you are not, and never have been, a believer in the team approach. You think that team building is a waste of time and is just a way for ineffective managers to cover up their incompetence and avoid taking responsibility for their own mistakes. You have friends in other organizations who work this way and they report problems with it. You know that it will take a lot of extra time and effort to set this team business in motion. Besides, you do not feel comfortable in suggesting things to other managers in their areas of expertise, and you do not want some outsider telling you how to run your department. Furthermore, you do not like, respect, or trust some of the others who will be on the team and would prefer not to work closely with them.

The vice president has scheduled the first meeting with the team in ten minutes. You plan to deal with this issue at the outset.

RESISTANCE RATING SHEET

Vice President   A   B
(Circle the appropriate letter)

Having just left the first meeting of the new management team, please indicate your impressions of the team and the vice president on the sheet below:

1. To what extent do you trust the vice president as your team's leader?

1	2	3	4	5	6	7

Not at all   **To a great extent**

2. How do you feel now about working with the other team members?

1	2	3	4	5	6	7

Uncooperative   **Cooperative**

3. To what extent, if any, has your attitude toward team building changed?

1	2	3	4	5	6	7

More resistant   **More receptive**

4. How willing are you to give the team approach a chance—say for six months?

1	2	3	4	5	6	7

Totally resistant   **Very willing**

RESISTANCE ROLE SHEET: VICE PRESIDENT A

You recently have been promoted to executive vice president for internal affairs. You feel that management team building throughout the entire organization would produce tremendous results. You recently attended a seminar on team building and are convinced that the sooner a move is made in this direction, the better. As you see it, the main advantages of team building are:

1. Work can take advantage of the different skills of the team members.

2. It will provide a support system for managers, who are currently isolated in their own departments.

3. Managers will stimulate one another's thinking, thus becoming more creative.

4. It will create the flexibility needed to deal with a variety of problems.

5. It will provide the base for project management, should that be indicated.

6. In other companies that you know of, it has led to significant changes in corporate policy that were not otherwise easy to achieve.

You have informed the management team of your intention and today you are going to meet the managers for the first time as a team. You have heard through office gossip that there is a good bit of grumbling about this change. Your managers are sharp, effective people, but they are used to working almost totally independently. You expect to meet some strong resistance at this meeting.

Your Approach to the Team's Resistance

You are to do your best to influence as many team members as you can to accept the concept of team building. Your goal is to break down or work around the resistance that the managers will offer.

In addition to making points that appeal to professional pride, feel free to influence the managers with facts and figures, an appeal to loyalty and fair play, your own power and status, guilt, and self-interests and benefits.

Use any other methods that fit for you. Keep in mind that it would be very helpful to get most if not all of the managers "on board" at this meeting because this is the most prestigious group in the company. If you can get them to join you, it will influence others who are ambivalent or negative to the approach.

Resistance Role Sheet: Vice President B

You recently have been promoted to executive vice president for internal affairs. You feel that management team building throughout the entire organization would produce tremendous results. You recently attended a seminar on team building and are convinced that the sooner a move is made in this direction, the better. As you see it, the main advantages of team building are:

1. Work can take advantage of the different skills of the team members.

2. It will provide a support system for managers, who are currently isolated in their own departments.

3. Managers will stimulate one another's thinking, thus becoming more creative.

4. It will create the flexibility needed to deal with a variety of problems.

5. It will provide the base for project management, should that be indicated.

6. In other companies that you know of, it has led to significant changes in corporate policy that were not otherwise easy to achieve.

You have informed the management team of your intention and today you are going to meet the managers for the first time as a team. You have heard through office gossip that there is a good bit of grumbling about this change. Your managers are sharp, effective people, but they are used to working almost totally independently. You expect to meet some strong resistance at this meeting.

Your Approach to the Team's Resistance

Your main aim for this session is to help the managers to express all their reservations. Try to elicit the most frank statements you can from each manager.

Give arguments in favor of team building only when the managers directly and specifically ask. Do not talk about future action steps until you are convinced that the managers have expressed all of their objections and negative feelings.

Although it would be very nice if you could obtain agreement and clear support in this first meeting, you realize that the likelihood of that happening is rather small. If the resistance you anticipate cannot honestly be reduced to a workable level, you are much better off leaving things as they are for now. The very last thing you want or need is a lot of "yeses" now and no support once you have made the changes. So, while you maintain your opinion, you realize that it is better not to force the issue.

RESISTANCE DATA ANALYSIS CHART

Question	Vice President	Subgroup 1	Subgroup 2	Subgroup 3
1	A			
	B			
	Change			
2	A			
	B			
	Change			
3	A			
	B			
	Change			
4	A			
	B			
	Change			
5	A			
	B			
	Change			

12

Neutral Corner:
Deciding on an Issue

Linda Raudenbush and Steve Sugar

Goals

- To learn why others hold the views they do about a current issue.

- To create a platform and an ongoing dialogue about different perspectives on an issue.

- To allow members who hold positive, negative, or neutral views on a topic to identify and explain their rationale.

- To present one's own view in a clear, logical, persuasive manner.

Group Size

Fifteen or more, to guarantee at least three participants in the three subgroups.

Time Required

Approximately ninety minutes.

Materials

- Scoring ballot sheets on a flip chart and also on 3" x 5" cards for each subgroup, prepared in advance by the facilitator.
- A newsprint flip chart and felt-tipped markers.
- One sheet of newsprint paper and felt-tipped markers for each subgroup.
- A stack of 3" x 5" index cards for each subgroup.
- Paper and pencils for each subgroup.
- Masking tape.
- Reference materials and handouts (as necessary for the lecturette topic.)
- A Neutral Corner Scoring Example for the facilitator.

Physical Setting

Any room in which subgroups can work in relative isolation.

Process

1. In preparation for the workshop, write one word each on three separate sheets of newsprint: "For," "Against," and "Undecided." Post the prepared sheets of newsprint in three different corners of the room. Set up a table with paper and pencils, index cards, and felt-tipped markers near each sheet of newsprint.

2. After participants arrive, present, without giving your own opinion, a brief lecturette, giving both sides on a current, semi-controversial issue, such as increasing the driving age to eighteen, lowering the barriers to trade with China, or something within the experience of the group if they are from the same organization. Ideally, the issue should be pertinent and interesting to all members of the group. (Five minutes.)

3. After you have finished, briefly answer any questions about the information you presented to clarify the issue completely, but do not allow discussion of the actual issue at this point. Each participant will be allowed time to consider the issue thoughtfully after this clarifying phase, so do not allow any side discussions to take place. (Five minutes.)

4. Tell participants to decide individually where they stand on the issue—for, against, or neutral. Give everyone a few minutes to consider, then ask everyone to move to the sheet of newsprint that most nearly represents his or her views of the issue.

5. When everyone is in place, define the task by saying:

   "Using the paper and pencils provided, each of the three subgroups has ten minutes to identify the five most important reasons why the members chose the subgroup they did, that is *why* they agree, disagree, or are undecided on the issue."

   (Ten minutes.)

6. Call time at the end of ten minutes, make sure that each subgroup has identified five reasons for its view, and then have each subgroup rank its list of reasons from "1" (most important) to "5" (least important) in private. Be sure no subgroup can be overheard by other subgroups. (Five minutes.)

7. After a few minutes, tell each subgroup to write its list on the paper provided, ranked from the most important (1) to the least important (5), and to give the sheets of paper to you.

8. After you have collected the sheets of paper, give a sheet of newsprint to each subgroup and tell participants to write their lists of five items, this time in random order, onto the newsprint sheet with felt-tipped markers and then to post their sheets on the wall with masking tape. (To ensure that the subgroups do not prematurely write their lists on the newsprint paper, delay the distribution of the felt-tipped markers until after you have received all of the paper-and-pencil ranked listings.)

9. Have people remain in their subgroups and explain the task by saying:

   "Using your index cards as ballots, each subgroup will have seven minutes to determine how each of the other two subgroups ranked their reasons for either agreeing, disagreeing, or remaining neutral. After you have determined a ranking for each of the other subgroups, decide which *key words* from each of their items helped you determine the ranking. List these on your ballot using the format I have drawn on the flip chart."

   (Ten minutes.)

10. Post the ballot form you have previously prepared, shown below. To expedite scoring, prepare two index card ballots for each subgroup in the same format:

Ballot Form

Voting Subgroup's Name:

Name of the Subgroup Being Assessed:

Ranking 1 (key words):

2 (key words):

3 (key words):

4 (key words):

5 (key words):

Sample Completed Ballot 1

Voting Subgroup's Name: For

Name of Subgroup Being Assessed: Against

Ranking 1 (too prompt)

2 (too much data)

3 (lacks finesse)

4 (stubborn)

5 (unlawful)

Sample Completed Ballot 2

Voting Subgroup's Name: For

Name of Subgroup Being Assessed: Undecided

Ranking 1 (negative ads)

2 (many feelings)

3 (unclear standards)

4 (regional issues)

5 (sentimental)

---

11. Call time at the end of seven minutes and collect two ballots from each subgroup.

12. Compare the ballots against the actual rankings for each of the other subgroups, scoring as follows:

- 10 points for identifying the Number 1 choice correctly
- 7 points for identifying the Number 2 choice correctly
- 5 points for identifying the Number 3 choice correctly
- 3 points for identifying the Number 4 choice correctly
- 1 point for identifying the Number 5 choice correctly.

Tally the score from all the ballots and post the results on the flip chart. (Ten minutes.)

13. Give each subgroup five minutes to select a spokesperson and prepare a three-minute presentation on the rationale for their selection and ranking order of their own subgroup's reasons. (Five minutes.)

14. When they are finished, have each subgroup deliver its presentation. (Three minutes per subgroup.)

15. After the last presentation, tell each subgroup to vote for the best presentation (not their own) by using another 3" x 5" card, distributing five points for each of the three criteria below (15 total points):

- Logic = 5 possible points
- Clarity = 5 possible points
- Persuasiveness = 5 possible points

16. Collect the ballots and tally the 15 points awarded by each subgroup on a piece of flip-chart paper. Add up the scores. The subgroup with the most points wins. The winning subgroup could conceivably have 30 points (all 15 from each of the other two subgroups). The final tally may reveal a sudden point "swing" and a new winner. This shows the importance of logic, clarity, and persuasiveness of each subgroup's presentation. (Ten minutes.)

17. Using broad open-ended questions, invite all participants to identify and share their reactions to the activity.

- What is your reaction to what just happened?
- How do you feel at this time about the issue we discussed?
- What do you think about the "for," "against," and "undecided" positions now?
- Have your feelings/thoughts changed during or as a result of listening to others' opinions?

- During what phases of the activity were you more emotional? More thoughtful? Why?

(Ten minutes.)

18. Using specific questions that focus on the process, invite all participants to review, interpret, and share what happened.

    - What occurred as you determined your reasons for your position and prioritized them?

    - As you voted on one another's rankings?

    - As you presented your group's point of view to the other groups?

    - What happened first within your group? What role did each group member play during the various phases of the process? Who said what? Who responded next?

    - What did you learn about your own position on the issue?

    - Did you modify your viewpoint? Why? Why not?

    (Twenty minutes.)

19. Using broad open-ended questions, encourage participants to relate the experience to their own reality.

    - How does your experience of this activity relate to your behavior in the real world?

    - What situations in your world are similar to what happened here?

    - When/how do you discuss differing opinions on a controversial subject in the workplace?

    - When/how do you attempt to understand the views of others?

    - When/how do you try to help others understand your point of view?

    - How will you use what you learned during this activity?

    - What was your most valuable learning? How will it change your behavior? When/how will you use this new behavior?

    (Ten minutes.)

Originally published in< The 2001 Annual, Vol. 2, Consulting.

NEUTRAL CORNER SCORING EXAMPLE

The other subgroups' guesses about the "for" subgroup's ranking and their reasons are listed in the chart below:

In the presentation round, both the "against" and "undecided" subgroups selected the "for" subgroup's presentation as the best presentation. The "for" subgroup selected the "against" subgroup's presentation as the best presentation.

		For	Against	Undecided
"For"	logic	0	3	2
	clarity	0	4	1
	persuasiveness	0	3	2
"Against"	logic	5	0	0
	clarity	5	0	0
	persuasiveness	4	0	1
"Neutral"	logic	5	0	0
	clarity	4	1	0
	persuasiveness	5	0	0
	Final Tally	28	11	6

Subgroup "for" is declared the winner with 28 points.

Communication Games:
Eliminating Unproductive Behavior
During Performance Reviews

Don Morrison

Goals

- To help participants understand the types of dysfunctional communication games that are often "played" in performance review discussions.

- To help participants recognize communication games and avoid or stop playing them.

Group Size

Any number of participants.

Time Required

Two hours.

Materials

- One copy of the Communication Games Descriptions for each participant.
- One copy of the Communication Games Work Sheet for each participant.
- One copy of the Communication Games Answer Sheet for the facilitator.

- One copy of the Communication Games Tips for Improving Feedback and Oral Communications for the facilitator.

- One copy of the Communication Games Guidelines for Useful Feedback for each participant.

- A pencil for each participant.

Physical Setting

A room with sufficient space to complete and discuss the work sheet in small groups. Writing surfaces should be provided.

Process

1. Distribute the Communication Games Descriptions to participants, allow them time to read the content, and then discuss each of the various communication games listed on the handout with the group. Solicit real-life examples and comments from participants. (Thirty minutes.)

2. Distribute the Communication Games Work Sheet and pencils and tell participants they will have fifteen minutes to complete it. (Fifteen minutes.)

3. When everyone has completed the work sheet, bring the large group together and ask for volunteers to name the communications game for each statement. Use the Answer Sheet to ensure correct answers are provided. Encourage participants to comment about their results and discuss their answers. (Fifteen minutes.)

4. Use an interactive discussion as you present the Communication Games Tips for Improving Feedback and Communications. (Thirty minutes.)

5. Provide one copy of the Communication Games Guidelines for Useful Feedback to each participant. Have participants pair off and practice giving reassuring and remedial feedback during a performance appraisal. Tell them to "Use a situation in which you have received several complaints from other employees or customers that suggest your employee does not have the necessary skills or knowledge for the job. Tailor it to your job situation." (Fifteen minutes.)

6. Wrap up with a total group discussion of what participants have learned. Use the following questions to focus the discussion:

   - What did you learn from this activity?

- How will you apply your knowledge to communication on the job?
- What will you do differently during performance reviews in the future?

(Fifteen minutes.)

Variation

- Use an observer during the practice session to detect any communication games that are being played.

Reference

Blanchard, K., & Johnson, S. (1981). *The one minute manager.* New York: Berkley Books.

Originally published in The 2000 Annual, Vol. 1, Training.

COMMUNICATION GAMES DESCRIPTIONS

Unfortunately, feedback sessions, like all forms of human communications, are subject to the games people play, which can interfere with open and honest communication. Everyone plays these games at some time—whether as the giver or the receiver of feedback. Such behavior is particularly harmful to both the employee and the organization when used in a performance review session.

We all need to know the different types of games, how to recognize them, and how to avoid or stop playing them altogether. The communication games played by the sender in the performance feedback situation include:

- *It's My Obligation.* In this game, the sender makes it clear that he or she is giving feedback out of an obligation to the process, with little commitment to sharing observations, solving problems, or using the performance review as a way to improve individual or work unit productivity. The obligatory forms are filled out and used as a shield. The receiver will find the review cold, impersonal, and often negative.

- *Hiding the Real Message.* In this game, the sender avoids direct and clear communication, hiding the real message with verbal qualifiers, reservations, and excess words. By the time the sender gets to the point, the receiver is lost in all the extra verbiage. This game makes it difficult, if not impossible, for the receiver to understand the message.

- *This Isn't Serious.* Sometimes, after giving negative feedback, senders decide they don't want to "hurt" the receivers, so they decide to rescue them. The sender will throw out a comment such as, "Well, don't worry about it; it wasn't important anyway" or "Don't worry; you aren't the first and you won't be the last to make that mistake." The result is that the receiver is led to believe the feedback and the poor performance were unimportant.

- *Leading Questions.* Here, the sender acts like Perry Mason and asks leading and unnerving questions. While this may be all right for Mr. Mason in his efforts to trap a criminal, it is not a good practice in a performance feedback session. The results are mistrust, suspicion, and increased defensiveness on the part of the receiver.

- *Guess What I'm Really Thinking.* In this game, the sender delivers indirect messages and expects the receiver to determine the hidden meaning from nonverbals. This game is commonly played by supervisors, and the employees are expected to divine the true meaning of the message.

The Pfeiffer Book of Successful Conflict Management Tools © 2003 John Wiley & Sons, Inc.

These games are all ways for the sender to avoid giving direct and clear feedback. They allow senders to avoid making disclosures and saying what they really mean. The solution is for senders to learn how to say what they mean and mean what they say.

Games can also be played by the receiver. Receiver games are primarily designed to obscure the message, particularly during a performance review session. These games include:

- *Make the Sender Feel Guilty.* During this game, the receiver attempts to make the sender feel guilty by interpreting the feedback to apply to a much broader range of behavior or results than the sender intends. The receiver looks and acts hurt, pouts, and even sulks for days. This type of guilt trip can ruin open, direct communication.

- *Divert Attention.* During this game, the receiver doesn't check for understanding or details, but quickly changes the subject whenever a sensitive issue is broached. The results are that the feedback session goes nowhere because no conclusion is reached and action planning never take place.

- *I'm Not the Only One.* Here, the receiver uses the rule of "safety in numbers." He or she tries to show that the feedback is in error by explaining how many other people are doing the same thing. The result is that the receiver will miss chances for growth and improvement by not "owning" the feedback.

- *Be a Masochist.* In this game, the receiver punishes someone (usually himself or herself) so the sender (usually the supervisor) won't have to. This game is often played by overachievers. It is designed, in part, to force the sender into giving only positive feedback. The result is that the receiver spends so much time in self-talk that the useful feedback may never by heard.

Most of these feedback games are smoke screens to keep the receiver from hearing and acting on feedback. In a performance feedback session, the employee suffers in the long run from these communication games.

COMMUNICATION GAMES WORK SHEET

Directions: Identify each statement below with the letter of the type of communication game being played, as follows:

A = It's My Obligation   D = Leading Questions   G = Divert Attention
B = Hiding the Real Message E = Guess What I'm Really Thinking H = I'm Not the Only One
C = This Isn't Serious   F = Make the Sender Feel Guilty I = Be a Masochist

_____ 1. Joe, why are you always putting me down?

_____ 2. It's company policy to do these performance reviews.

_____ 3. I knew I blew it. Perhaps I should resign.

_____ 4. You're not measuring up, and I think you know why.

_____ 5. Let's not discuss it now. Let's use the time to review the Becker project.

_____ 6. Did you really correct the numbers? Who can confirm that? Do I need to audit your work? Interview staff?

_____ 7. Everybody takes extended breaks.

_____ 8. I think you may tend to get a little too busy and don't always check things out. Not always, but enough to raise questions about your work. The point is, your calculations are often inaccurate.

_____ 9. Don't take this too seriously; it's no big deal.

_____ 10. I work my tail off, and what thanks do I get?

_____ 11. I think everyone in the work group would disagree.

_____ 12. Let's get this over with so we can get back to work.

_____ 13. How many times were you late this month? Do you know everyone's complaining? Can't you get here on time?

_____ 14. Taking that approach can lead to big trouble, if you know what I mean.

_____ 15. Why do you think I gave you this rating on the project?

_____ 16. That's your opinion. Anything else you want to say?

Communication Games Answer Sheet

A = It's My Obligation   2

B = Hiding the Real Message   8

C = This Isn't Serious   9, 12

D = Leading Questions   6, 13

E = Guess What I'm Really Thinking   4, 14, 15

F = Make the Sender Feel Guilty   1, 10

G = Divert Attention   5, 16

H = I'm Not the Only One   7, 11

I = Be a Masochist   3

COMMUNICATION GAMES TIPS FOR IMPROVING FEEDBACK AND ORAL COMMUNICATIONS

Feedback is an intense form of communication for both the supervisor and the employee. The supervisor needs to communicate conclusions about performance to employees. On the other hand, employees want to know where they stand, but may find some or all of the feedback hard to take. Feedback must be specific and clear enough that the employee can accept it and make a commitment to an appropriate course of action.

Both the supervisor and the employee must be committed to giving and receiving clear feedback whenever they can. The following five tips, which are expanded below, can help you make the feedback process work:

1. Know what's in it for you;

2. Develop your feedback skills;

3. Don't play communication games;

4. Remember that feedback occurs between human beings;

5. Focus on goals (accomplishments), knowledge, skills, and style.

Know What's in It for You

Feedback is often viewed as either positive or negative, but another way to see performance management is as supportive of employees. Even when feedback is positive, it can produce stress and anxiety. Thinking about the long-term payoffs of successful feedback helps put this short-term discomfort into perspective.

Some of the payoffs for giving quality supportive feedback are:

1. The satisfaction of helping another grow and develop.

2. Working with integrity and in a way that shows respect for others in the workplace.

3. Being open and honest with people.

4. Producing the quality and quantity—bottom-line results.

5. Meaningful interpersonal relations based on open, clear, and supportive feedback.

Develop Your Feedback Skills

During feedback sessions, both the supervisor and the employee give and receive feedback. Both, therefore, need to use key feedback skills. Three of these skills—listening, empathizing, and questioning—are responsive.

To be responsive, a person must be receptive and non-evaluative. The other two—concluding and describing—are assertive. To use these skills, a person must be proactive, be willing to take risks, and be able to evaluate what is heard.

The responsive and assertive skill groups are two different ways of thinking and acting. Most people think only of the assertive feedback given by the supervisor in performance management, but responsive skills are also critical in these situations. Both the supervisor and the employee must use all five skills from both groups. The ability to "shift gears" from using responsive skills to using assertive skills and back again is the real "art" of effective feedback.

Listening is a vital skill in all areas of human communications; in a performance management session, it is critical. Both the supervisor and the employee must listen! They must set aside their personal opinions, feelings, and biases so they can hear the other person's point of view. They must be able to paraphrase the other's observations and conclusions.

A point of view is kind of like a belly button—everyone has one! Your point of view contains all your values, biases, feelings, emotions, and needs as you view the world around you. In a feedback session, your point of view must be "defused" or "suspended" for you to understand the other person and to empathize with him or her. Listening for and acknowledging feelings can help remove personal blocks or defensiveness that often threaten a feedback session.

Empathizing occurs when either the supervisor or the employee:

- Asks for information about the other's feelings;

- Shares his or her own similar experiences;

- Make statements that show understanding of the feelings and values of the other person; and

- Avoids evaluating the other's feelings and values.

Empathizing and empathic listening keep communication from being a mechanical process.

Both the supervisor and the employee also need questioning skills to gain understanding of one another's points of view. Questioning shows interest in what the other person is saying. This interest should also be supported through nonverbal behavior. The best questioning technique is to ask open-ended questions, such as "Tell me why that happened," "What do you think about that?" or "How did you proceed?"

The major purpose of performance feedback is to make sure that an employee's performance is on target. During the process, both the supervisor and the employee must judge that performance. Supervisors are paid to judge others' performance, but employees must engage in continuous self-evaluation of their own performance. This process involves:

- Judging the quality, quantity, timeliness, and appropriateness of behavior across a variety of situations and against established goals;

- Making judgments about the strengths and weaknesses of accomplishments, knowledge, skills, ability, and style;

- Controlling personal biases; and

- Determining whether success or failure is due to the individual's behavior or to factors beyond the individual's control.

Supervisors first draw conclusions, then decide what feedback to give, how to evaluate the employee's performance, what additional training or development is needed, what additional work assignments to give, and what support is needed to meet or exceed goals.

Simply observing performance and drawing conclusions is not enough. Both the supervisor and the employee must be able to describe the performance in a clear, concise, and concrete way. This involves:

- Describing the observed behavior, actions, and results;

- Being specific about the time, place, behavior, actions, and results observed;

- Describing one's own reactions and personal feelings about the behavior and the results; and

- Tailoring the timing and the amount of feedback.

The Pfeiffer Book of Successful Conflict Management Tools © 2003 John Wiley & Sons, Inc.

Don't Play Communication Games

We all need be able to recognize and avoid communication games. Sender games include:

- It's My Obligation
- Hiding the Real Message
- This Isn't Serious
- Leading Questions
- Guess What I'm Really Thinking

   Receiver games include:

- Make the Sender Feel Guilty
- Divert Attention
- I'm Not the Only One
- Be a Masochist

Remember That Feedback Occurs Between Human Beings

Performance feedback occurs between two human beings, so it will always be a somewhat subjective process. It cannot be effectively computerized or otherwise mechanized. It will always involve judgment, questioning, empathy, and personal commitment.

   It is important for both the supervisor and the employee to try to be as objective, detailed, and concrete as possible. Each must try to avoid playing communication games. They both must be willing and able to give and receive feedback. But they are both human, with their own concerns, opinions, and reactions.

Focus on Goals (Accomplishments), Knowledge, Skills, and Style

What individuals do from day-to-day has both short-term and long-term implications. Evaluating and discussing performance is a complex process. All aspects of the employee's performance should be covered—not only the goals themselves, but also how the goals were accomplished and the impact of the employee's performance on others inside and outside of the organization.

This means discussing the knowledge and skills used by the employee or the absence of critical knowledge and skills. It also means discussing the effectiveness of the employee's style.

Both the supervisor and the employee must be willing to discuss all aspects of performance. There will be short-term anxieties, but the long-term payoffs—an open, honest relationship, strengthened communications, and improved performance—more than offset any short-term anxiety.

Types of Feedback

One of the most important tools a supervisor has for maintaining control and developing employees is the proper use of feedback. Feedback can be either verbal or nonverbal. Nonverbal feedback sends a message, although perhaps not what is intended. For purposes of this discussion, we will focus on verbal feedback. Verbal feedback has often been categorized as either positive or negative, but another way of viewing it is as *reassuring* feedback (reinforcing ongoing behavior) or *remedial* feedback (indicating that a change in behavior is needed). In this sense, all feedback can be considered positive, in that it is for the growth and development of the individual.

Reassuring Feedback.   One of the most damaging and erroneous assumptions that supervisors make is that good performance and appropriate behavior are to be "expected" from the employee and that the only time feedback is needed is when the employee does something wrong. Supervisors operating under this assumption rarely give supportive feedback, although in reality it is the more important of the two types of feedback. An axiom of effective supervision (Blanchard & Johnson, 1982) it to "catch them doing something right and let them know it." Use reassuring feedback to reinforce behavior that contributes to organizational goals and values.

If you focus on what employees are doing well, then they will come to value excellent work and see their work in terms of performing as well as possible. What is reinforced has a tendency to become stronger. What is not reinforced has a tendency to fade away, so excellence should be actively reinforced and errors simply mentioned so that employees will focus on excellence. The following example of the two types of feedback illustrates the difference.

Focus on Errors: "The last four letters you typed were replete with typos. I cannot have that kind of sloppy work going out of my office."

Focus on Excellence: "The written communications this week have looked good, except for the last four letters, which contained a number of typos. Perhaps your fingers get ahead of themselves. Please take these back and retype them. Thanks."

Fortunately, however, no one has to make a choice between using only reassuring or only remedial feedback. Both are important and useful, and it is important to understand how each works so that the maximum benefit can be obtained.

Remedial Feedback. Remedial feedback is as essential to the healing and growth process as is reassuring feedback. It should be thought of as a remedy, a prescription for improved health and performance, used to alter behavior that is ineffective.

A remedial feedback session, although not harmful if done correctly, is not always an enjoyable experience for the receiver. Even under the best of circumstances, the subordinate will probably feel a little defensive or embarrassed. There is no need to apologize for giving remedial feedback. Remedial or otherwise, feedback is a contribution; apologies will discount its importance and lessen its impact. Nevertheless, remedial feedback must be given in a way that does not lessen the recipient's dignity and sense of self-worth.

The supervisor should always have an option ready to explore with the employee. Presenting a behavioral option that the employee might never have considered can be effective and powerful in altering and "healing" bad behavior. The option should be presented immediately after the remedial feedback to help the employee move quickly to a more comfortable position. This reinforces the intrinsic worth of the employee and helps him or her focus on the possibilities and prospects for positive growth.

The following example shows how an option could be presented when giving remedial feedback: "When you criticized Bob during the staff meeting, he seemed very intimidated and upset. When you choose to criticize others' input, it's less disconcerting for everyone to discuss it with the person privately after the meeting."

Guidelines for Giving Effective Feedback

The following guidelines are helpful for anyone who is trying to improve feedback skills:

Be Specific. Being specific is the most important rule in giving any type of feedback. Unless the feedback is specific, very little learning or reinforcement is possible. The following examples show the difference between general and specific feedback:

General: "I'm happy to see that your work is getting better."

Specific: "I'm happy that you turned in every report on schedule this month."

Although a supervisor's approval ("I'm pleased to see. . . .") or disapproval ("I'm upset that. . . .") can give emphasis to feedback, it should be supported by specific evidence in order to effect a change in behavior.

Center on Actions, Not on Attitudes. Although subordinates should always be accountable for their actions, it is much more difficult to hold them accountable for their attitudes or feelings. Of course, attitudes and feelings are important, yet they are difficult to quantify, so discussing them leads to generalities and may lead to defensiveness. Just as feedback must be specific and observable in order to be effective, it must be nonthreatening in order to be accepted.

One attitude that managers often try to measure is loyalty. Certain employee actions that seem to indicate loyalty or disloyalty can be observed, but loyalty is a result, not an action. The following highlights the difference between giving feedback on actions and giving feedback on attitudes:

Feedback on attitude: "You have been showing disrespect for Tammy again."

Feedback on actions: "You refused to help Tammy with the month-end report, threw the printout down on her desk, and swore at her."

The more that remedial feedback is molded in terms of attitude, the more it will be perceived as a personal attack and the more difficult it will be to deal with the employee's reactions. The more that remedial feedback is cast in specific, behavioral terms, the more likely that it will be accepted by the receiver. The more that reassuring feedback is given in terms of specific actions, the higher the likelihood that those actions and behaviors will be repeated.

Give Feedback as Close to the Actual Event as Possible. Feedback of either type works best if it is given as soon as possible after the behavior occurs. Waiting decreases the impact that the feedback will have on the behavior. The passage of time may make the behavior seem less important to both parties and may mean that specific details are forgotten.

On the other hand, dwelling on something for a long period can cause it to be blown out of proportion. From the subordinate's point of view, the longer the wait for the feedback, the less important it must be. The following example illustrates this point:

Delayed feedback: "Several times last year you didn't submit your monthly capital improvement progress reports."

The Pfeiffer Book of Successful Conflict Management Tools © 2003 John Wiley & Sons, Inc.

Immediate feedback: "It's July 3 and you haven't turned in your capital improvement progress reports for June."

Pick an Appropriate Time.   Enough time should be allotted for the feedback session to deal with the issues completely. A manager can undermine the effectiveness of feedback by watching the clock and hurrying through the session. Picking the right time and place is a matter of mixing a little common sense with an awareness of organizational values and the significance of the message.

Do Not Mix Your Agenda.   Frequently, other issues surface during a feedback session. When reassuring feedback is being given, no topic that does not relate to the specific feedback should be discussed if it would undercut the message. For example, the manager could destroy the good just accomplished by adding, "Oh, before I forget, even though you did a great job on the facility plan, I'd like you to pay closer attention to your monthly progress reports. The last one was pretty sloppy." When the parting comment is negative, it has a lingering effect and can completely overshadow and negate the positive.

When remedial feedback is given, however, the situation is different. The feedback should be absorbed as soon as possible, with the employee's negative feelings lasting no longer than necessary. Any reproving should be accompanied by an immediate show of concern and reassurance. As soon as the feedback has been understood and acknowledged, and a commitment has been secured to improve, the manager may want to solicit the employee's input on something else or make some other reassuring statement that reaffirms the employee's intrinsic worth and value. Obviously, the supervisor should not concoct a situation just to provide this type of feedback.

In certain situations, it is appropriate to give both reassuring and remedial feedback at the same time. This is true for training sessions, performance review meetings, and when experienced employees are being assigned new and challenging tasks.

When the situation is appropriate for giving both types of feedback at the same time, don't use the word "but" to connect the two thoughts. The word will dampen nearly everything that was said before it. If it is fitting to give reassuring and remedial feedback within the same sentence, the clauses should be connected with "and." This allows both parts of the sentence to be heard clearly and sets the stage for a positive suggestion. Here are some examples of these sentence structures:

Connected with but: "Your output the first quarter was high, but your second quarter performance should have met the same high standard."

Connected with and: "Your first report was on time, and your others should have been also."

Connected with but: "You were late this morning, but the chief called to tell you what a great job you did on the budget."

Connected with and: "You were late this morning, and the chief called to tell you what a great job you did on the budget."

Alternate the reassuring and remedial feedback. When considerable feedback is being given at the same time, it is frequently better to mix the reassuring feedback with the remedial feedback than to give all of one type and then all of the other.

Regardless of which category comes first, whatever is said last will be remembered the most clearly. If someone with low self-esteem is first given reassuring feedback and then only remedial, he or she is likely to believe the reassuring feedback was given just to soften the blow. Alternating between the two types will make all the feedback seem more genuine.

When feasible, do use reassuring feedback to soften the remedial feedback. When both types of feedback are appropriate, there is usually no reason to start with reassuring. However, this does not mean that remedial feedback should be quickly sandwiched in between reassuring statements. Use reassuring statements as a good teaching aid for areas that need improvement. This is especially true if the employee has done a good job in the past and then has failed under similar circumstances.

Using Feedback Effectively

When using feedback, "seek first to understand, then seek to be understood." The person giving the feedback is responsible for helping the recipient to understand what is being said. Because we all see the world differently, it is important for the recipient to understand the giver's perspective before responding.

Feedback should always be used to develop the employee and support positive growth, not to destroy the individual. The object of giving feedback is not to critique the other person, but to relate what was seen and heard and what effects that behavior has had. One's personal approval or disapproval, even if important, is secondary.

Remedial feedback should be given directly to the person for whom it is intended. If others are present, they should not become an audience. Good eye contact with the recipient is essential.

The Pfeiffer Book of Successful Conflict Management Tools © 2003 John Wiley & Sons, Inc.

Receiving Feedback

Just as giving feedback properly requires skill and understanding, so does receiving it. When receiving feedback, many people tend to argue, become defensive, refuse to believe, or discredit the information. Statements such as, "I didn't say that," "That's not what I meant," and "You don't understand what I was trying to do" are attempts to convince the person giving the feedback that he or she is wrong.

However, the recipient must understand that the observer—whether manager, peer, or subordinate—is simply relating what he or she experienced as a result of the recipient's behavior. Right or wrong, perceptions are important and affect behavior. Of course the giver and receiver have different viewpoints, but the purpose of feedback is to give a new view or to increase awareness.

As a rule of thumb, the appropriate response is to acknowledge and thank the person for the feedback. It is also appropriate, of course, to ask for clarity or more detail on any issue—seeking to understand before seeking to be understood.

Feedback can be thought of as food. It is necessary to grow, develop, and sustain life. When people are hungry, food is what they need; but when they are full, food is the last thing they want or need. The same applies to "swallowing" feedback. When people have had enough, they should stop. Attempting to swallow all the feedback that might be available, or that various people would like to give, is like taking another helping just because someone says, "Have some more."

It is reasonable for the receiver to expect specificity in feedback. No feedback should be given or accepted as legitimate if it cannot be clearly demonstrated by an observable behavior. For example, if someone says, "You're not a team player," an appropriate question would be, "What specifically have I said or done to cause you to think that?"

If that response is countered with "I don't know; I just feel that way," then the accusation should be immediately forgotten.

It is impossible to change to meet everyone else's expectations, and the situation becomes more complicated as more and more people express differing expectations or feedback. A single act can generate disparate feedback from different people who observe it. For example, failure to contribute at a staff meeting could be viewed as uncooperative by one person, shyness by another, or merely uninformed by a third. Each person will see it from his or her unique perspective.

Even though an individual is the best authority on himself or herself, there are still parts of each person's behavior that are more obvious to others. Only the individual can decide whether or not to change the behavior. For feedback to be effective, the receiver must hear what the giver is saying, weigh it, and then determine whether or not the information is relevant.

Although people may be the best judges of their own attitudes and intentions, they are better able to grow and develop if they pay attention to the feedback they receive from others, even if the feedback is uncomfortable to receive.

Effective Strategies for Giving Feedback

The strategies below offer one approach to giving feedback during a performance review. First, decide on the desired future objective, whether in the next ten minutes after the session or three years later. Pay attention to the ultimate outcome. Focus on the desired results, not on following the system. Change your methods or even modify your original strategy if conditions change or unforeseen events occur. After you decide on an approach, keep the following rules in mind:

- Be clear about what you want in terms of specific, identifiable outcomes for yourself, your subordinate, and the organization.

- Outline what you expect to say and how you intend to conduct the meeting.

- Have a strategy in mind as you meet with the individual, but don't have it out in the open.

Giving Reassuring Feedback

The following are some suggested strategies for giving reassuring feedback:

- Acknowledge the specific action and result you are reinforcing. Immediately let your subordinate know that you are pleased about something he or she did. Be specific and describe the event in behavioral terms. ("You finished the project on time!")

- Explain the accomplishment and state your appreciation. The person must be able to see the effects of his or her behavior in specific, observable ways. Your appreciation is important, but as an additional reinforcing element. The main reinforcement is the effect. ("It was a major factor in getting the contract, and I am pleased with your outstanding work.")

- Help the subordinate to take full responsibility for the success. If the employee acknowledges the feedback, this step is accomplished. If the employee seems overly modest, more work is needed. Unless he or she can internalize the success and receive satisfaction from it, very little growth will occur.

- Ask how the success was accomplished or if any problems were encountered and how they were overcome. In talking about what happened, the employee is likely to realize how much he or she was really responsible for. It is important for both of you to hear how success was accomplished.

- Ask if the subordinate wants to talk about anything else. While the employee is feeling positive and knows that you are appreciative and receptive, he or she may be willing to open up about other issues. The positive energy created by this meeting can be directed toward other work-related issues, so take advantage of the opportunity.

- Thank the subordinate for the good performance. This assures that your appreciation will be remembered as he or she returns to the work setting.

Giving Remedial Feedback

The following steps are suggested as a strategy for giving remedial feedback:

- Relate clearly in specific, observable, and behavioral terms the nature of the failure or behavior and the effect of the failure or behavior on the work group or organization. If you can say something appropriate to reduce the employee's anxiety, the employee is more likely to accept the feedback nondefensively.

- Before assuming that the subordinate is at fault, ask what happened. In many instances, the subordinate is not at fault or is only partially responsible.

- Help the employee take full responsibility for his or her actions. The more time spent in finding out what happened, the easier this will be. The employee needs to learn from the experience in order to reduce the probability of a reoccurrence, but unless this step is handled effectively, the employee will feel defensive.

- After the employee has accepted responsibility, the next step is to decide what to do to rectify the situation. Jointly devise a plan that will help eliminate errors.

If you both want the same thing (i.e., better performance), then both of you are obligated to do something about it. This is also an excellent opportunity to build on the employee's strengths. ("I'd like you to develop a purchasing policy with the same quality as the investment policy you wrote.")

- Once the issue is resolved, end the session by stating your confidence in the ability of the employee to handle the situation. The object is to allow the employee to re-enter the work setting feeling as optimistic as the situation permits. The employee must also understand that you will follow up and give additional feedback.

COMMUNICATION GAMES GUIDELINES FOR USEFUL FEEDBACK

- Useful feedback is descriptive rather than evaluative. By avoiding evaluative language, it reduces the need for the receiver to respond defensively. The receiver may choose to use or reject the feedback on its own merits.

- Useful feedback is specific rather than general. For example, being told that one is "autocratic" and "domineering" will probably not be as useful as to be told, "Just now when we were discussing the issue, you did not listen to what others said, and I felt forced to accept your arguments or to face attack from you."

- Useful feedback takes into account the needs of both the receiver and the giver. Feedback can be destructive when it serves only the giver's needs.

- Useful feedback is directed toward behavior the receiver can change. Frustration is only increased when a person is reminded of a shortcoming over which he or she has little or no control.

- Useful feedback is solicited rather than imposed. Feedback is most useful when the receiver asks a question that those observing him or her can answer.

- Useful feedback is well-timed. In general, feedback is most useful when given as soon as possible after the observed behavior, depending, of course, on the person's readiness to hear it, on support available from others, etc.

- Useful feedback is checked with the sender. The receiver should rephrase the feedback he or she has received to ensure clear communication.

- Useful feedback is checked with others in the group. In a training group, particularly, both giver and receiver can check their feedback with others for agreement.

14

The Company Task Force:
Dealing with Disruptive Behavior

Susanne W. Whitcomb

Goals

- To help the participants to become aware of the roles and behaviors that are disruptive in meetings, the degree to which they are disruptive, and the positive as well as negative consequences associated with each.

- To offer the participants an opportunity to develop strategies for dealing with disruptive roles and behaviors.

Group Size

Any number of subgroups of seven to nine participants each.

Time Required

Two and one-half hours.

Materials

- A copy of The Company Task Force Background Sheet for each participant.

- One set of The Company Task Force Role Sheets 1 through 9 for each subgroup. Each subgroup member is to receive a different sheet; Sheet 8 and/or Sheet 9 may be eliminated for any subgroup consisting of fewer than nine members. (The facilitator may also want to have an extra copy of each role sheet available for distribution during step 13.)
- Blank paper and a pencil for each group leader.
- A clipboard or other portable writing surface for each group leader.

Physical Setting

A room large enough so that each subgroup can be seated in a circle and can work without disturbing the other subgroups. In addition, a separate room should be provided for the use of those subgroup members who are designated as most obstructive.

Process

1. The facilitator tells the participants that they are to be involved in a role play and explains the goals of the activity.

2. Subgroups of seven to nine participants each are formed, and the members of each subgroup are asked to be seated in a circle.

3. Copies of The Company Task Force Background Sheet are distributed, and the participants are asked to read this handout.

4. A set of role sheets is distributed to each subgroup in such a way that each member receives a different sheet. All participants are asked to read their sheets and are advised that they must maintain their roles during the role play.

5. The facilitator requests that the subgroup leaders start their meetings.

6. After fifteen minutes the facilitator stops the meetings and instructs all subgroups to remain intact. The members of each subgroup are asked to spend ten minutes determining which role was the most obstructive.

7. Each participant who is designated most obstructive by his or her subgroup is asked to join the others so designated, to form a separate subgroup in another room, and to await instructions.

8. The remaining participants are told that when the role play resumes, they are to assume new roles as cooperative, insightful people who are seriously working on the task-force problem. The facilitator then instructs

The Pfeiffer Book of Successful Conflict Management Tools © 2003 John Wiley & Sons, Inc.

each subgroup to spend fifteen minutes establishing two strategies for dealing with its most obstructive member when that person returns; one strategy is to serve as the primary plan, and the other is to be used only if the first is unsuccessful.

9. While the majority of the participants are working on their strategies, the facilitator asks the participants who were designated most obstructive to reflect on the positive aspects of their behaviors within their subgroups. (For example, The Rambler relieves tension, and The Organization Man/ Woman provides valuable reminders of various obstacles to be overcome.) It is explained that when they return in approximately ten minutes, their subgroups will use specific strategies to deal with them. They are told to be sensitive to these strategies: If they are approached with humane attitudes, they are to respond in kind and adjust their behaviors to be more reasonable; however, if they are approached with aggression or in a demeaning way, they are to be creative in responding negatively and in character so that their subgroups can learn from their reactions. Finally, the obstructive members are asked to discuss ways to manifest their behaviors quickly when they return so that their subgroups can use the chosen strategies as soon as possible.

10. After the allotted time has passed, the obstructive members are asked to return to the main assembly room and to rejoin their subgroups. Then the facilitator instructs the subgroups to resume their meetings.

11. After fifteen minutes the facilitator asks the subgroups to stop their role plays. Each subgroup is instructed to discuss the experience; the nonobstructive members are asked to concentrate on whether the primary or backup strategy worked and how well, and the obstructive member is asked to concentrate on his or her reactions to the strategy(ies). Blank paper, pencils, and clipboards or other portable writing surfaces are distributed to the individual subgroup leaders, who are asked to take notes during the discussions so that reports can be presented to the total group. (Fifteen minutes.)

12. The total group is reconvened, and the facilitator asks the subgroup leaders to take turns sharing the results of the discussions. (Ten minutes.)

13. The subgroups are reassembled. Each subgroup is assigned one or two roles and is asked to determine the following for each role:

- Positive features;
- Negative features;

- Interventions that might be used when dealing with this type of behavior in meetings; and

- Ways in which these interventions might or might not be helpful.

  (Twenty minutes.)

14. The total group is reconvened for a discussion of the results of the previous step and for summarizing. The following question is useful in concluding the experience: If you were to give advice on handling disruptive people, what would it be?

Variations

- The activity may be shortened by eliminating step 13.

- After step 12, copies of the lecturette entitled "Dealing with Disruptive Individuals in Meetings" (page 73) may be distributed and the subgroups' strategies compared with those presented in the lecturette.

- In step 14 each participant may be asked to select a partner, to discuss with the partner a disruptive person with whom he or she must interact, and to develop a strategy for dealing with this person.

- The role play may be enacted in a group-on-group configuration, with the majority of participants observing as one subgroup conducts its meeting. Subsequently, the observers report on the factors listed in step 13.

Originally published in A Handbook of Structured Experiences for Human Relations Training, Volume IX *(1983).*

THE COMPANY TASK FORCE BACKGROUND SHEET

You are an employee of Organic Foodstuffs, Inc., a company that has been manufacturing vitamins and food supplements in the town of Belmont Shore since 1913. Gradually the residential areas of the town have encircled the company's factory, and complaints from those who live nearby have been escalating over the last few years. These complaints generally involve air and water pollution, residential-parking abuses, the piercing sound of the 8:00 a.m. whistle, and lunch-time littering. The company president has recently joined the Community Service League and since then has become aware of the extent of the factory's unpopularity. Consequently, the president has appointed a task force of employees to address the company's poor image. You are a member of this task force, which is meeting today to determine recommendations to be submitted to the president immediately afterward.

The Company Task Force Role Sheet 1

The Leader

You have been appointed by the company president to be the leader of the task force. As the leader, your basic responsibilities are to accomplish the following:

- Keep the discussion flowing and on track;
- Control the members who try to dominate the discussion; and
- Ensure that the session results in specific recommendations for ways to improve the company's image.

At the beginning of the meeting, you introduce yourself as the officially appointed leader, emphasize the seriousness of the task at hand, and elicit ideas for image improvement.

Do not show this role description to anyone.

The Company Task Force Role Sheet 2

The Power Monger

You want to usurp the leadership role from the officially appointed leader and make a big impression on the other task-force members. You have no real interest in the task at hand; instead, your objective is to obtain some of the power you need in order to bring to fruition your "pet" project: convincing the company to open a branch office in Tahiti. Once you have assumed control of the task force, your plan is to switch the focus of the meeting to your project. At this point you hope to gain support for the project by emphasizing its positive points. For example, opening the branch office will attract worldwide publicity, show the company's concern for world affairs, and bring fame to Belmont Shore.

Do not show this role description to anyone.

THE COMPANY TASK FORCE ROLE SHEET 3

The Pain in the Neck

You are the negative member of the task force. The other members appear to be extremely poorly organized, and you fail to see how anything can be accomplished in this meeting. In fact, you do not understand why you were appointed to the task force; you have nothing to contribute, and you resent the fact that you have to take time from your busy work schedule to attend. You are hoping to convince the others that the task is impossible and should be abandoned.

Do not show this role description to anyone.

THE COMPANY TASK FORCE ROLE SHEET 4

The Idealist

You have a deep, spiritual commitment to eliminating pollution. You feel that the entire focus of the task force is wrong; the appropriate task is not to reverse the company's negative image, but to put an end to the abuses for which the complaints have been received. It is important to you that the company be concerned not only with its own welfare, but also with that of the entire world.

Because you cannot compromise your values by helping to complete the assigned task, you try to persuade the other members to adopt your viewpoint and work on solving the real problem.

Do not show this role description to anyone.

THE COMPANY TASK FORCE ROLE SHEET 5

The Rambler

In this meeting, as in all others that you attend, you cannot stay focused on the subject at hand. You have an active but undisciplined mind, and the comments made at meetings frequently remind you of unrelated anecdotes and bits of news or information that your gregarious nature compels you to share aloud.

Do not show this role description to anyone.

THE COMPANY TASK FORCE ROLE SHEET 6

The Organization Man/Woman

You are highly conscious of the formal organizational hierarchy; during your career with the company you have always been careful to proceed through the "right channels," obey the rules, and adhere to the established norms. Your instinct for professional survival makes you extremely cautious; in fact, you refuse to act on any idea until you are certain that it meets the company standards. Consequently, you maintain a wary stance throughout this meeting. You feel responsible for reminding the others that trying to change the company's regular operating procedures may be dangerous and that those in authority must make the ultimate decisions.

Do not show this role description to anyone.

The Pfeiffer Book of Successful Conflict Management Tools © 2003 John Wiley & Sons, Inc.

THE COMPANY TASK FORCE ROLE SHEET 7

The Mediator

You cannot stand conflict and you believe that compromise is always possible. Consequently, during the meeting you make a concerted effort to maintain harmony among the members of the task force. You feel compelled to remind the others when appropriate that all viewpoints are worth hearing, that most positions on issues are not so very different, and that everyone should have a chance to participate in the process of establishing recommendations.

Do not show this role description to anyone.

THE COMPANY TASK FORCE ROLE SHEET 8

The Veteran

You have been employed with the company twice as long as any other member of the task force. In your opinion, the current situation with the company's image does not warrant operational changes. During your long period of employment, you have seen a number of practices implemented and then abandoned; you believe that changes arising from the image problem will fall into the same category. In addition, over the years you have learned why certain approaches have failed and why they will continue to fail in the future. Consequently, you feel it is important to let the others know when they suggest alternatives that have proven ineffective.

Do not show this role description to anyone.

THE COMPANY TASK FORCE ROLE SHEET 9

The Silent One

Attending meetings is always difficult for you because you are too shy and reserved to participate actively. You are professionally insecure and believe that your opinion, even when elicited, is not worth stating. When the others ask for your input, you are forced to tell them that although you find the discussion interesting, you are present only to listen and to learn.

Do not show this role description to anyone.

Conflict and the Organization

This section offers six experiential learning activities—all role plays—that confront participants with conflict on a wider scale: interdepartmental budget fights, culture clashes in a merger, and more. Two exercises, "Crime Fighting Task Force" and "Piccadilly Manor," take participants outside the workplace altogether for a taste of the sort of infighting that goes on in community politics. The learning points, however, are very much back to business.

- Budget Cutting: Conflict and Consensus Seeking"—Realistic role play involving an interdepartmental clash over company resources.
- Winterset High School: An Intergroup Conflict Simulation—Role play illustrating conflicts that arise from "occupational stereotyping" (the white-collars vs. the blue-collars).
- Crime-Fighting Task Force: Understanding Political Tactics in Groups— Role players try to recognize and cope with vested interests and hidden agendas of relative strangers in a decision-making situation.
- Piccadilly Manor: Improving Decision Making in a Political Milieu—An equally well-thought-out exercise in which players must deal with the values and agendas of people outside their own work group.
- Merger Mania: Understanding Intercultural Negotiation—The "cultures" at issue being those of two fictitious companies at odds during a merger.
- Lindell-Billings Corporation: A Confrontational Role Play—Centered on a question of business ethics that pits executives against middle managers.

15

Budget Cutting: Conflict and Consensus Seeking

Terry L. Maris

Goals

- To experience the dynamics of consensus seeking in a decision-making group.
- To provide experience in establishing priorities.
- To explore methods for resolving conflict in decision-making groups.
- To examine individual ways of handling conflict in groups.

Group Size

Subgroups of six members each.

Time Required

Approximately two and one-half hours.

Materials

- A set of six name tags labeled A, B, C, D, E, and F for each subgroup, one for each member of the subgroup.

- One copy of the Budget Cutting Instruction Sheet for each participant.
- A set of six different Budget Cutting Priorities Sheets (A, B, C, D, E, and F) for each subgroup, one for each member of the subgroup, corresponding to the member's name tag.
- One copy of the Budget Cutting Key Facts Sheet for each participant.
- Blank paper and a pencil for each participant.

Physical Setting

A room large enough to accommodate a table for each subgroup, and enough space so that the subgroups can work without distraction.

Process

1. The facilitator divides the participants into subgroups of six members each and directs the members of each subgroup to count off alphabetically, i.e., "A," "B," "C," etc. The facilitator announces that each member within a subgroup is the manager of one of six plants within a company; member A being the manager of Plant A, and so on. Name tags are distributed, and each member wears the letter designation of his or her plant. (Five minutes.)

2. The facilitator distributes to each participant a copy of the Budget Cutting Instruction Sheet, the appropriate Budget Cutting Priorities Sheet (A, B, C, D, E, or F), a copy of the Budget Cutting Key Facts Sheet, blank paper, and a pencil.

3. The subgroups are seated at their tables, and the participants are instructed to read all their handouts and to prepare themselves to participate in a budget meeting. The facilitator answers participants' questions and ensures task clarity. (Fifteen minutes.)

4. The facilitator instructs the participants to cease their budget meeting preparations and to begin their subgroups' budget meetings. (Forty-five minutes.)

5. The facilitator calls time and instructs the participants to share their reactions to the experience within their subgroups. (Ten minutes.)

6. The participants are instructed to discuss their budget sessions, identifying key aspects of their subgroups' functioning. The following questions may be used to guide this discussion:

- What was the general tone of the meeting?
- Did conflict generally evolve into cooperation? What did or did not help this to happen?
- What ways of dealing with the problem did members evidence or introduce?
- Which methods were most effective in achieving the subgroup's stated objective?
- Were priorities established? How was this done?
- Did the demand for consensus help or hinder the resolution of the problem?
- What was the outcome of the subgroup's deliberations?

Key aspects then are shared across subgroups in brief, verbal reports, and similarities noted. These may be listed on newsprint. (Twenty-five minutes.)

7. The participants are directed to meet again in their subgroups to discuss the following:

- How could priorities be set most effectively in a group of this type?
- What procedures for resolving the conflict would be most effective in a group of this type?
- How might consensus be achieved most easily in a group of people with apparently conflicting objectives?

(Twenty minutes.)

8. The subgroups report their suggestions to the total group, and major points are listed on newsprint. These points are then related by the members to actual situations in which what was learned from the experience might be applied. (Twenty minutes.)

Variations

- The facilitator can designate a leader or cast one participant as the president to conduct the meeting within each subgroup.
- Observers can be designated to record the decision-making procedures utilized in the subgroups.

- The facilitator can give a brief lecturette prior to this activity on factors that influence attitudes toward consensus. Participants then can process this aspect of their behavior during the budget session.

- The budget meeting and/or group discussions can be videotaped and re-played for the participants' later examination.

Originally published in The 1982 Annual Handbook for Facilitators, Trainers, and Consultants.

Budget Cutting Instruction Sheet

The Ace Manufacturing Company, in which you are employed as the manager of one of six facilities (plants), *must* cut $500,000 from its budget for the next fiscal year. Although a tentative budget had been agreed to by all plant and corporate managers, this drastic adjustment now must be made because of a recent legal judgment against the company.

The president of Ace Manufacturing has called a special meeting of all plant managers; the meeting will convene soon and will last only forty-five minutes. Consistent with the president's style of management, you and your colleagues have been given complete freedom to decide how the budget cuts will be allocated. The only requirement is that *all* managers *must* agree to the final decisions, whatever they may be, and that the decisions on how the cuts will be allocated must be made at today's meeting.

You and your staff have reconsidered the financial requirements for your plant and have decided that you should attempt to use this opportunity to improve the position of your plant relative to the others. In this budget meeting, you intend to see to it that your plant will receive the smallest possible budget cut, while you attempt to support the financial interests of the company as a whole and the president's request for a decision on the budget-cut allocations.

Your copy of the Budget Meeting Priorities Sheet represents the new expenditures for your plant that had been agreed to in the draft budget. You may use any or all of this information in the discussion, but you may not read verbatim from the sheet.

Budget Cutting Key Facts Sheet

The Ace Manufacturing Company has 2,446 nonunionized employees located in six plants throughout the country. All the plants produce the same product (widgets) for comparable markets. The reasons for having six geographically dispersed facilities are to minimize transportation costs and to serve regional markets better. The company has been in business for twelve years and for the past several years has held approximately 11 percent of the national market share. In the next three to five years, business is expected to expand steadily.

Plant

	A	B	C	D	E	F
Number of Employees:	405	399	412	395	420	415
Annual Employee Turnover (%):	15	10	13	9	12	10
Average Hourly Earnings:	$7.35	$8.40	$7.85	$8.65	$8.15	$8.50
Worker Days Lost Due to Accidents:	187	133	215	150	141	175
Annual Production (in millions):	2.315	2.107	2.410	2.110	2.323	2.349
Cost per Unit:	$7.75	$8.05	$7.65	$8.15	$7.80	$7.70
Price per Unit:	$8.05	$8.20	$7.90	$8.20	$8.00	$7.95

 The Pfeiffer Book of Successful Conflict Management Tools © 2003 John Wiley & Sons, Inc.

BUDGET CUTTING PRIORITIES SHEET
(Plant A)

1. **Warehouse Expansion** *Estimated cost: $500,000)*

   Because of steadily increasing production and frequently inclement weather, our present warehouse needs to be expanded by 25 percent to accommodate a larger finished-goods inventory. Three times this past year, severe snow storms have prevented the shipment of finished goods on schedule. Also, because of the limited warehouse capacity, widgets (which must be protected from the elements) had to be stored temporarily in the production area. Consequently, production had to be cut back and some employees were laid off. An addition to the present warehouse would permit the temporary storage of widgets during inclement weather. This addition is necessary, not only for present needs, but also to accommodate the expansion of the plant in future years.

2. **Purchase of Semitrailer Trucks** *(Estimated cost: $200,000)*

   The trucking firms that have been transporting both our raw materials and our finished goods have been disrupting our operations lately with increasingly frequent strikes. These strikes appear to be the result of rather severe internal conflict within the union. Several local unions in the area have refused to obey the order of their top officials to refrain from illegal strikes during the life of existing labor-management agreements. Although it is not our desire to antagonize union truckers, we feel that we no longer can sit idle while the unions fight among themselves. We have calculated that with the purchase of four trucks at $50,000 each, we will be able to handle our shipments ourselves during these strikes. If and when we no longer need to haul our own goods, we can lease the trucks to another company.

3. **Consulting Contract** (Estimated cost: $70,000)

   In recent months, our plant has been the target of union organizers. Although we are convinced that our employees have always been compensated well and treated fairly, we are concerned about the possibility that the union's efforts may prove to be successful. If they are, it would affect the entire company—not just our plant. For these reasons, we feel that it is imperative that we do everything within our power to resist unionization. A well-known consultant has proposed a plan designed to resist the unionization of our employees. The consultant says that because the union effort is in an early stage, with the benefit of consulting services, we would have better than a 50 percent chance of keeping the union out. Additionally, the proposal calls for extensive training of our supervisors, which, in itself, would be quite valuable to us.

Budget Cutting Priorities Sheet
(Plant B)

1. **Expansion of Production Capability** *(Estimated cost: $400,000)*

We urgently need to expand our production capability by adding a second assembly line. For the past several months, orders for our product have far exceeded our ability to fill them, even though we have been operating at full capacity. Not only did we lose approximately $600,000 in sales last year, we also have lost several good customers to our competitors. If we do not increase our output in the near future, we run the risk of irretrievable losses in our market share, both regionally and nationally. We estimate that it would cost about $400,000 to expand our production area and equip it with the necessary machinery.

2. **Purchase of Overhead Crane** *(Estimated cost: $200,000)*

When our plant was built five years ago, corporate headquarters decided that it would be too expensive to install an overhead crane to handle materials. At that time, the company was expanding rapidly, and capital was very tight. Although to install such equipment then would have added only $125,000 to the construction budget, the money just was not available. However, the board promised that as soon as cash flow improved, we would be able to add a crane to our production facility. Because of inflation and improved technology, the crane necessary for our operations now will cost about $175,000, plus $25,000 for installation and testing. Because we are the only plant that does not have a crane—and because that has hurt our production—we have strong feelings that one must be purchased.

3. **Security Contract** *(Estimated cost: $80,000)*

Three times within the past year, our plant has been the target of vandalism and theft. Although other facilities in the city also have been affected, we are particularly vulnerable because of our location and our general lack of safeguards. To provide minimal security, it will be necessary to install various detection devices around our plant and hire at least four full-time security guards. A local security firm has offered us a contract that would provide both types of protection. It is willing to install the necessary equipment for the price of $40,000 (a one-time cost) and provide us with four trained security guards for an additional $40,000 annually. Considering that we already have lost approximately $31,000 this past year because of vandalism and theft, we believe that the proposed security contract will be well worth its cost.

BUDGET CUTTING PRIORITIES SHEET
(Plant C)

1. **Purchase of Building** *(Estimated cost: $575,000)*

   The opportunity recently has arisen for us to purchase an abandoned warehouse and the six acres of land on which it is located, near our plant. Because our production output is the highest in the company and is constantly increasing, we soon will need additional storage facilities for both raw materials and finished goods. Our present storage facilities are adequate, but the price and location of the property for sale are too good to pass up. If we do not purchase the property soon, it is highly likely that it will be bought by someone else.

2. **Purchase of Forklifts** *(Estimated cost: $125,000)*

   To increase our capability in handling both raw materials and finished goods, we must purchase five new forklift trucks. Although we have two older models, they are not sufficient to meet our needs. Both have a lift capacity of only one ton, and one of them needs to be overhauled. The newer forklifts have a lift capacity of five tons each and normally sell for $30,000 each. If we agree to purchase a minimum of five and trade in our two older models, we can buy new ones for only $25,000 each. This offer will remain open only so long as the equipment dealer has the current inventory in stock. Because the equipment dealer is trying to move out the present stock to make room for a new shipment of more expensive forklifts, we must act now if we intend to take advantage of the offer.

3. **Safety Study** *(Estimated cost: $75,000)*

   Our plant has lost more days of work because of accidents this year than any other plant in the company. We have tried to isolate the source of this problem, but so far we have been unsuccessful. Because of our inability to reduce the number of accidents, we were prompted to seek outside assistance. In response to our inquiries, we received proposals from several consulting firms that specialize in industrial safety. After carefully reviewing each proposal, we decided to sign a contract with J.B. Smith and Associates for a study to be conducted over a period of approximately six months. Although the figure quoted was only an estimate, the company guaranteed that the cost will not exceed $75,000. We have not yet signed the contract, but would like to do so as soon as possible.

BUDGET CUTTING PRIORITIES SHEET
(Plant D)

1. **Replacement of Metal Trimmers** *(Estimated cost: $450,000)*

   The ten metal trimmers in our plant have been fully depreciated and are now in need of replacement. Not only have maintenance expenses on these machines been increasing, but we are the only plant in the company that still is using this old, first-generation equipment. Five of the newer models—which have twice the capacity of our old machines—can be purchased for $90,000 each. In addition to the increased efficiency and safety of this newer equipment, it requires less space, thus permitting additional uses for a portion of the production area.

2. **Parking Lot/Landscaping** *(Estimated cost: $185,000)*

   We have an immediate need for an employee parking lot. Since our plant was built four years ago, our employees have been forced to park in a field adjacent to the building. Although we cover the field with gravel annually (at great expense), in the spring it becomes a swamp. On several occasions, cars have become mired up to their axles, and a few have sustained damage. A local contractor has surveyed the area and estimates that the problem could be solved for approximately $165,000. For this price, the contractor will regrade the land and haul in fill dirt where needed, construct a five-hundred-car asphalt lot, install appropriate lighting, and plant trees and shrubs for aesthetic effect. We believe that we should implement this project to raise the morale of our employees and increase the value of our property.

3. **Feasibility Study** *(Estimated cost: $65,000)*

   One of the engineers in our plant has developed a plan for the improvement of our production process that calls for the design of a full-scale working model of a major piece of equipment. Our production manager was quite impressed with the proposal and urged our senior staff to obtain funding for a feasibility study. As a result of our effort, corporate headquarters became convinced that the project was worth funding. The principal reason for approval of our request was headquarters' belief that our proposed modification would be beneficial not only to our plant but also to other plants in the company. If the funds for this study are withdrawn, it will have a negative impact on the entire company.

BUDGET CUTTING PRIORITIES SHEET
(Plant E)

1. **Acquisition of Land** *(Estimated cost: $465,000)*

   Land adjacent to our plant has been offered for sale. The parcel consists of approximately 150 acres with 1,000 feet of waterfront. Although we have no immediate need for that amount of land, we are extremely interested in obtaining the two deep-water docks that are part of the property. Just recently, we received our first overseas order (from South America); this will make it necessary for us to ship some of our goods by sea. To be able to unload raw materials and load finished goods from our own docks would greatly reduce our handling expenses and increase our chances of obtaining a greater foreign market for our product. The portion of the new property that we will not develop immediately could be leased to offset the cost of the acquisition; however, no figures are available yet to substantiate the financial feasibility of such action.

2. **Personnel Acquisition** *(Estimated cost: $210,000)*

   In order to maintain our increasing production output, it was necessary for us to expand our work force. As a result, we have hired a new assistant plant manager, two more engineers, and four new supervisors. Within the next month, we hope to add three or four more on-line employees. The total labor cost to our plant for these new workers is estimated to be $210,000. These additions are for the purpose of adding a special process to our production operation. A new customer has signed a five-year contract with us for an annual minimum of 250,000 widgets. Our part of the agreement, however, calls for the design, manufacture, and attachment of an additional device onto our finished product. The increase in our work force is necessary, therefore, to serve the unique needs of our new customer. Without these employees, we probably would lose the contract to a competitor.

3. **Waste-Treatment Study** *(Estimated cost: $50,000)*

   For the past several months, a local ecology group and residents in our area have been criticizing our waste-treatment efforts. It has been their contention that we are not concerned about protecting the environment. The negative publicity that these people are causing our plant could prove to be quite damaging. Because there is some truth to their claims (our pollution control equipment is not very effective), we feel that we must initiate immediate action to curb these attacks. We have solicited bids from several engineering firms that specialize in pollution control. The lowest bid proposes a six-month study of our operations, complete with specific recommendations and estimated costs for improvement. By authorizing this study now, we can publicize our intentions and thereby calm our critics. We have built up a great deal of goodwill in the community and we do not want to lose it.

Budget Cutting Priorities Sheet
(Plant F)

1. **Modification of the Assembly Line** *(Estimated cost: $485,000)*

   The assembly line in our plant no longer is suitable to our needs. Because we took over the existing facility of a company that went out of business, our plant was not designed to meet the specifications of our product. In the year since we have been in operation, we have done very well with some modifications and now, in fact, are second in the company in the quantity of widgets produced. However, we feel that further increases in production no longer will be possible because of the inefficiency of our assembly line. We know that, with the proper equipment, we could lead the company in production. It is not fair to deny us the opportunity to achieve the higher levels of production that currently are enjoyed by the five other plants. Our building (and much of our equipment) is older than that of four of the company's other plants.

2. **Correction of Violations** *(Estimated cost: $190,000)*

   A little over six months after we occupied our present facility, it was inspected by the county fire marshal. The report cited numerous violations of the industrial fire code. We explained that we were new occupants of the old building and would correct all deficiencies in time, and the fire marshal informed us that "substantial improvements" would have to be made within six months—at which time we would receive another inspection. Our budget already has been depleted by necessary modifications to the production line, and our engineers have estimated that the correction of all violations will cost approximately $190,000 (the largest expense is for an automatic sprinkler system). What makes our situation even more urgent is that the fire marshal has a reputation for harassing violators and has had two factories shut down pending corrections of violations. We really have no choice but to comply as quickly as possible.

3. **Training and Development** *(Estimated cost: $85,000)*

   Because of the location of our plant, we do not have a large labor pool from which to hire workers. The labor market in our area provided us with the minimum number of employees needed to start production a year ago, but we have suffered all along from a serious shortage of skilled workers. Our only alternative is to establish a program within our plant to upgrade the skills of selected employees. The emphasis at first would be remedial and for a select group of workers in critical production jobs, but eventually we hope to be able to expand the program to all employees. We estimate that, for the first year of operation, this program will cost approximately $40,000 for a training director and staff, plus $45,000 for equipment and materials.

16

Winterset High School:
An Intergroup-Conflict Simulation

Charles E. List

Goals

- To provide participants with an opportunity to practice a conflict-management strategy.

- To examine ways that occupational stereotyping can contribute to organizational conflict.

Group Size

One or more subgroups of seven to fifteen members each.

Time Required

Approximately two and one-half hours.

Materials

- A copy of the Winterset High School Background Sheet for each participant.

- A copy of the Winterset High School Principal's Role Sheet for each participant who plays the role of principal.

- Enough copies of the Winterset High School Guidance Counselor's Role Sheet for approximately half of the participants.

- Enough copies of the Winterset High School Maintenance Staff's Role Sheet for the remaining participants.

- A pencil and several sheets of blank paper for each participant.

- A clipboard for each participant.

- A newsprint flip chart and a felt-tipped marker for the facilitator and for each team of guidance counselors and each team of maintenance personnel.

- Masking tape for posting newsprint.

Physical Setting

Movable chairs for participants and a room that is large enough to allow the subgroups to work without disturbing one another.

Process

1. The facilitator explains the goals of the activity.

2. Each participant is given a copy of the background sheet and is asked to read it. (Five minutes.)

3. The total group is divided into subgroups consisting of seven to fifteen members each. The subgroups select one of their members to play the role of principal. The facilitator assigns about half of the others to the role of guidance counselor, and the remaining participants are assigned to the role of maintenance staff. (From three to seven people can participate as guidance counselors, and from three to seven people can participate as maintenance personnel.)

4. Each participant is given a copy of the appropriate role sheet, a clipboard, a pencil, and several sheets of blank paper and is asked to read the role sheet. Counselors and maintenance people are asked to write down some additional suggestions for solving the problem. (Ten minutes.)

5. The guidance counselors in each subgroup are instructed to discuss the conflict and plan a strategy for resolving the conflict, and the maintenance staff in each subgroup is instructed to meet separately and plan its strategy.

6. While the counselors and maintenance staffs are planning their strategies, the facilitator meets in a separate area with all the principals to explain and clarify the process of the activity. A newsprint flip chart and a

felt-tipped marker is given to each principal. The facilitator instructs the principals to copy the questions from their role sheets onto newsprint. Each principal copies the list twice (once for the counselors and once for the maintenance staff).

7. About ten minutes into the discussion, the facilitator interrupts the counselors and asks each counseling team to meet with its principal. The maintenance staffs continue with their planning. Each principal meets with his or her counselors in a separate area and tries to persuade them to participate in an intergroup-development program with the maintenance staff. Each principal presents the team of counselors with the questions on newsprint. As the counselors respond to the questions, their answers are listed on the newsprint, and the newsprint is given to the counselors for further study and elaboration of answers. (Twenty minutes.)

8. The principals are instructed to meet with their maintenance staffs and make their presentations while the counseling teams continue their discussions. Principals try to persuade the maintenance staffs to participate in the intergroup-development program. They also present the staffs with the same questions on newsprint that they presented to the counseling teams. Answers are listed on the newsprint, and each principal gives the newsprint to the maintenance staff. (Twenty minutes.)

9. Each counseling team exchanges newsprint with the corresponding maintenance staff. Each subgroup works independently and makes notes on similarities and disparities in the answers proposed by the two subgroups. Members of each subgroup are allowed to ask for clarification from the other subgroup. Principals facilitate the clarification process. (Fifteen minutes.)

10. Each principal meets jointly with the team of counselors and the maintenance staff. The participants review the list of questions and determine which answers they can agree on and which remain as obstacles. (Ten minutes.)

11. The total group is reassembled. As each subgroup of counselors and maintenance staff presents its agreed-on answers, the facilitator lists them on newsprint. The results are tabulated or summarized. (Five minutes.)

12. As each subgroup presents its conflicting answers, the facilitator lists them on newsprint. Each subgroup is assigned one of these conflicting answers and is instructed to try to resolve the conflict. Principals ask their subgroups to consider the five items that are listed under item 6 of the principal's role sheet. (Fifteen minutes.)

13. The total group is reassembled. As each subgroup presents its solutions, the facilitator posts them on newsprint. The facilitator leads a discussion of the following questions:

- How would you describe your behavior and the behavior of others in this conflict situation?

- What was the most difficult part of arriving at solutions that were acceptable to both factions? The easiest?

- What was similar to or different from your experience in actual conflict situations?

- How did occupational stereotyping contribute to the difficulty in arriving at solutions? In what other kinds of ways might such stereotyping cause or add to organizational conflict? What can be done to decrease occupational stereotyping?

- What insights or methods arising from this activity might you be able to use in future conflict resolution?

(Fifteen minutes.)

Variations

- Some of the counselors can be instructed to agree with the maintenance staff, and some members of the maintenance staff can be instructed to agree with the counselors.

- One participant from each subgroup could be assigned to play the role of a graduate student. The student would be instructed by the facilitator to try to persuade the maintenance staff that the project was worth the Saturday work.

Originally published in The 1987 Annual: Developing Human Resources.

WINTERSET HIGH SCHOOL BACKGROUND SHEET

Several graduate students from the sociology department of State University asked the principal of Winterset High School for permission to conduct a research project at the school. They wanted to open the school on Saturdays to teach remedial reading, writing, and mathematical skills to children who were having problems in these areas and to semiliterate adults.

Although no government funding was available for the project, the graduate students had been promised that school supplies would be donated by a local business. The graduate students would take turns bringing food that could be stored in the refrigerator and heated on the stove in the school cafeteria. Fifteen classrooms would be needed, and graduate students would volunteer their time to teach the classes.

The principal was delighted with the offer and told the graduate students that the school's guidance counselors would have to be consulted but an answer would be forthcoming shortly. The principal wanted the counselors to coordinate the program with the graduate students.

The counselors liked the idea and developed an action plan and check list for implementing the program. One of the items on the check list was to arrange for the maintenance staff to provide necessary services (e.g., unlocking and locking the doors and cleaning the facilities at the end of the day) on Saturdays. They made an appointment to discuss the program with the supervisor and several other members of the maintenance staff.

When the counselors presented the proposal, the response from the maintenance staff was hostile. The maintenance staff refused to work on Saturdays and would not budge from this position.

After the counselors reported the maintenance staff's position to the principal, several meetings were scheduled. The principal was confident that the intergroup conflict could be resolved in a cooperative and collaborative manner. First, the principal would meet with the counselors; then the principal would meet with the maintenance staff; later, the principal would meet together with both groups.

WINTERSET HIGH SCHOOL PRINCIPAL'S ROLE SHEET

You hope that the counselors and maintenance staff can work out an acceptable solution and that the remedial school program can be implemented. However, you do not want to force either group to make concessions. Your objective is to facilitate a mutually agreeable solution.

As you review some notes you took in a consulting-skills laboratory, you notice the following paragraph, which expresses the way you feel:

> Lawrence and Lorsch[1] in their differentiation-integration model, have clearly demonstrated that units of organizations are and should be different. When units have differing tasks, goals, personnel, time constraints, and structures, the functioning of these units is bound to be different. The issue is not how to make all the units the same, but how to develop an integrated process that allows these contrasting units to work together. One strategy for developing greater integration between work units is an intergroup-development program.

You plan to speak with each group individually and to persuade each group to participate in an intergroup-development program. In planning the program, you devise the following intervention:

1. Establish the following ground rule: Both groups should agree to adopt a problem-solving stance, rather than to accuse or fix blame.

2. On newsprint, copy the following list twice for separate presentations to the two groups:

   - What actions did the other group engage in that created problems for us in this Saturday-program situation?

   - What actions did we engage in that might have created problems for the other group regarding the Saturday program?

   - What characteristics have been evident in the other group's behavior in this problem?

   - What characteristics have been evident in our group's behavior in this problem?

---

[1]P.R. Lawrence and J.W. Lorsch (1969). *Developing Organizations: Diagnosis and Action.* Reading, MA: Addison-Wesley.

The Pfeiffer Book of Successful Conflict Management Tools © 2003 John Wiley & Sons, Inc.

- How do we think the other group will describe our behavior in this problem?

- What would each group need to do to enable both groups to work together effectively?

3. Answers formulated by each group will be listed on newsprint, and the two groups will exchange newsprint.

4. Each group will review the work of the other group and may ask for clarification on any point. Each group will note which answers from the other group are in agreement with its own answers and which are different.

5. Both groups and the principal will meet jointly to identify the answers on which both groups agree. Answers that still need work will be considered jointly by members from both groups.

6. As the groups work jointly on solutions to answers that were different, they should consider the following items:

- What the problem is,

- What actions should be taken,

- Who will be responsible for each action,

- What the schedule is, and

- What can be done to keep the problem from recurring.

You plan to use all of your facilitating skills to make this intervention a successful one.

WINTERSET HIGH SCHOOL GUIDANCE COUNSELOR'S ROLE SHEET

You hold a master's degree and are one of several guidance counselors for Winterset High School. You not only counsel students about vocational opportunities, but you counsel problem students with whom the teachers are not qualified to deal. Therefore, you and the other counselors consider yourselves a special group of professionals. You do not teach any classes and enjoy a great deal of flexibility in your schedule. Your supervisor, who is referred to as your "group coordinator," reports directly to the principal of the high school. All the counselors consider themselves as liberals, and they advocate change that will benefit all the citizens in the community. You are enthusiastic about the proposed Saturday program.

You think the maintenance staff is overpaid. You perceive these employees as too conservative and believe they have an unsympathetic attitude toward disadvantaged citizens. Your private opinion of them is that they are "prejudiced common laborers."

Nevertheless, you expected them to welcome the opportunity to be paid overtime wages for working on Saturdays. After all (so you imagine), the extra money would help to pay for many of the things they must be striving for. You feel angry and frustrated about their refusal to work on Saturdays.

You, of course, would not be working on Saturdays and would not be present to deal with the maintenance people if they were forced to do the Saturday work. Therefore, you are concerned about problems they might create for the graduate students. You perceive these people as being arrogant because they belong to a union that is different from the teachers' union and are exempt from some of the requirements imposed on the teachers.

When the principal of Winterset High School asks for a meeting with the guidance counselors, you are obligated to attend. As the counselors search for a resolution to the problem, the following suggestions will probably be considered:

1. Make the maintenance staff understand the financial benefits of working on Saturdays.

2. Persuade the maintenance staff that the Saturday students are serious students who will not create a lot of work for the maintenance people.

3. Schedule only two maintenance people to work on Saturdays and hire high school students to assist.

The Pfeiffer Book of Successful Conflict Management Tools © 2003 John Wiley & Sons, Inc.

4. Rotate the Saturday work so that no maintenance person will have to work every Saturday.

5. Use disposable plates, cups, and forks so that dishwashing is not necessary.

6. Give the maintenance staff a free lunch on Saturdays.

Winterset High School Maintenance Staff's Role Sheet

You are a high-school graduate who has a well-paying job as a maintenance person at Winterset High School. The union you belong to is different from the teachers' union, and you do not consider yourself part of the school staff.

You think that the school staff is too liberal and that the students should be controlled. No one seems to care how the building is left at the end of the day. Everyone knows that the maintenance staff will clean it thoroughly before morning. Whenever you catch students writing on the wall or otherwise damaging the school, the counselors simply talk to them sympathetically and send them on their way.

This job was not your first choice, but you do not resent putting in five days a week in order to make a good living. But now the counselors are wanting you to work on Saturday. You will not even consider such a possibility. After all, the Saturday classes would be available to the worst type of people—problem students and adults who did not have enough initiative to complete their education. And when you think about how liberal the present teachers are, you wonder what might happen when those young "radical" university students try to teach the classes . You cringe when you imagine the condition of the school at the end of the Saturday classes. You are even more resentful when you realize that these liberal counselors—who are insisting that you put in the extra time—are not even planning to be there on Saturdays. And their nerve—insinuating that you would do *anything* for a little extra money!

When the principal of Winterset High School asks for a meeting with the maintenance people, you are obligated to attend. As the maintenance staff searches for a resolution to the problem, the following suggestions might be considered:

1. Arrange for the counselors to clean the school on Saturdays.

2. Ask the graduate students to clean the school.

3. Hire an extra union person to work on Saturdays.

4. Schedule the classes for a weekday and limit the number so that the few vacant classrooms will accommodate these special students.

5. Hold the classes for one hour per day five days a week immediately following the close of the regular school.

6. Tell the graduate students to find facilities on their campus.

The Pfeiffer Book of Successful Conflict Management Tools © 2003 John Wiley & Sons, Inc.

17

Crime-Fighting Task Force: Understanding Political Tactics in Groups

R. Bruce McAfee and Robert A. Herring III

Goals

- To familiarize participants with the various political tactics that may be encountered in groups.
- To offer participants an opportunity to observe or experience the effects of hidden agendas and political tactics on group decision making.

Group Size

A minimum of fifteen participants, six of whom serve as role players. All participants who are not role players serve as observers; consequently, the maximum size of the total group is dictated by the number of participants who can sit closely enough to the players to see and hear the role play.

Time Required

Approximately one hour and fifteen minutes.

Materials

- One copy of the Crime-Fighting Task Force Situation Sheet for each participant.

- One copy of the Crime-Fighting Task Force Political Tactics Sheet for each participant.
- One copy of the appropriate Crime-Fighting Task Force Role Sheet for each role player.
- One copy of the Crime-Fighting Task Force Observer Sheet for each observer.
- A clipboard or other portable writing surface for each observer.
- A pencil for each observer.
- Six name tags—one for each role player—filled out as follows:
  - Retired Army Officer
  - Guidance Counselor
  - Farmer
  - Manager in Retail Store
  - Owner of Office-Supply Store
  - Chairperson

Physical Setting

A room with sufficient space and movable chairs to accommodate all participants. The observers must be seated around the role players.

Process

1. Announce the goals of the activity.

2. Give each participant one copy of the Crime-Fighting Task Force Situation Sheet and a copy of the Crime-Fighting Task Force Political Tactics Sheet. Ask the participants to review the material contained in these handouts, then elicit and answer questions. (Ten minutes.)

3. Ask six volunteers to role play the members of the Crime Fighting Task Force. Give each volunteer one of the Crime Fighting Task Force Role Sheets and the appropriate name tag. Ask each role player to put on the name tag and to read and study his or her role for the next few minutes.

4. As the role players are studying their roles, meet with the remaining participants in a different part of the room. Give each a copy of the Crime-Fighting Task Force Observer Sheet, a clipboard or other portable writing

The Pfeiffer Book of Successful Conflict Management Tools © 2003 John Wiley & Sons, Inc.

surface, and a pencil. Explain that they are to observe the role play, complete their Observer Sheets, and then share the contents of these sheets with the total group. Ask them to read their sheets; then elicit and answer questions. (Ten minutes.)

5. Have the role players sit in a circle with the observers seated around them. Announce that the Crime-Fighting Task Force has twenty minutes to decide how it should spend the $425,000, and ask the role players to begin. (Twenty minutes.)

6. After twenty minutes ask the role players to stop. Review the contents of the Observer Sheet with the total group, asking the observers to report their findings. (Five to ten minutes, depending on the number of observers.)

7. Ask the task-force members to take turns sharing the contents of their role sheets. Point out each role player's hidden agenda. (Five minutes.)

8. Lead a concluding discussion based on the following questions:

   ■ How satisfied were the role players with the way they worked together? How satisfied were they with the results of their work on the task?

   ■ What generalizations can you make about the effects of hidden agendas and political tactics on group decision making?

   ■ When might you have a need to uncover hidden agendas or be aware of political tactics?

   ■ How can you use this information on the job?

   (Fifteen to twenty minutes.)

Variations

■ One or two observers may be assigned to a single role player and report specifically on that player's interactions with the others.

■ The role play may be completed a second time with the role players abandoning their hidden agendas and political tactics. In this case, processing would concentrate on the differences in both process and outcome between the two role plays.

Originally published in The 1999 Annual, Vol. 2, Consulting.

CRIME-FIGHTING TASK FORCE SITUATION SHEET

Six citizens have been appointed by the City Manager to serve on the Crime-Fighting Task Force. This task force has received a $425,000 one-year grant to help solve your city's crime problems. The grant stipulates that "grant funds must be spent in such a manner that crime will be reduced in the least amount of time." The purpose of today's task-force meeting is to determine how the $425,000 should be spent. Five programs are potential recipients of the money:

Program A: Establishing more drug-treatment/counseling centers to treat drug addicts and alcoholics.

Program B: Conducting crime-prevention training for homeowners and business owners. (Individuals would be trained and sent out to homes and businesses to teach crime-prevention techniques.)

Program C: Hiring more police officers.

Program D: Establishing a first-offenders' program. (Counselors would work with first-time criminals with the goal of reducing the number of repeat offenders.)

Program E: Contracting with consultants who would advise the task force on how to spend the money.

The members of the task force may choose one or more of the five, but they must reach a consensus on how to spend the money.

The Pfeiffer Book of Successful Conflict Management Tools © 2003 John Wiley & Sons, Inc.

CRIME-FIGHTING TASK FORCE POLITICAL TACTICS SHEET

The following are political tactics that are commonly used in group situations:

Building a Favorable Image: This strategy involves dressing appropriately, drawing attention to one's successes, name dropping, expressing enthusiasm about the organization, adhering to group norms, and exhibiting an air of confidence about one's abilities.

Presenting Information Selectively: This strategy consists of withholding unfavorable information from others, presenting only the information that supports one's own view, and interpreting information in a way that is favorable to oneself or one's position.

Blaming and Attacking: People who use this strategy further their own interests by blaming others for their own failures. They make sure that they will not be blamed when something goes wrong and that they will receive credit when something goes right.

Relying on Outside Experts: As experts outside of a group can be found to support almost any position, some people influence group decisions by quoting experts or inviting them to express their opinions at group meetings.

Forming Coalitions or Alliances: When one or more group members realize that they do not individually have sufficient power to control the decision-making process, they can increase their power by forming a subgroup and imposing their will on other members.

Compromising: This strategy involves giving up part of what one wants in exchange for receiving something of value from others.

Manipulating the Rules: People who use this strategy interpret group rules in such a way as to advance their own personal interests. For example, a manager might refuse one employee's request on the grounds that it is against company policy, but grant an identical request from a favored employee on the grounds that it is a "special circumstance" or that the rule does not apply in this particular case. As most rules can be interpreted in a number of ways, this strategy often succeeds.

Ingratiating Oneself: People try to increase their power by gaining the favor of others. They may, for example, praise others excessively or show excessive support.

Controlling the Meeting's Agenda: One can increase one's power by controlling the agenda of a meeting. One can manipulate the items that appear on the agenda, as well as the order in which they appear.

CRIME-FIGHTING TASK FORCE ROLE SHEET 1

Retired Army Officer

Do not tell anyone the contents of your role sheet until the facilitator asks you to do so.

You are a retired army officer and are running for city council in the elections being held in fourteen months. You are trying desperately to win in what you know will be a tough race. You feel your chance of winning will be the greatest if the task force decides to spend all or almost all of the funds on Program C (hiring additional police to arrest criminals). You realize that the citizens really want the crime problem eliminated now and they want the hoodlums put behind bars. By spending money on more police and having them make arrests, you can claim that "your task force" has solved the city's crime problem. Besides, it will help you to establish a record of being tough on crime, which will certainly help you be elected.

During the role play you must push hard for Program C. You are to use the political tactic of *manipulating the rules.* In presenting your view, keep reminding the task force members that the grant states, that "grant funds must be spent in such a manner that crime will be reduced in the least amount of time." Argue that hiring more police will clearly reduce crime in the least amount of time, as there will be fewer criminals around—at least in the short run.

CRIME-FIGHTING TASK FORCE ROLE SHEET 2

Guidance Counselor

Do not tell anyone the contents of your role sheet until the facilitator asks you to do so.

You are a guidance counselor in one of your city's high schools. You hate your present job and would really like to find a new one. In order to do this, you would like the task force to implement Program A (establishing more drug treatment counseling centers) and spend most of its money on it. As you have had many years of counseling experience, you will be the logical choice to head at least one of these new centers.

During the role play, you are to use the political tactic of *compromising*. Offer to everyone who supports other programs that you will vote for that person's program if he or she will also vote for yours. However, try to have as many new centers established as possible, as that will enhance your chances for finding a new job.

CRIME-FIGHTING TASK FORCE ROLE SHEET 3

Farmer

Do not tell anyone the contents of your role sheet until the facilitator asks you to do so.

You own 1,000 acres and 800 hogs. You really wanted to serve on this task force and lobbied to be appointed. You have a straightforward reason for wanting to serve—you have over ten acres planted in marijuana and don't want to be caught. Your goal in serving on this task force is to persuade the chairperson to like you. If you can convince the chairperson to like you, you will be able to exert influence over him or her in the future, thereby ensuring that your marijuana plants will be safe. Therefore, you are going to use the political tactic of *ingratiating oneself*. During the role play praise the chairperson frequently on techniques used to conduct the meeting or any other behaviors. It is important that you block any efforts to support Program C (hiring more police officers), as it might make your situation more precarious. You would like to hire consultants, conduct numerous pilot studies, or do anything that the chairperson seems to favor (except Program C). Hiring consultants is particularly desirable, as they will slow the process down and allow you more time to exert your influence with the chairperson.

The Pfeiffer Book of Successful Conflict Management Tools © 2003 John Wiley & Sons, Inc.

CRIME-FIGHTING TASK FORCE ROLE SHEET 4

Manager in Retail Store

Do not tell anyone the contents of your role sheet until the facilitator asks you to do so.

You are the manager of the clothing department in the city's largest retail store. In addition you have counseled runaway teenagers for five years. You would like the task force to spend most, if not all, of its money on Program D (establishing a first-offenders' program). If all $425,000 were spent, at least eight counselors or social workers would have to be hired, and your favorite cousin, who earned a college degree in social work but has not been able to find a job, would have a good chance of being hired.

During the role play, argue that a first offenders' program is better than any of the other alternatives because it will educate people who are most likely to commit criminal acts—past criminals. In presenting your arguments, use the political tactic of *relying on outside experts*. Thus, you will want to cite experts who agree with you. For example, tell the committee the following:

- Dr. Susan Barnes, a world-wide authority and a professor of criminal justice at UCLA, has stated that 86 percent of the crimes committed in the U.S. are committed by repeat offenders. Based on a review of many studies, she has concluded that first-offender programs are more effective than any other method for crime reduction.

- A report published by the U.S. Attorney General's office entitled, "A Statistical Analysis of Crime in America," concludes that first-offender programs have the best cost/benefit ratio of any crime-fighting technique.

- Bernard Crowley, who is perhaps the leading authority on crime in the Midwest, reported on the TV program *NightLine* that most riots could be prevented if cities were to spend their money on first-offenders' programs.

(*Note:* None of this "expert" information is true, but the task-force members will not know that.)

CRIME-FIGHTING TASK FORCE ROLE SHEET 5

Owner of Office-Supply Store

Do not tell anyone the contents of your role sheet until the facilitator asks you to do so.

      You are the owner of an office-supply store in your city. Your goal during this meeting is to impress all of the other task-force members so that they will shop at your store. Also, some of the grant money will have to be spent on office supplies, and you want it to be spent at your store. In order to impress others during the role play, use the political tactic of *building a favorable image*. Therefore, appear very interested in the discussion and nod affirmatively when others make suggestions. State how pleased you are with what the group is trying to accomplish—reducing crime. When opportunities arise, be sure to drop names. Mention that you know the mayor of the city, the city treasurer, and the city chief of police. Mention that, as a store owner, you are an expert on the shoplifting problem. Remember that you really don't care how the grant money is spent; you only care about increasing business.

Crime-Fighting Task Force Role Sheet 6

Chairperson

Do not tell anyone the contents of your role sheet until the facilitator asks you to do so.

You are the task-force chairperson. It is your job to assist the task force in arriving at the best possible decision—the one that will be most effective in resolving the city's crime problem. You are to begin by explaining the purpose of the meeting. Be sure to state that there are five alternatives for spending the $425,000 grant, but that the money can be divided among various programs.

You are to conduct an orderly meeting and help the committee arrive at a consensus. Assist the members in defining the problem, developing alternatives, weighing the pros and cons of each alternative, and ultimately making the best decision. Keep in mind that your job is to assist the members, not to dictate to them.

CRIME-FIGHTING TASK FORCE OBSERVER SHEET

Instructions: You are to observe the role play closely and write answers to the following questions:

1. Which political tactics are being used by each of the role players?

- Retired Army Officer:

_____

_____

_____

- Guidance Counselor:

_____

_____

_____

- Farmer:

_____

_____

_____

- Manager in Retail Store:

_____

_____

_____

- Owner of Office-Supply Store:

_____

_____

_____

- Chairperson:

_____

_____

_____

The Pfeiffer Book of Successful Conflict Management Tools © 2003 John Wiley & Sons, Inc.

2. When one of the role players uses a political tactic, how do the others respond? (Describe two instances.)

_____

_____

_____

_____

_____

_____

_____

_____

3. What behaviors helped the role players to stay on task? What behaviors led them off track?

_____

_____

_____

_____

_____

_____

_____

4. How effective are the role players in reaching the goal of achieving consensus about how to spend the money?

_____

_____

_____

_____

_____

_____

_____

Piccadilly Manor: Improving Decision Making in a Political Milieu

A. Carol Rusaw

Goals

- To study conditions under which rational and nonrational decisions are often made.

- To examine the use of rational and nonrational decision-making concepts when resources are limited, political stakes are high, and group goals are diverse.

- To develop skills for reaching consensus in a diverse group.

Group Size

Up to thirty-six participants in groups of eight or nine.

Time Required

Approximately two hours.

Materials

- Copies of the Piccadilly Manor Rational and Nonrational Decision Making Handout for all participants.

- Copies of the Piccadilly Manor Background Sheet for all participants.
- Copies of the Piccadilly Manor Case Study and Roles Sheet for all participants.
- Copies of the Piccadilly Manor Observer Sheet for all observers.
- A flip chart and felt-tipped markers for each small group.
- Masking tape distributed for use by each of the small groups.
- Pencils or pens and writing paper for participants.

Physical Setting

A room large enough for participants to move into small group discussions easily. Hard surfaces for writing.

Process

1. Explain that making decisions is a crucial skill for group leaders and that, in general, group decisions may be rational or nonrational. Say that the purpose of this activity is to enable group members to examine the conditions that favor making rational decisions. (Five minutes.)

2. Give all participants copies of the Piccadilly Manor Rational and Nonrational Decision Making Handout and summarize the key points by writing them on the flip chart as participants follow along. Note that participants will be asked to discern how the different models are represented in a case study and then they will take part in a group decision-making exercise. (Ten minutes.)

3. Divide the participants into small groups of eight or nine and give each participant a copy of the Piccadilly Manor Background Sheet and a copy of the Case Study and Roles Sheet. Each group should have six role players and at least two observers.

4. Ask participants to read the Background Sheet, study the Case Study and Roles Sheet individually, determine the decision-making styles being used, and then to decide as a group who will play what role and who will act as observers. (Fifteen minutes.)

5. Hand out paper and pens or pencils and ask participants to write down some key points about their roles so they can stay in character. (Five minutes.)

The Pfeiffer Book of Successful Conflict Management Tools © 2003 John Wiley & Sons, Inc.

6. Give observers in each group copies of the Piccadilly Manor Observer Sheet. Then tell the participants playing Mayor Jackson in each small group to begin the discussion and to act as the facilitator and recorder during the discussion, jotting down ideas for resolving the management problem and alternative funding sources on the flip chart. (Twenty minutes.)

7. After announcing the end of the discussion period, tell the "mayors" to facilitate a discussion to reach a consensus on solutions. Ask the mayors to write a summary of the decisions made on the flip chart for later reporting to the large group. Say that each mayor must be prepared to state the criteria on which the group's decisions were made, the reasons for the choices, and the decision-making model(s) that were predominate. Tell mayors to post their charts on the wall. (Twenty minutes.)

8. Announce that time is up and ask the mayors to read and explain their groups' decisions to the large group. (Fifteen minutes.)

9. Ask participants to reflect on the decision-making process in their groups and note whether and how the diversity of interests helped or hindered creativity. Have observers report what they saw in each group. (Ten minutes.)

10. Lead a discussion on these questions:

   - What type of decision-making model did members of your group use? What conditions affected the type of model used?

   - How did members create options for solving the administrative problems?

   - What criteria did your group use to evaluate the suggestions of group members? How did they establish these criteria?

   - How did differences among the interests and goals of group members affect the process of decision making?

   - How did the differences among members affect your group being able to come up with novel solutions?

   - How were political differences resolved?

   - How satisfied were members of your group with the solutions chosen?

   (Twenty minutes.)

Originally published in The 2000 Annual, Vol. 1, Training.

Piccadilly Manor
Rational and Nonrational Decision Making Handout

Helping a group to make a decision is difficult for leaders, not only because of constraints of time and other resources, but also because of the difficulty of finding ways to meet different needs and interests. Often, leaders must reconcile different points of view, even among people from a homogeneous work environment. In addition, the "best" decision that leaders could make in terms of efficient and effective use of resources may not be accepted by the group. Leaders must examine all the possible decisions and how they may affect others.

In general, decision-making processes in a group can take two forms: rational and nonrational.

Rational Decision Making

Rational decision making involves defining, sorting, and prioritizing alternatives and then selecting one that maximizes outputs. Coalitions of group members often use rational methods, but the aim is to promote their own interests rather than the multiple interests of others. A dominant subgroup often has an abundance of resources, talents, and power strategies to enable its own interests to be met.

Rational decision making succeeds when people can agree on goals, objectives, and desired outcomes and when they have discretion in obtaining and allocating resources. Rational decision making follows a step-by-step process for reaching a "best" decision. Aldag (1991) describes them as:

1. *Investigate the problem.* Using rational decision-making methods, groups conduct an in-depth investigation into the issue confronting them. Typically, groups spend much time defining the problem. This is a difficult stage because what may attract a person's attention and may appear to be the core of a "problem" may be only a symptom of a larger problem.

   To illustrate, a noticeable increase in employee turnover may suggest a problem with employee dissatisfaction, inadequate salary and benefits, or structural problems that interfere with satisfactory performance, such as duplicate functions. It is important to examine the problem from different points of view and investigate how it might be linked with other areas.

2. *Identify decision objectives.* This step involves seeing what the situation will be like once the problem has been solved: What is the ideal state to be

achieved (i.e., fewer turnovers)? It requires determining what *must* be done versus what *should* be done.

3. *Diagnose causes.* Rational decision making involves investigating possible symptoms, contributors, and linkages to other problems.

4. *Develop alternatives.* Rational decision making uses creative problem-solving techniques, such as brainstorming, to generate as many alternatives as possible.

5. *Evaluate alternatives and select the best one.* In assessing alternatives, people use two important criteria: (a) How realistic the alternative is in terms of goals and resources of the organization, based on the information available and on their own imperfect judgment, and (b) how well the alternative will solve the problem, given the essential conditions and what would be ideal for optimal effects or results.

6. *Implement and follow up.* To put the best alternative into action requires the group to establish a structure and process. The leader sets up critical milestones, obtains necessary resources, such as staff and budgets, and sets up ways to track progress.

Deterrents to Rational Decision Making

1. *Uncertainty and risk.* Uncertainty may exist when external conditions are beyond the leader's control and when the leader lacks adequate access to information.

2. *Cognitive and perceptual limitations.* Perceptual and cognitive processes such as reliance on short-term memory, limited computational abilities, unarticulated doubts about outcomes, and stress may interfere with effective decision making.

3. *Turf wars.* A primary difficulty with rational decisions that dominant coalitions within groups make is that the solution selected often satisfies only that particular coalition. Dissatisfaction with the decision may give rise to competing groups; "turf wars" are frequent consequences.

Nonrational Decision Making

Nonrational decision making, on the other hand, is focused on the immediate interests of all group members, who examine a limited range of alternatives that seem to resolve a problem or issue, find common grounds for creating alternatives, and select a decision that each group member can accept. Nonrational methods use resources that are available and use bargaining and negotiating as tools for reaching consensus. Nonrational decision making integrates multiple viewpoints and results in decisions that the majority of participants can accept in principle. Nonrational decisions work best when situations involve uncertainty, disagreement among people, and use of scarce resources.

Three common nonrational models have been described as:

The "Muddling Through" Model

Lindblom (1959) suggests that because of the number of constraints within it, the rational model of decision making is indeed limited. He believes that it does not adequately describe what actually occurs. Instead, he offers the model of incremental decision making, which is based on limited, successive comparisons to existing policies.

This model has five central assumptions:

1. The decision calls for only small changes to existing conditions or policies. No new structures are formed.

2. The decision is noncomprehensive. It considers only the range of limited choices available to the decision maker at that particular moment.

3. The decision takes into consideration choices made in sequence over time, never one decision made once and for all.

4. The decision considers outcomes that are sufficient, but not optimal because of limited resources.

5. The decision does consider the pluralist nature of groups.

Satisficing and Garbage Can Approaches

Two variations of Lindblom's incremental approach are Simon's (1947) "satisficing" approach and March and Olsen's (1984) "garbage can" method of decision making. Simon maintains that individuals will make decisions that meet bare minimal criteria or that "satisfice" conditions. Decisions that "satisfice" or use "bounded" rationality frequently are put into effect when cost and time constraints prevent optimizing.

March and Olsen's "garbage can" model is appropriately called "organized anarchy" because both the problem definition and the solution emerge from unstructured group deliberations. When crises or periods of ambiguity arise, individuals are uncertain about what constitutes the problem because goals are unclear, group membership changes often, and the technologies are poorly understood or change rapidly. In the garbage can methodology, people may find bits and pieces of solutions and put them together. The exact nature of a problem or issue comes out of their collective knowledge and discussion.

Conclusion

Group decisions may entail using well-thought-out processes or using processes that do not seem to follow any systematic design. The "logic" groups use depends on several conditions, such as clear premises for making a decision, the degree of group member agreement and support of goals, discretionary use of available resources, how much situations change, and possible impacts of decisions on group members. When leaders have commitment of the group to attaining shared goals; abundant knowledge; technological, financial, and staff resources; and control over how people and resources attain agreed-on goals, they may follow rational processes to set and achieve goals. However, the greater the group diversity; degree of conflict; scarcity of time, money, and technical knowledge; and volatility of outcomes, the more the leader may rely on incremental decision processes.

Whether they use rational or nonrational models, however, leaders must cultivate group member participation. By remaining open to the ideas of others and incorporating their viewpoints in setting and reaching objectives, leaders can facilitate decisions that are both sound and acceptable to others.

References

Aldag, R.J. (1991). *Management* (2nd ed.). Cincinnati, OH: Southwestern.

Lindblom, C. (1959). The science of "muddling through." *Public Administration Review, 19*(1), 77–99.

March, J.G., & Olsen, J.P. (1984). The new institutionalism: Organizational factors in political life. *American Political Science Review, 78,* 734–749.

Simon, H.A. (1947). *Administrative behavior: A study of decision-making process in administrative organization.* New York: Macmillan.

Piccadilly Manor Background Sheet

During the last fifty years, the federal government has created nearly two million public housing units for low income people. Although most newer units offer well-constructed homes and provide adequate property management services, most of the units over twenty-five years old were built in the inner cities and suffer from poor maintenance. As home dwellers moved to the suburbs in the 1950s and thereafter, many simply abandoned their homes. As the number of abandoned properties increased, decay took hold. Over time, the older units received fewer funds for upkeep.

Those still living in older units tend to be elderly; many of them are also disabled. Their average yearly income is less than $7,000 per year. The majority receive public assistance, which often fails to provide adequate health care, job training, remedial education, or recreation programs. Local community agencies or other local, state, or federal agencies provide additional, but limited, funds.

City governments oversee most inner city housing units through an independent, appointed board. Following federal grant guidelines, city councils develop an annual budget and delegate administration of the project to this independent board. The board determines tenant eligibility, participation in services, and rental rates. The board's director, who is usually appointed by a mayor, is responsible for the overall administrative operations. The city council makes all major decisions affecting the housing project.

The board creates a housing authority to provide day-to-day administration of the housing facilities. Typical responsibilities include maintenance and custodial work; purchasing and inventory; finance and accounting; processing tenant applications; personnel and training; security; and social services.

Housing authority employees range from unskilled to professional and legal personnel, depending on the extent of services they provide. Most of the housing authorities have personnel management systems that are not subject to civil service structures and benefits. Often, there is little protection for employees, morale is low, and performance is marginal. Many housing authorities both use unionized employees and contract with residents to oversee functional operations.

The control of a housing project is determined by "cooperation agreements" between the housing authority and HUD (Housing and Urban Development). The cooperation agreements affect both revenue available and services provided. Under the terms of the agreements, the municipal government waives normal real estate taxes but requires a payment in lieu of taxes equal to 10 percent of the rent received. This is less than the amount of taxes that would normally be paid. The cooperation agreement also commits the local jurisdiction to provide usual services and utilities, such as fire and police protection. However, in some areas, safety personnel are reluctant to enter housing projects. The absence of direct city government complicates this issue and worsens the isolation in which housing projects exist.

The public housing manager is subject to constant scrutiny, particularly because fiscal problems are often linked with inefficient management; demands for services usually outstrip available financial resources. Federal subsidies do not fill the gap between actual operating costs and rental income. In addition, federal block grants for housing have declined steadily over the last twenty years.

Piccadilly Manor Case Study and Roles Sheet

Background

Piccadilly Manor is a public housing complex that sits in the middle of Springvale, a Northeastern city of 800,000. Nearly 60 percent of the 40-year-old complex of 700, three-story units are empty. Of the 280 occupied units, 174 (or about 62 percent) are occupied by single tenants aged 65 and over. The remaining tenants are single parents and their children. Nearly all residents receive public assistance, usually less than $7,000 per year.

Funding

Springvale and the U.S. Department of Housing and Urban Development (HUD) have signed a cooperation agreement that outlines the amount of federal funding allocated for specified public housing services based on formulas that match, dollar for dollar, the amounts raised with local funding, including tenant rent. For this fiscal year, HUD has allocated $7,000,000 for Piccadilly Manor. Funds are to be used to subsidize rent as well as to repair or maintain the structures. No funds have been allocated for renovation.

The $7,000,000 is a significant drop from the $12,000,000 peak funded in the early 1980s. In fact, for nearly two decades, federal subsidies have deteriorated. Because of the decline in funding, the Springvale City Council has decided against expensive upgrades to the units, postponed scheduled maintenance, and asked residents to help with the grounds upkeep. Springvale pays these residents minimal wages from other general assistance fund sources. To offset the expenses, moreover, Springvale has waived residents' normal real estate taxes, but required dwellers to pay the city 10 percent of the rent subsidy in lieu of taxes.

According to the cooperation agreement, Springvale must provide the usual municipal services and utilities, such as fire and police protection. In addition to finding a way to pay these expenses in the face of dwindling revenue, the city has encountered problems with city fire and police personnel. Because of the high crime rate in Piccadilly Manor, public safety employees are reluctant to answer resident calls. Their slowness to respond makes residents feel even more isolated from mainstream Springvale residents and more vulnerable to fires and to crime.

Piccadilly Manor Administration

Mayor and City Council

Primary responsibilities for running Piccadilly Manor are shared by a nine-member city council and an at-large mayor. To find alternative ways of funding Piccadilly Manor has been a primary goal of the council for the last four years. Various ideas have been explored, such as forming alliances with businesses, civic groups, and nonprofit organizations with interests in Piccadilly Manor. But the council terms are only two years long, which makes running for re-election a top priority for both council members and the mayor. This has prevented any serious long-range planning. Five of the nine current council members were elected at the same time last November.

Housing Authority Board

When Springvale built Piccadilly Manor in the early 1950s, the city council appointed a Housing Authority Board to oversee administration of government funds and to provide efficient day-to-day maintenance and security services. The Housing Authority Board determines tenant eligibility, participation, and rental rates. The board's current director, Kelly Wilson, was appointed by Mayor Jackson and reports to the city council.

The board also employs technical and professional civil-service personnel to carry out specialized services, such as maintenance and custodial work; purchasing and inventory; finance and accounting; processing of tenant applications; personnel and training; security; and social services. Although technical and professional employees are hired under Springvale's civil-service laws, the majority of Piccadilly Manor employees are residents who receive minimum wage public assistance funds. The technical and professional workers often argue with the employee-residents over work roles and responsibilities; "turf battles" have divided the two groups and have produced widespread poor morale and marginal performance. Moreover, employee-residents decry the fact that they have virtually no benefits and can be terminated without notice. They resent the benefits the city employees' union provides to the technical and professional employees.

Resident Complaints and Funding Issues

Resident complaints have escalated over the last two years. The most recent was an angry letter to the mayor and city council describing many residential frustrations. In the letter, Piccadilly Manor residents complained of rats in the buildings, improperly wired electrical systems, leaking toilets, drug dealers pitching gun battles on the streets, and inadequate public transportation services to suburban shopping centers, medical offices, and vocational training facilities.

Dealing with Complaints

It is now January and the new city council members have begun their terms. The highest priority items on their agenda are the angry resident letter and the continuing frustration of finding adequate funds for improving the administration of Piccadilly Manor. The mayor has convened a task-force meeting, which has been declared as a beginning step in dealing with the issues. The task force consists of Mayor Jackson; one incumbent and two new council members; Kelly Wilson, director of the Housing Authority Board; and two Piccadilly Manor residents. Jackson hopes the task force will find creative ways to address the administrative crises by thinking "out of the box." Frustrated with past strategies that, for various reasons, never bore fruit, Jackson wants to "re-invent" the way Piccadilly Manor is managed. By bringing residents together with those who can steer decisions through to actions, Jackson is confident the new council will take creative action.

Task Force Membership

The task force comprises the following members:

Mayor Terry Jackson

The mayor would like to accommodate the variety of interests on the board. Because Jackson will begin campaigning for re-election later this year, it is important to cultivate the support of both residents and interest groups associated with housing. The mayor believes that this can be achieved by offering several financial incentives, such as tax breaks to businesses and nonprofit organizations. The mayor is eager to show voters that the Manor's financial management is sound and has improved the well-being of residents.

Council Member Taylor Jones

Jones is a newly elected liberal who believes that the housing project should be moved from the inner city to the suburbs. The reasoning is that tax receipts will be higher there, services will be more abundant, and the quality of life will be improved for the residents, especially for families with school-aged children. Jones proposes financing the move through a variety of means, such as grants, nonprofit funds, and grass-roots fund-raisers. Jones was friends in college with a person who is the head of a popular rock group and has asked the person to donate the proceeds from a concert to help a relocation funding.

Council Member Tracy Smith

Smith, a returning member of the council, is a pessimist who thinks that moving tenants to the suburbs will solve nothing. In fact, Smith is sure it will create more problems and that suburban property values will tumble, crime rates will increase, and "white flight" will escalate. Smith believes that existing housing is generally structurally sound, based on recent studies, and that tenants are opposed to moving. Smith believes that some upgrading of the Manor is necessary, but cannot count on major sources of revenue. Smith thinks that what money does come in may be best diverted to self-help programs in which tenants learn to manage their units' upkeep, security, and services.

Council Member Cam Brown

Brown, a local business owner and first-time council member, strongly believes that inefficient management should be eliminated. The solution, Brown thinks, is to contract out essential services at a cost lower than is spent for civil service employees currently. In this scenario, the council would be responsible for direct oversight of contracted work and would pinpoint and correct deficiencies quickly, easily, and efficiently. Brown does not believe the council should invest more money in the existing system because that system does not work.

Worker-Resident Pat Davis

Davis is a Piccadilly Manor tenant and worker-resident who has been active in obtaining support for public housing from several neighborhood, legal, medical, religious, and charitable nonprofit organizations. Davis is rumored to have had ties with militant groups in the late 1960s and has a style that is direct and confrontational. Davis believes that other council members are insensitive to the needs of housing tenants and are perpetuating racial, ethnic, and economic bias by refusing to commit additional resources to tenant management.

Tenant Chris Gomez

Gomez, like Davis, is a Piccadilly Manor resident. Gomez voices the frustrations of many other tenants: lack of consistent and adequate plumbing and heating, poor medical and protective services, and escalating rent. Gomez also favors additional council financial and social service aid, but is less militant than Davis. Gomez would like to have tenants trained in community organizing and leadership skills, as well as in maintenance. Gomez believes that a strong community can take care of itself and is committed to creating awareness and support for mutual help from within.

Housing Authority Board Director Kelly Wilson

Before adjourning last May, the Springvale City Council appointed Wilson to replace Corky Corcoran, who was implicated in an article in the Springvale *Times* in a real estate scandal involving use of federal housing funds. Corcoran resigned and took a job as finance director in another city. Wilson, a former political science professor and director of a nonprofit, self-help organization, is knowledgeable about administrative reform and is eager to lead the board in providing first-rate services. Wilson wants to expunge the political influences in the board and promote more participation from a mix of citizens, residents, and civic and community leaders who would help in determining policy.

PICCADILLY MANOR OBSERVER SHEET

Directions: You are to observe the role play and then give members of the group your feedback and invite reactions from them. Some questions to keep in mind during the role plays are:

1. What were some differences in points of view that emerged among players? How did participants manage these differences?

2. How did different task force members facilitate creative problem solving? What words or behaviors encouraged this? What words or behaviors discouraged creativity?

3. How did member interaction set the stage for the type of decision model (rational or nonrational) that the task force adopted?

4. What were some criteria task force members used in making their decisions? What values were revealed during the decision-making process?

19

Merger Mania:
Understanding Intercultural Negotiation

John Chesser

Goals

- To provide an opportunity for participants to experience the effects that different organizational cultures have on negotiation.

- To allow participants to experience how personal attitudes can obstruct the negotiation process.

- To offer participants a chance to practice or observe an important skill in negotiation: uncovering the deeper issues beneath the surface facts.

Group Size

At least twelve participants: four *company representatives*, four *negotiators*, and four *observers*. Additional participants may be accommodated as observers or as suggested in the first item under "Variations."

Time Required

Two hours and five to ten minutes.

Materials

- One copy of the Merger Mania Memo for each participant.
- One set of Merger Mania Role Sheets A through D for the company representatives (a different sheet for each of the four representatives).
- One copy of the Merger Mania Stipulation for each company representative.
- One copy of the Merger Mania Observer Sheet for each observer.
- A name tag for each participant:
  - Four labeled "Negotiator";
  - One labeled "Company Representative, Sun";
  - One labeled "Company Representative, Conglomerate";
  - One labeled "Company Representative, Grand Baton";
  - One labeled "Company Representative, Ajax"; and
  - Four (or more) labeled "Observer."
- A clipboard or other portable writing surface for each participant.
- A pencil for each participant.
- Several sheets of paper for each negotiator.
- A newsprint poster prepared in advance with the following information:

Function	Time
Negotiators' Strategy Session 1	10 minutes
First Meeting with Company Representatives	10 minutes
Negotiators' Strategy Session 2	15 minutes
Second Meeting with Company Representatives	15 minutes
Negotiators' Strategy Session 3	15 minutes
Third Meeting with Company Representatives	15 minutes

- A newsprint flip chart and a felt-tipped marker.
- Masking tape for posting newsprint.
- A stopwatch for the facilitator's use in timing the steps.

Physical Setting

A room large enough for four subgroups to work without disturbing one another. In addition, a hallway or a separate room should be available so that the facilitator can meet privately with the company representatives. Movable chairs should be provided.

Process

1. The facilitator states that the upcoming activity offers the participants an opportunity to experience the effects that different organizational cultures and different personal attitudes have on the process of negotiation. Then each participant is given a copy of the Merger Mania Memo and is asked to read it. After everyone has finished reading, the facilitator displays the prepared newsprint poster and clarifies the activity process with the following comments, referring to the poster as needed:

   "This activity simulates a merger of four companies. Four of you will play *company representatives,* each with his or her own predetermined character and motives. Four others will serve as *negotiators,* whose purpose is to resolve the differences among the company representatives and complete the merger agreement. All remaining participants will be *observers.*

   "The negotiators will begin with a strategy session. After that session, there will be separate meetings, each involving one negotiator and one company representative and observed by one (or more) observers. There may be as many as three strategy sessions and three meetings between negotiators and company representatives. Once the meetings start, the same subgroups of negotiators, company representatives, and observers will meet throughout the simulation."

   (Ten minutes.)

2. Four volunteers are chosen to be negotiators and four to play the roles of company representatives. The remaining participants are designated as observers.

3. The facilitator accompanies the observers to a separate part of the room. Each observer is given a name tag labeled "Observer," a set of role sheets, a copy of the Merger Mania Stipulation, a copy of the Merger Mania Observer Sheet, a clipboard or other portable writing surface, and a pencil. The facilitator asks the observers to read all handouts so that they can become familiar with the entire role-play situation as well as their own task.

4. The facilitator accompanies the negotiators to a different part of the room. Each negotiator is given a "Negotiator" name tag, a clipboard or other portable writing surface, several sheets of paper for making notes, and a pencil. The facilitator explains that soon the negotiators will begin their first strategy session, during which they will determine *how to gather information from the company representatives that will help in figuring out a solution that is agreeable to all four representatives.*

5. As soon as the observers have finished reading their handouts, they are asked to gather around the negotiators to observe the first strategy session. Then the negotiators are instructed to begin the session and to spend ten minutes developing a strategy. (Ten minutes.)

6. After telling the negotiators to begin, the facilitator accompanies the company representatives to a hallway or a separate room. Each is given one of the four name tags for company representatives, the role sheet that matches the tag, a copy of the Merger Mania Stipulation, a clipboard or other portable writing surface, and a pencil. After the representatives have read their handouts, the facilitator answers their questions and briefly helps them to develop their roles. (The facilitator monitors time so that this step concludes at the same time that the strategy session ends.)

7. After the ten-minute period has elapsed, the facilitator calls time and accompanies the company representatives back to the main room. The participants are instructed to form subgroups consisting of one company representative, one negotiator, and one or more observers. (This process is monitored so that extra observers are divided approximately equally among the four meeting subgroups.) Then the facilitator announces the start of the first meetings between negotiators and company representatives. (Ten minutes.)

8. After ten minutes the facilitator calls time. The negotiators gather for their second strategy session while the observers observe. The company representatives meet with the facilitator in the hallway or separate room to discuss the outcomes of the previous meetings, whether to make adjustments in the way they play their roles, and what such adjustments might be. (The representatives may want to become more candid in their discussions if the negotiators are having extreme difficulty, or they may want to withhold more if the negotiators are progressing toward a solution too easily.) (Fifteen minutes.)

9. After fifteen minutes the facilitator returns to the main room with the company representatives and calls time. The facilitator announces the

start of the second round of meetings between negotiators and company representatives, reminding the participants that:

- They must meet with the same subgroups as before; and
- The negotiators must work toward a solution that is agreeable to all company representatives.

(Fifteen minutes.)

10. The second round of meetings continues for fifteen minutes, after which the facilitator calls time.[1] The facilitator then announces the start of the final strategy session. While the negotiators are working on their final strategy, with the observers observing, the facilitator and the company representatives again meet in the hallway or separate room to discuss progress made thus far and whether to make further adjustments in the way they play their roles. (Fifteen minutes.)

11. After fifteen minutes the facilitator returns to the main room with the company representatives, calls time, and announces the start of the final meeting with company representatives. (Fifteen minutes.)

12. At the conclusion of the fifteen-minute meeting, the facilitator reconvenes the total group. The observers are asked to take turns sharing the information they wrote on their observer sheets. As the observers report, the facilitator records salient points on newsprint and calls attention to themes. (Ten to fifteen minutes.)

13. The facilitator leads a concluding discussion based on the following questions:

- What was it like to be a company representative? How did your assigned personal attitudes affect discussions with the negotiator?
- What was it like to be a negotiator?
- What did you learn about how cultural differences between organizations affect negotiation?
- What have you learned about negotiation that you can use on-the-job?

(Fifteen minutes.)

---

[1] If the negotiators have arrived at a solution that is agreeable to all company representatives, the facilitator should skip the rest of this step as well as step 11 and proceed to step 12.

Variations

- The activity may be used with twenty-four or more participants by conducting two role plays simultaneously (two sets of negotiators, company representatives, and observers). Additional participants could still be accommodated as extra observers.

- If no solution has been reached after the second negotiation meeting, the facilitator may suggest that the negotiators probe for underlying issues during the next meeting.

- If no solution has been reached after the third meeting, the negotiation may be resumed after Step 13 so that the participants have a chance to use any new strategies brought up during the discussion.

Originally published in The 1997 Annual, Vol. 2, Consulting.

MERGER MANIA MEMO

The following memo was sent to a consulting firm assigned to mediate a dispute between four companies involved in a merger:

Memo to: Chris Wilson, Consultation Associates
From: Pat Stewart, United Securities

We've recently run into a problem, and we hope you can help. United Securities maneuvered into position as lead underwriter on a large international merger of chemical companies: *Sun, Conglomerate, Grand Baton,* and *Ajax* are to become Worldwide Chemical Industries. This is our first externally leveraged buyout, so we knew it would be difficult. Now the deal is foundering on an argument about employee compensation.

The first attempt to resolve the compensation issue went very badly. The only thing the four company representatives could agree on was that all four companies should adopt the same compensation scheme. Ultimately the representatives stormed out of the meeting, vowing never to speak to one another again.

The good news is that the four company representatives have agreed to talk to your negotiators. The bad news is that they still won't meet each other face-to-face. They want a negotiator assigned to each of them; the four negotiators will act as go-betweens in working through this dispute.

I believe that holding a series of meetings will work best: Your negotiators discuss strategy; after the strategy session, your negotiators meet in four separate groups with the four representatives (one negotiator per company representative); then your negotiators hold another session to discuss strategy; and so on. I figure we'll have time for three strategy sessions for the negotiators and three meetings between the negotiators and the company representatives.

Unless we can resolve this dispute quickly, we'll either lose the deal (and all the fees), or the companies will merge painfully and we won't be able to sell the $725 million in high-yield bonds resulting from the merger. *Your negotiators' objective is to help the four company representatives find a solution that is agreeable to all of them, so that the merger can proceed.*

MERGER MANIA ROLE SHEET A: COMPANY REPRESENTATIVE, SUN

Important: **Do not allow the negotiators to see this sheet!**

You have been asked to play the role of a company representative. You have received the Merger Mania Memo, which tells about the problem at hand; this role sheet, which covers facts and motives unique to your role; and a Merger Mania Stipulation, which offers information not covered in the memo and not given to the negotiators. For example, the stipulation provides additional information about the previous merger meeting and its results, including acknowledged facts, hidden but common motives, and fears shared by all four company representatives.

Your Position

Your employer, Sun Chemical Corporation, has a reputation for quality and efficiency. It sells commodity chemicals as well as specialized plastic and rubber products to the automobile industry. It dominates the Asian market.

Sun bases pay on length of service. Job titles are relatively unimportant because the company is very egalitarian. All workers are eligible for large bonuses based on company profits. At the first merger meeting, you said little, but winced every time the Grand Baton representative spoke about a hierarchical pay plan. Your position is that the compensation plan should be Sun's: *pay based on people's length of service.*

Issues

Sun had hoped to become dominant in the chemical industry until a political-bribery scandal sent its stock price plummeting. The board of directors saw a merger as the only way to obtain the capital needed for worldwide expansion. Sun views the other companies in the merger as mere conduits for its chemical products. Eventually, it hopes that the new company will concentrate all production with Sun. Naturally, it would be best if the production workers were to be paid the way they always have been paid: the Sun Chemical Corporation way.

Sun's biggest worry is that the other companies will lose money and thereby jeopardize the bonuses. Sun would rather keep its own compensation system and have its profitability measured independently so that bonuses could continue.

Your Strategy

As the company representative for Sun Chemical Corporation, you are accustomed to decision making by dialogue and consensus. At the first merger meeting, you adopted a wait-and-see attitude. Unfortunately, the more you waited, the less you liked what you saw. You were very upset at the outbursts that occurred and were the first to walk out. Unless there is evidence of genuine agreement among the parties during this meeting, you think that many more meetings may be necessary before agreement is reached. *Your strategy is to agree only if the other three agree first.*

MERGER MANIA ROLE SHEET B:
COMPANY REPRESENTATIVE, CONGLOMERATE

Important: Do not allow the negotiators to see this sheet!

You have been asked to play the role of a company representative. You have received the Merger Mania Memo, which tells about the problem at hand; this role sheet, which covers facts and motives unique to your role; and a Merger Mania Stipulation, which offers information not covered in the memo and not given to the negotiators. For example, the stipulation provides additional information about the previous merger meeting and its results.

Your Position

Your employer, Conglomerate Holdings Company, is a hot new organization formed by several young graduates of the Buckminster MBA program, all from wealthy, cosmopolitan families. Conglomerate's approach is based on sophisticated economic analysis coupled with international marketing expertise. Foreign investors have provided Conglomerate with all the investment capital it has needed to become not only the dominant chemical conglomerate in Latin America, but also a force in Spain, Italy, and North Africa. Conglomerate has provided its investors with returns that are the envy of those who hold stock in other chemical companies.

Conglomerate is so confident of its ability to expand to the U.S. market that it actually opposed the inclusion of the U.S.-based Ajax in the merger. In the first merger meeting, you made no secret of your lack of respect for Ajax. You also don't respect the scientific skills of Grand Baton and the productive efficiency of Sun; you think both companies could use a dose of Conglomerate's marketing wizardry.

Conglomerate's pay system (which you designed) is based on the theory of paying people according to the value they add to the company's products. It uses a sophisticated econometric model that pays "work units" (employees) on the value they add to the product at each stage of production. This information is easy to obtain in your company because your accounting department must gather information to pay a value-added tax (VAT). A computer program that calculates the value added by divisions, departments, work teams, and individual workers determines workers' pay. Your position is that the compensation plan should be Conglomerate's: *pay based on value added.*

Issues

Imagine your chagrin when, after the first merger meeting, you fed the Ajax pay scheme into your computer and found that it is the only system of the four that is feasible in a world marketplace. Only the Ajax plan is based on market wage rates, and this is the only kind of information available in all markets. Worse yet, you found that the Ajax pay system was designed by the star economics professor at Buckminster University and the mentor of Conglomerate's young owners. Now you are faced with a dilemma: How can you ever admit that Ajax has the best plan? You are concerned about saving face and protecting your company's image of using the newest and most sophisticated ideas.

Your Strategy

You decide you will still argue that Conglomerate has the best plan, but will admit that the Ajax plan is your second choice.

Merger Mania Role Sheet C:
Company Representative, Grand Baton

Important: **Do not allow the negotiators to see this sheet!**

You have been asked to play the role of a company representative. You have received the Merger Mania Memo, which tells about the problem at hand; this role sheet, which covers facts and motives unique to your role; and a Merger Mania Stipulation, which offers information not covered in the memo and not given to the negotiators. For example, the stipulation provides additional information about the previous merger meeting and its results, including acknowledged facts, hidden but common motives, and fears shared by all four company representatives.

Your Position

Your employer, Grand Baton Inc., considers itself the "Chanel No. 5" of chemical companies—with some justification: One of its most profitable lines of business is processing expensive perfumes for top cosmetics companies. The company is also on the cutting edge of biotechnology and pharmaceutical product development, having expanded from its traditional base of agrichemicals.

The company is based on a strict hierarchy of "the best and the brightest," the "best" being determined almost entirely on educational qualifications. Compensation is based on a rigid hierarchy, with a fixed percentage difference in pay between job levels. At the first merger meeting, you argued that your pay system was the best because "the cream will rise to the top, while the dregs will slide to the bottom." Your position is that the compensation plan should be Conglomerate's: *a fixed percentage difference in pay between job levels.*

Issues

Naturally, you feel smugly superior, although you are a bit worried that Sun will prove superior at production. You view the other companies as needing help from Grand Baton, including assistance with management and with compensation systems. In fact, you are full of helpful advice on a whole range of topics (not limited to the chemical business), and you think it is very important to demonstrate how intelligent you are.

At the first merger meeting, you developed a dislike for the Sun representative, who seemed unimpressed by Grand Baton and who threatens your superiority. You can't tell what this person thinks and you are bothered by that fact. On the other hand, you secretly admire the Conglomerate representative, who is well educated and highly cultured, and you want to impress this person. You have a slight concern that Conglomerate may be a threat to your own company because both Grand Baton and Conglomerate draw from the pool of the best and brightest. You understand the value of Conglomerate's compensation system because it rewards employees, as does your own company's plan.

Your Strategy

If you can find a way to agree with the Conglomerate representative without losing face, you will.

Merger Mania Role Sheet D: Company Representative, Ajax

Important: **Do not allow the negotiators to see this sheet!**

You have been asked to play the role of a company representative. You have received the Merger Mania Memo, which tells about the problem at hand; this role sheet, which covers facts and motives unique to your role; and a Merger Mania Stipulation, which offers information not covered in the memo and not given to the negotiators. For example, the stipulation provides additional information about the previous merger meeting and its results, including acknowledged facts, hidden but common motives, and fears shared by all four company representatives.

Your Position

Your employer, Ajax Corporation, is a purveyor of commodity chemicals that has been dragged unwillingly into the merger by reform-minded external directors. Its fossilized corporate culture is appropriate to the atmosphere of the headquarters town, where people are seen as commodities, just like the inks and paint pigments that Ajax sells to its slowly shrinking list of customers. Therefore, the Ajax pay plan has been to calculate the market wage for similar jobs in its industry and pay 5 percent more than that.

Last year, though, the compensation committee of the board of directors hired some upstart professor to adjust the pay system for entry into world markets. The professor refined the system by linking it with a database in Geneva, Switzerland, run by the Organization for Economic Cooperation and Development. The system now calculates a wage for five hundred different chemical-industry jobs in any location in the world. You maintained at the first merger meeting that Ajax's new pay system was "world class—the best." Your position is that the compensation plan should be Ajax's: *the world-market, base-pay plan.*

Issues

However, you do not really understand how your new pay system works or why Ajax might need it. You don't care about world markets, and you don't want to be merged into Worldwide Chemical Industries. You worked your way

The Pfeiffer Book of Successful Conflict Management Tools © 2003 John Wiley & Sons, Inc.

up through the ranks from factory supervisor and became a personnel manager because you get along well with the rank-and-file employees.

You also share the rank-and-file employees' view of "outsiders": You are afraid of them and do not trust them. You worry now that the business press is comparing Ajax unfavorably with the other three companies: Sun is more efficient, Grand Baton more inventive, and Conglomerate more adept at marketing. The *Wall Street Journal* says that the only reason Ajax was included in the merger at all was to give Worldwide Chemical Industries access to the huge U.S. market.

Your Strategy

You plan to take out your frustrations on the others by refusing to agree to any compensation plan other than the one used by Ajax.

Merger Mania Stipulation

Important: Do not allow the negotiators to see this sheet!

The point of this activity is for the negotiators to try to delve into the underlying corporate cultural biases and personal fears that have obstructed negotiations for the merger of four companies. Therefore, playing your role requires you to keep in mind two different kinds of information:

- "Facts" (the position you take); and
- "Reality" (the underlying issues).

"Facts" are things you have argued before and will pretend to believe until the negotiators delve into "reality" and question these facts. The negotiators have to dig beneath superficial facts to the underlying reality to solve the problem. Your job is to give them the reality *only* if they ask questions that show an increasing awareness of the role that organizational biases about culture as well as personal animosities have played in the situation.

There are two general lines of questioning that will, if pursued by the negotiators, lead to a solution of the problem. Both require that the negotiators ignore the details of the four pay plans and *question* your position, trying to persuade you to reject these previously agreed-on "facts." When the negotiators start asking the right questions, then you may want to give them clues (body language, a pained expression, more talk) that they have hit the right button.

The first line of questioning might be as follows:

"Fact" 1. All four company representatives agreed at the first merger meeting that the newly formed company should have a single, uniform pay system throughout the world. The four agreed that a uniform system would be simpler to administer, would appear fair, and would help build a strong corporate culture.

"Reality" 1. The reasons cited for adopting a single system are just diversions. Actually, you are afraid that retaining separate pay plans will undermine the unity of the new company. Unfortunately, you and the other company representatives do not respect one another's organizational cultures enough to compromise. Instead, you each hope that your own system is adopted. In your view, "strong organizational culture" means "my corporate culture." However, if the negotiators question this "fact," you will open

up and admit the fears you have about this agreement. You will also admit that it might make everyone more comfortable to keep the four systems intact. If this happens, the problem is solved and the role play ends.

The second line of questioning might be as follows:

"Fact" 2. Each of the four company representatives argued at the first merger meeting that his or her pay plan was better than the other three and should be used by all.

"Reality" 2. You do not necessarily believe this. You are just trying to be a tough negotiator to impress your own company. In fact, only the Ajax representative is opposed to any other system. Sun will accept any system agreed on by the other three. Grand Baton will follow the lead of the Conglomerate representative (although Grand Baton must be told that Conglomerate recommends the Ajax plan).

Conglomerate's computer analysis shows that the Ajax system is the best. Each negotiator must question this position to get a company representative to reveal his or her strategy. The negotiators have to determine what the Conglomerate representative's "second choice" would be and then present the Ajax system to the other company representatives as a possible solution. If this happens, the result will be agreement, thus ending the role play.

MERGER MANIA OBSERVER SHEET

Instructions: Observe the upcoming activity on negotiation, and record your observations by answering the questions below.

1. What happened in the negotiators' strategy sessions? What changes occurred over the two (or three) sessions?

2. How did the negotiators adapt to the cultural needs of their company representatives? How did they represent those needs during the strategy sessions?

3. How did the negotiators uncover the "realities" beneath the surface "facts" that were motivating the company representatives? What did the negotiators do with this information?

4. If agreement on a solution was reached, what contributed to the success? If not, what contributed to the failure? What could have been done differently?

Lindell-Billings Corporation:
A Confrontation Role Play

Thomas H. Patten, Jr.

Goals

- To provide an opportunity to practice confrontation.
- To explore design considerations in using confrontation inside an organization.
- To examine and develop skills in intergroup conflict, negotiation, and problem solving.

Group Size

A minimum of fifteen participants. Several groups may be directed simultaneously.

Time Required

Approximately three hours.

Materials

- A copy of the Lindell-Billings Corporation Case Sheet for each participant.
- A copy of the Lindell-Billings Corporation Organization Chart for each of the participants.

- Newsprint, masking tape, and felt-tipped markers.
- Role-name and role-title signs, if there is a large audience.

Physical Setting

A room large enough for teams to meet privately.

Process

1. The facilitator explains to the participants that a confrontation meeting will be staged through role playing.

2. The facilitator establishes two teams. Team A—top management—consists of seven people (Lindell, Billings, Mahoney, Thayer, Diamond, Gomez, and Jamieson) who will be confronted as a group. Team B—the staff team—consists of eight staff vice presidents, whose roles are shown on the Lindell-Billings Corporation Organization Chart. If there are more than fifteen participants, the remainder are assigned as observers.

3. The facilitator distributes a copy of the Lindell-Billings Corporation Case Sheet and a copy of the Lindell-Billings Corporation Organization Chart to each participant. After allowing five minutes for reading these materials, the facilitator explains that participants will have one hour to prepare for a confrontation based on their team roles. During this time they are to reach a consensus about the issues in the case and their feelings about them and then to write the consensus on newsprint. The facilitator indicates that in the top-management team Lindell will be the chairperson and that the staff team's first task is to select a chairperson for itself.

4. The facilitator consults with the teams to answer any questions and to keep the activity moving. The respective teams are encouraged to have their newsprint ready within an hour, but they are not to post it until the other team has also reached a consensus.

5. When both teams have reached a consensus and written it on newsprint, they simultaneously post their sheets of newsprint. The teams are allowed five minutes to read the other team's consensus. Then the chairperson of the top-management team (Lindell) explains that team's consensus, and the chairperson of the staff team does likewise. They answer any questions asked by other participants. The facilitator acts as a moderator, if needed. At this time, the observers, if any, report on their observations

of individual and team behavior. The total reporting and debriefing takes approximately one hour.

6. Both teams meet again and take one-half hour to decide consensually what action they propose to take next as a consequence of the confrontation. They write their course of action on newsprint.

7. Following the team meetings, step 5 is repeated. This second confrontation should take about one-half hour.

8. The facilitator leads the entire group in a discussion of the dynamics of the activity from a design standpoint, emphasizing how the features of the confrontation meeting can be applied to a wide range of problems in organizations. Participants may be asked to suggest examples of application. The total discussion time should take about five to fifteen minutes.

Variations

- Real organizational data can be substituted for the role-play case when the experience is used inside an organization.

- Instead of a confrontation meeting, the case can be studied by several groups. Their analyses of the issues can be compared within the total group.

Originally published in The 1975 Annual Handbook for Group Facilitators.

LINDELL-BILLINGS CORPORATION CASE SHEET[1]

Robin R. Lindell and Dale K. Billings are, respectively, chairperson and president of the Lindell-Billings Corporation, one of the most aggressive mini-conglomerates in the world. The company, which manufactures rubber and woven hose products, was founded by Lindell's father about forty years ago. It has, in the past decade, acquired a small life insurance company (the Rush Life Insurance Company), a chain of eighteen quick-service restaurants (Chihuahua Tacos), twenty ultramodern gas stations located off interstate highways (Plus Gasoline), and it is considering taking over the Ranchero Motel chain.

Lindell-Billings' top management consists of Lindell, a hard-driving businessperson who progressed from a manufacturing position in the rubber-hose division of the business; Billings, a shrewd financier who was chairperson of Rush before moving to the parent corporation; Lou Mahoney, manager of the Rubber and Woven Hose Products Division; Terry Thayer, general manager of the Rush Life Insurance Division; Chris Gomez, general manager of the Chihuahua Tacos Division; Pat Jamieson, general manager of the Plus Gasoline Division; and Kelly Diamond, executive vice president of the staff group. This team works well together and is extremely entrepreneurial in its outlook.

Beneath the top-management team are managerial groups that direct the day-to-day operations of the various divisions. Lindell-Billings provides these managers with considerable autonomy but looks for inputs from Kelly Diamond's staff group when it considers long-range business planning. Diamond's staff vice presidents and managers have in-depth expertise in such fields as finance, personnel, engineering, marketing, purchasing, public relations, advertising, and legal and tax affairs. It should be emphasized that the staff group reporting to Diamond contains a number of highly competent and highly paid executives who have approximately the same status as the divisional general managers.

Lindell and Billings have just pulled off a financial coup that has Diamond's staff upset and concerned. Several are threatening to resign, to report data to the Justice Department or the Securities and Exchange Commission,

---

[1]Based on a problem reported by R.L. Heilbroner, *The Worldly Philosophers,* New York: Simon and Schuster, 1953, 202–203. The design was adapted from Richard Beckhard, "The Confrontation Meeting," *Harvard Business Review,* March–April 1967, 149–155; and from J.K. Fordyce and R. Weil, *Managing with People,* 1971, 93–97, by Addison-Wesley Publishing Co., Reading, MA. Reprinted by permission of Addison-Wesley Publishing Co., Inc.

The Pfeiffer Book of Successful Conflict Management Tools © 2003 John Wiley & Sons, Inc.

or otherwise to disrupt the business. On the other hand, the top-management group (including Diamond) stands solidly behind Lindell and Billings, who have hired an OD (organization development) consultant to conduct a confrontation meeting with the staff group.

These are the issues that concern the staff group:

- Lindell and Billings gave a check for $39 million to wheeler-dealer J.J. LaVerne for the purchase of the Ishpeming Copper Company, on the condition that the check would be deposited in the National City Bank and left untouched for a specific period. LaVerne has a controlling interest in the Ishpeming Copper Company and is answerable to virtually no one.

- Lindell and Billings then set up a "paper" organization known as the LB Copper Corporation, with the names of certain members of the staff group as dummy directors, and had the LB Copper Corporation buy Ishpeming Copper—not for cash, but for $75 million in LB Copper stock that was conveniently printed for the purpose.

- Lindell and Billings then borrowed $39 million from the National City Bank to cover the check they had given to LaVerne. As collateral for this loan they used the $75 million in LB Copper stock.

- They then sold the LB Copper Corporation stock on the market (first having touted it through their brokers) for $75 million.

- With the proceeds, Lindell and Billings retired the $39 million loan from the National City Bank and subsequently reported $36 million as the parent company's profit on the deal.

LINDELL-BILLINGS CORPORATION ORGANIZATION CHART

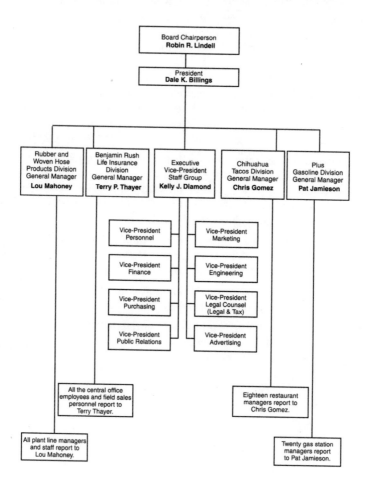

Board Chairperson
Robin R. Lindell

President
Dale K. Billings

| Rubber and Woven Hose Products Division General Manager **Lou Mahoney** | Benjamin Rush Life Insurance Division General Manager **Terry P. Thayer** | Executive Vice-President Staff Group **Kelly J. Diamond** | Chihuahua Tacos Division General Manager **Chris Gomez** | Plus Gasoline Division General Manager **Pat Jamieson** |

Vice-President Personnel

Vice-President Marketing

Vice-President Finance

Vice-President Engineering

Vice-President Purchasing

Vice-President Legal Counsel (Legal & Tax)

Vice-President Public Relations

Vice-President Advertising

All the central office employees and field sales personnel report to Terry Thayer.

Eighteen restaurant managers report to Chris Gomez.

All plant line managers and staff report to Lou Mahoney.

Twenty gas station managers report to Pat Jamieson.

Part 3
Inventories, Questionnaires, and Surveys

The instruments in this final section of the handbook are data-gathering tools. They can provide a range of useful information to organizations, workshop participants, intact teams, or individuals—not to mention trainers and consultants.

How does a department or an organization commonly deal with employees who rock the boat? How well does a work team handle conflicts involving goals or procedures or personalities? How effectively do individuals cope with their own anger, never mind other people's? And here's a huge one for any group of humans trying to work together productively or to benefit from "constructive" criticism: How much do you folks actually trust one another?

Surveys can produce insights that help participants view themselves and their surroundings more objectively. They can cough up hard evidence to break through denial that a problem exists. Just as helpfully, they can offer evidence that no problem exists, at least not in the form the trainer had in mind, and that a contemplated training program probably would be a waste of time and money.

As with the material in the rest of the handbook, we submit these instruments as the cream of the crop from three decades of the Pfeiffer *Annuals*. They approach issues of trust, communication, and conflict from several different angles, so choose a survey with a specific end in mind. Each includes the background information necessary to understand it, use it, and interpret it. Scoring sheets and scales are provided, as are data provided by the survey's authors about its reliability and validity.

Are you planning an experiential learning activity in which a team works through its actual problems and issues? One of these questionnaires, administered beforehand, could give the group real data to work with, helping them to focus on particular trouble spots. Are you teaching techniques for coping effectively with interpersonal conflict in general? How much value could you add with a self-evaluation that gives participants new and maybe surprising insights into how they cope with conflict now?

However you apply them, these eight tools are knowledge catchers. And knowledge is something you can't catch enough of.

- **Conflict Management Climate Index**—Takes an organization's temperature with respect to the way power is used, feelings are expressed, and disagreements are handled.

- **Cornerstones: A Measure of Trust in Work Relationships**—Assesses the level of trust between individuals in the same work group or organization.

- **The Team Effectiveness Critique**—Addresses the ways that an intact work team currently handles conflict, solves problems, communicates, achieves clarity on its goals, and more.

- **Trust Orientation Profile**—Surveys the "trust climate" in a team or organization. To what degree do you people trust one another, and how does it show?

- **Conflict Management Style Survey**—Measures the individual participant's habitual responses to various types of conflict involving different kinds of people.

- **Communication Audit: A Pairs Analysis**—How effectively does an individual communicate with his or her supervisor, with senior management, and with others at work and elsewhere?

- **Inventory of Anger Communication**—How well does an individual cope with and express his or her own anger?

- **The Defensiveness Inventory**—How does an individual habitually respond to criticism?

1

Conflict Management Climate Index

Bob Crosby and John J. Scherer

There are factors in the "climate" of any organization that can help or hinder third-party efforts to address and manage conflict. Although these climate conditions do not themselves create or resolve conflict, they can be powerful variables in determining how effective an intervention will be. When these factors are favorable, even a moderately skilled third-party consultant, working with moderately skilled participants, can be effective. When they are not favorable, even a highly skilled consultant, working with highly skilled individual participants, is likely to be frustrated.

USES OF THE INSTRUMENT

Because these climate conditions are so critical, it may be impossible to help a given organization unless the climate conditions are first adjusted. For this reason, it is imperative that these factors be identified and analyzed in terms of the organization in question before a commitment is made to a method of third-party intervention. The Conflict-Management Climate Index presented here is useful in the following initial steps of the consulting process:

1. *Deciding Whether to Accept the Conflict-Management Assignment.* By collecting a sampling of opinion (using the instrument presented here) from organizational members regarding these climate factors, the consultant can generate very useful data to be used in establishing expectations with the client. Whether or not the consultant decides to accept the job, in sharing the instrument data with the client, he or she can provide a great deal of useful information to the organization. This information frequently will

indicate a need for deeper, long-term organization development work, beyond the particular crisis intervention.

2. *Sensing Interviews.* The instrument can be used in the sensing-interview stage to collect and organize attitudes of organizational members prior to the introduction of any conflict-management intervention and is an excellent method of gathering data in a new or "cold" group.

3. *Diagnosis of Needs.* Once the data have been collected, the categories themselves become self-explanatory diagnostic guides, thus enabling the third-party consultant to focus on factors that need attention during initial discussions with key members of the client system.

4. *Training Intervention.* The instrument also can be used as a teaching device to introduce the concept of conflict-management climate to members of an organization in such a way that they can learn something about conflict management at the same time that they are diagnosing the organization. This is a very powerful combination of input and output and increases the value of both.

5. *OD Program.* Obviously, the particular crisis for which the third-party consultation is needed can be a symptom of larger, more profound issues in the organization. It is possible for the consultant to use the data generated by the instrument to explain to decision makers why these crises may continue unless something is done about the climate to make it more supportive of effective conflict management.

Thus, when asked to "come and do something on conflict management" for an organization, the consultant can use the instrument to elicit data that will help to determine the significant issues that need to be addressed and the best interventions by which to address them.

A Few Notes on Scoring

The lower the score on this instrument, the less likely conflict-management efforts will be to succeed, unless some climate-changing activities are first carried out. It generally would not be advisable to engage in conflict-resolution projects in organizations in which average scores on this instrument were lower than thirty, without clear and strong commitment on the part of top management to attempt to understand and change the climate factors operating within the organization.

Many of the items on the instrument are derived from Richard Walton's work in the field (Walton & Dutton, 1969), and the authors recommend his book as a companion piece to the use of this measurement device.

Reference

Walton, R.L., & Dutton. J.M. (1969). The management of interdepartmental conflict: A model and review. *Administrative Science Quarterly, 14,* 73–84.

Originally published in The 1981 Annual Handbook for Group Facilitators.

CONFLICT-MANAGEMENT CLIMATE INDEX

Bob Crosby and John J. Scherer

Your Name _____

Organizational Unit Assessed _____

Instructions: The purpose of this index is to permit you to assess your organization with regard to its conflict-management climate. On each of the following rating scales, indicate how you see your organization as it actually is right now, not how you think it should be or how you believe others would see it. Circle the number that indicates your sense of where the organization is on each dimension of the Conflict-Management Climate Index.

1. Balance of Power

1	2	3	4	5	6

Power is massed either at the top or at the bottom of the organization.

Power is distributed evenly and appropriately throughout the organization.

2. Expression of Feelings

1	2	3	4	5	6

Expressing strong feelings is costly and not accepted.

Expressing strong feelings is valued and easy to do.

3. Conflict-Management Procedures

1	2	3	4	5	6

There are no clear conflict-resolution procedures that many people use.

Everyone knows about, and many people use, a conflict-resolution procedure.

4. Attitudes Toward Open Disagreement

1	2	3	4	5	6

People here do not openly disagree very much.

"Going along to get along" is the motto. People feel free to disagree openly on important issues without fear of consequences.

5. Use of Third Parties

1	2	3	4	5	6

No one here uses third parties to help resolve conflicts.

Third parties are frequently used to resolve conflicts.

6. Power of Third Parties

1	2	3	4	5	6

Third parties are usually superiors in the organization.

Third parties are always people of equal or lower rank.

7. Neutrality of Third Parties

1	2	3	4	5	6

Third parties are never neutral, but serve as advocates for a certain outcome.

Third parties are always neutral as to substantive issues and conflict-resolution methods used.

8. Your Leader's Conflict-Resolution Style

1	2	3	4	5	6

The leader does not deal openly with conflict but works behind the scenes with those involved to resolve it.

The leader confronts conflicts directly and works openly to resolve them.

9. How Your Leader Receives Negative Feedback

1	2	3	4	5	6

The leader is defensive and/or closed and seeks vengeance on those who criticize him/her.

The leader receives criticism easily and even seeks it as an opportunity to grow and learn.

10. Follow-Up

1	2	3	4	5	6

Agreements always fall through the cracks; the same problems must be solved again and again.

Accountability is built into every conflict-resolution agreement.

11. Feedback Procedures

1	2	3	4	5	6

No effort is made to solicit and understand reactions to decisions.

Feedback channels for soliciting reactions to all major decisions are known and used.

12. Communication Skills

1	2	3	4	5	6

Few, if any, people possess basic communication skills or at least do not practice them.

Everyone in the organization possesses and uses good communication skills.

13. Track Record

1	2	3	4	5	6

Very few, if any, successful conflict-resolution experiences have occurred in the recent past.

Many stories are available of successful conflict-resolution experiences in the recent past.

CONFLICT-MANAGEMENT CLIMATE INDEX
SCORING AND INTERPRETATION SHEET

Instructions: To arrive at your overall Conflict-Management Climate Index, total the ratings that you assigned to the thirteen separate scales. The highest possible score is 78 and the lowest is 13.

Then compare your score with the following conflict-resolution readiness index range.

Index Range	Indication
60–78	Ready to work on conflict with little or no work on climate.
31–59	Possible with some commitment to work on climate.
13–30	Very risky without unanimous commitment to work on climate issues.

Find your lowest ratings and study the following descriptions or interpretations of the thirteen separate dimensions. As you read the descriptions, think about what specifically might be done (or changed) in other activities described, in order to increase your organization's readiness to manage conflict more effectively.

CLIMATE FACTORS AFFECTING CONFLICT MANAGEMENT IN ORGANIZATIONS

1. *Balance of Power.* Simply stated, is power spread appropriately and realistically throughout the organization, or is it massed at either the top or bottom levels? The ideal is not for everyone to have equal power, but for a general feeling among most members of the organization that they have sufficient influence over the most significant aspects of their work lives. This may include the power to obtain a fair hearing and a realistic response from someone in authority.

    This factor is important because it reflects the extent to which communication is likely to be distorted. Research evidence (Mulder, 1960; Solomon, 1960) seems to indicate that when two people perceive their levels of power to be different, they are likely to mistrust any communication that takes place between them. People who perceive themselves as being less powerful than the other party tend to perceive communication from that person as being manipulative or condescending. Those who see themselves as being more powerful experience communication from the less powerful as being devious or manipulative. Ironically, these more powerful persons also perceive collaborative behavior as an indication of weakness on the part of those whom they see as less powerful. These perceptions can make effective conflict resolution all but impossible.

In organizations in which power is massed at the top, it is extremely difficult for the third-party consultant to achieve the neutrality necessary to be effective without appearing to "take sides" with someone at the less powerful end of the organization. In organizations in which power is massed at the bottom, there is frequently so much disrespect for—or even disgust with—top management that it is difficult for the third-party consultant to encourage the more powerful workers to respect or even attend to any collaborative actions that top management may take.

Because an appropriate balance of power within an organization is relatively rare, the third party and the participants involved in the conflict will need to collaboratively seek ways to create a balance of power within the limits of the conflict-resolution episode. The two persons or parties in conflict must understand that the more powerful member is to lend some skills or status to the weaker member for the duration of the intervention and also that the more powerful member may not use that power to punish the subordinate, regardless of the outcome of the conflict-resolution process.

The purpose of this balancing of power between the two parties in conflict is to facilitate the process of discussion and mediation, not to create institutional equals. When the consultation process is finished, the parties involved will return to their usual roles (e.g., the boss will still be the boss and the subordinate will still be the subordinate), and it is essential that everyone involved understand this.

2. *Expression of Feelings.* Conflict management is much easier to achieve in a climate in which open expression of members' feelings—especially when those feelings are strongly negative—is valued. In many organizations, a person will find the expression of strong emotions a costly experience and may be either subtly or openly ostracized or reprimanded for such conduct.

It is easy to see why conflict management is more likely to be successful in a climate in which feelings are valued. In the first phases of any conflict resolution, the expression of feelings on the part of the parties

The Pfeiffer Book of Successful Conflict Management Tools © 2003 John Wiley & Sons, Inc.

in conflict is extremely important; in fact, the success of the next two steps in the conflict-resolution process, differentiation and integration, is directly related to whether complete and honest communication of emotions has occurred.

3. *Conflict-Management Procedures.* In organizations in which there are clearly defined procedures or channels for conflict resolution, the work of a third-party consultant—whether internal or external to the organization—is obviously much easier. In a system in which there are no clearly defined ways to resolve conflict and in which people do not know what to expect or what to do when conflict arises, the work of the third party is made extremely difficult. When people feel safe in using conflict-resolution procedures, they are more likely to have confidence in the outcome. Conversely, if people in conflict feel that they are fumbling through it, they are not likely to put much faith in either the acceptability or the reliability of the procedure they have chosen to use. If top management seriously wants to support effective conflict management, then specific procedures must be made known to and accepted by members at all levels of the organization.

4. *Attitudes Toward Open Disagreements.* This factor reflects the attitudes of members of the organization about open disagreement over proposals or issues. Janis' book, *Victims of Groupthink* (1972), vividly describes decision making at the national level and shows how unexpressed reservations can lead to apparently consensual policy decisions with which few of the decision makers are in actual agreement.

In a system in which open disagreement about issues is viewed as disloyalty or insubordination, effective third-party conflict mediation is almost impossible. In such organizations, participants may pretend to agree or to work out differences of opinion without actually allowing themselves to find out how very far apart their views or positions are. Where differentiation is insufficient, integration or long-term conflict resolution is simply not possible.

Organizations that require creativity, such as advertising firms and think tanks, solicit and encourage differences of opinion because the discussions that result make possible insights and solutions that might never be thought of in a climate in which everyone agreed with the first idea suggested.

5. *Use of Third Parties.* A healthy conflict-management climate will encourage people to ask others in the system to act as third-party consultants when conflicts arise. Most organizations have, at least tacitly, established

the norm that conflict must be kept "in the family" and not "aired in public." This makes the work of the person who is called in to help extremely difficult. One of the first concerns, then, is to confront the reservations and resistances that people have about working with a third party. In particular, it should be made clear that the use of a third party is not a sign of weakness on the part of the persons in conflict. This can be reinforced merely by using third parties effectively.

6. *Power of Third Parties.* As Walton (1969) points out, it is difficult for someone with hierarchical power to be an effective third party. When subordinates feel that anything they say may later be used against them, it is highly likely that crucial information will not be shared during the confrontation episode. However, these data frequently are the keys to unlocking conflict situations. In a healthy conflict-management climate, a supervisor would encourage subordinates to seek third-party help from someone on their level or even lower in the organization. It is hard for most managers to do this, because they want to be seen as helpful and caring and also because they want to have some control over potentially explosive situations.

7. *Neutrality of Third Parties.* Third parties from within the organization must remain neutral about substantive outcomes, or at least suppress their biases sufficiently to be effective. When third parties are unskilled and biased about what the outcome of the conflict-resolution process should be, one of the people in conflict is likely to feel "ganged up on," and the person who wins may feel a little bit guilty. Such a "conflict-resolution" process may result in a defusing of the issue but also is likely to cause the significant feelings of the people involved to be submerged, to increase mistrust of management, and to make participants feel a lack of ownership of a solution that they may feel was imposed on them.

   In addition, past experience with a biased third party makes it difficult for members of the organization to trust the process in the future. Therefore, the third-party consultant may need to spend a great deal of time and energy in establishing his or her neutrality and credibility with the persons involved.

8. *Your Leader's Conflict-Resolution Style.* The senior people in any organization greatly influence the climate. Walton and Dutton (1969) showed that it is possible to characterize a general style of conflict management in an organization and that the people at the top of the organization set that style by their own behavior. In their "contingency theory" of organization, Lawrence and Lorsch (1969) found that not only could they

characterize the way people generally approached conflict but also showed that one particular approach, "confrontation," worked best and was associated with organizational effectiveness. In other words, these researcher/consultants found that the way people approach conflict is not a contingency factor but that there was a "best way": confrontation. It means that conflict is openly recognized when it occurs and the people involved proceed to deal directly with the conflict problem. It means *not* running away, *not* trying to "smooth over" real and important differences, *not* immediately trying to "split the difference," and *not* fighting a win-lose battle. Confrontation implies creative problem solving. When superiors confront conflicts, they are seen as strong and their behavior encourages others to deal directly with problems of conflict.

The model set by those in positions of power has effects on all sorts of subordinate behavior but especially influences how subordinates relate to one another when dealing with conflicts. Even when the supervisor's nonconfrontational style is successfully applied to solve a particular problem, it still weakens the organization's problem-solving and conflict-resolution capacity.

9. *How Your Leader Receives Negative Feedback.* In a conflict situation, there is always great potential for the expression of negative feelings. It is rare, even when conflict is dealt with very effectively, for no negative comments to have been expressed. Such comments may concern the content of the conflict ("I think your approach is unlikely to increase sales as much as mine would") or may relate to how the parties feel on an emotional level ("Your attempts to dominate our ad campaigns are signs of your inflated ego"). Grossly ineffective handling of conflict is associated with an inability to deal with either of these types of negative feedback. Even worse is when the leader or person in authority acts against the other party at a later date, thus gaining "vengeance." This kind of behavior is associated with other nonfunctional ways of handling conflict, such as not letting the other party know one's true feelings, never letting disagreements get out in the open, and trying to deal with conflict "behind the scenes." The type of persons using these strategies avoid showing anger or any expression at all. Their motto might be "Don't get mad, get even."

No healthy person actually enjoys negative feedback, on either the content or interpersonal level, but effective leaders are able to ignore or fail to respond in kind to personal attacks—while often openly recognizing the feelings expressed by the other party—and are likely to look at content criticism more objectively, to determine whether there really is a sound point to the critique. At our best, we may relatively quickly transfer the kernel of truth in a negative item into positive corrective action. A conflict, for example, over the leader's daily "checkup" on a delegated project might lead this leader to examine and correct the tendency to avoid really "letting go" of an important project.

10. *Follow-Up.* Follow-up procedures and methods of accountability should be built into all conflict-resolution decisions. It is possible to have a highly successful confrontation dialogue between two people, to have them reach intelligent resolutions, and then to have those resolutions disappear between the "cracks" in the relationship or in the organization's busy work schedule. It is extremely important that the last step in the conflict-resolution process specifies:

1. What has been decided?

2. What will be done next and by whom?

3. What checks are there on how and whether it is carried out?

4. What are the expected consequences?

5. How, when, and by whom will the effectiveness of these decisions be evaluated?

When people are used to making sure that planned outcomes are implemented, the work of a third party is made much easier. In places in which problems historically must be solved over and over again, it is necessary for the third-party consultant to train people in follow-up procedures before beginning the conflict dialogue.

11. *Feedback Procedures.* When communication channels exist that can be used to surface disagreements and conflicts, it is obvious that more conflict resolution is possible. This does not guarantee that conflicts are generally resolved effectively, but it is a prerequisite if such effective action is to take place at all. There are many ways by which members of an organization can be given access to and encouraged to use channels for feedback. When upper levels or those in power are responsive to feedback that indicates conflict problems, then even relatively simple "mechanistic" feedback approaches, such as the old-fashioned suggestion box, can work well. Some years ago, New England Bell Telephone Company instituted an "open lines" program whereby people at lower levels could raise problems by telephoning an anonymous executive ombudsman, with their own anonymity guaranteed. Certainly a situation in which the parties feel free to directly approach one another is the most preferable, but when the overall climate cannot support this, a mechanistic approach, if

The Pfeiffer Book of Successful Conflict Management Tools © *2003 John Wiley & Sons, Inc.*

used responsively, can be a useful and productive step toward changing the conflict-management climate.

One commonly touted action that may not work is the so-called "open-door policy." When lower-level or less powerful individuals actually try to use the open door, they find that the policy exists in name but not in fact—that it is not so easy to get through the door at all, and that, when it is done, the response is overtly or covertly a turn off or "cooling out" process. Furthermore, one is observed in the process and the person using the open door may be labeled as a telltale, a spy, someone who cannot handle his or her own problems, etc. All of these negative factors are characteristic of organizations with poor conflict-management climates, and would not, of course, apply to organizations with good climates, open expression of feelings and disagreements, clear procedures for dealing with conflict, effective use of third parties, etc. As it happens, it is the former type of organization in which a so-called open-door policy is likely to succeed, while such a policy would be laughably unnecessary in the latter type of organization.

12. *Communication Skills.* If people in an organization are accustomed to blaming, criticizing, projecting their own issues onto other people, and scapegoating; if they do not know how to make "I" statements (Gordon, 1970) that clearly communicate how to listen to their own positions; or if they cannot listen empathically (Milnes & Bertcher, 1980; Rogers & Farson, 1977) without forming opinions, then it probably will be necessary to prepare them for confrontation dialogues by training them in communicating and listening in high-stress situations. Of course, it is easier to do conflict-management work in an organization in which the members have received training in communication skills. In that case, the role of the third party is to help the participants to stay "on track" and to coach them in maintaining open communication.

13. *Track Record.* How successful were past attempts to resolve conflict equitably? If there is a history of people being reprimanded or fired for initiating an attempt to resolve a conflict, the third-party consultation may be perceived as "window dressing." On the other hand, nothing succeeds like success, and nothing helps the conflict-management consultant more than an organization with a history of useful and lasting involvement in dealing with conflict.

Conclusion

The conflict-management climate in organizations functions a great deal like the weather. When the weather is good, you can do many more things more enjoyably than when the weather is bad. In the middle of a storm, you can still do many of the things you could do when the weather was good, but it requires much more energy, and the risks of failure are increased. We believe that one of the major skill focuses of consultants to organizations trying to learn to manage conflict is in collaborating with top management in seeking innovative ways to change the weather in the organizations along the dimensions charted in the Conflict-Management Climate Index.

References

Gordon, T. (1970). *Parent effectiveness training.* New York: Wyden.

Harriman, B. (1974). Up and down the communications ladder. *Harvard Business Review, 52,*(5), 143–151.

Janis, J.L. (1972). *Victims of groupthink.* Boston: Houghton-Mifflin.

Lawrence, P.R., & Lorsch, J.W. (1969). *Organization and environment.* Homewood, IL: Richard Irwin.

Milnes, J., & Bertcher, H. (1980). *Communicating empathy.* San Francisco, CA: Jossey-Bass/Pfeiffer.

Mulder, M. (1960). The power variable in communication experiments. *Human Relations, 13,* 241–256.

Rogers, C.R., & Farson, R.E. (1977). Active listening. In R.C. Huseman, C.M. Logue, & D.L Freshley (Eds.), *Readings in interpersonal and organizational communication* (3rd. ed.). Boston: Holbrook Press.

Solomon, L. (1960). The influence of some types of power relationships and game strategies upon the development of interpersonal trust. *Journal of Abnormal and Social Psychology, 61,* 223–230.

Walton, R.L., & Dutton, J.M. (1969). The management of interdepartmental conflict: A model and review. *Administrative Science Quarterly, 14,* 73–84.

2

Cornerstones: A Measure of Trust in Work Relationships

Amy M. Birtel, Valerie C. Nellen, and Susan B. Wilkes

Abstract: Trust between co-workers in the workplace has been demonstrated to be a key component of effective management, organizational commitment, and job satisfaction. The Cornerstones Trust Survey can be used to assess the level of trust between individuals in organizational life and in work relationships. It measures three dimensions of trust: *competence* (the person's perceived ability to do the work), *credibility* (the person's consistency and predictability), and *care* (the other person's valuing of the respondent's needs and concerns).

Respondents answer fifteen questions regarding their level of trust for an identified colleague. Composite scores are obtained on the three dimensions. Instructions are included for using this instrument as a basis for personal feedback and action planning.

INTRODUCTION

The Cornerstones Trust Survey is designed to assist the professional in assessing the level of interpersonal trust among respondents who work together. The reasons for wanting to measure interpersonal trust are many and are supported by research emphasizing the importance of trust between individuals in the workplace. McAllister (1995) suggests that it is especially important for managers to be able to build trust with employees, as much of their work function involves acting as a conduit between people and/or systems. Mishra and Morrissey's (1990) study of employee/employer relationships found six main advantages for an organization when workers trusted their leaders: improved communication; greater predictability, dependability, and confidence; a reduction in employee turnover; openness and willingness to listen and accept criticism non-defensively; repeat business; and a reduction of friction between employees. Posner and Kouzes (1988), two highly regarded scholars of leadership, cite research in which the degree to which employees trusted their management directly affected their organizational commitment, job satisfaction, role clarity, and perceptions of organizational effectiveness. It thus seems evident that the ability to inspire interpersonal trust is an invaluable asset in the workplace and that evaluating it and finding ways to improve it are important in today's organizations.

There is a great deal of research on the situational antecedents of trust, and many of the findings are similar or related. For purposes of this instrument, many of the researchers' suggested antecedents were subsumed into three major categories: *competence, credibility,* and *care.* A similar grouping is seen in the work of Mayer, Davis, and Schoorman (1995). *Competence* refers to the ability of the individual in question to perform the task or activity on which the assessment of trust is being based. For example, if a person is thinking about allowing a doctor to perform heart surgery on him or her, the person must trust in the doctor's skill as a cardiac surgeon. In the same way, an employee must trust his or her co-worker or manager to carry out assigned duties in a highly effective way. *Credibility* is defined as a measure of the individual's consistency across situations. For example, one person's trust in another is strongly influenced by the degree to which that person's word matches his or her deeds, as well as by the predictability of the person's behaviors based on previous behaviors or statements. Finally, the construct of *care* provides an assessment of how much the individual in question has demonstrated a willingness to value the needs and concerns of the person who is thinking about trusting him or her. People are more likely to trust others if they have evidence to suggest that the others will consider their interests when taking actions that may affect them, especially important in employer/employee relationships.

Description of the Instrument

The Cornerstones Trust Survey is a self-scoring instrument with fifteen items, five on each of the three dimensions described above. Respondents use a seven-point Likert scale to rate the trust they hold in an identified colleague, co-worker, or supervisor. The instrument takes approximately five minutes to complete.

Respondents can calculate their own scores on this survey, using the Cornerstones Trust Survey Self-Scoring Sheet. After scores have been tabulated, they are plotted onto a grid provided on the scoring sheet. There are a number of potential uses for the results, described in the "Using the Results" section.

Administering the Survey

Explain to respondents that they will complete a brief survey to determine the level of trust they feel for an identified colleague. If the results will not be shared with the other person, assure the respondents that they do not need to write the person's name on the survey and that you will not be "sharing" their results with others or requiring them to do so. In this case, mention that some people do find it helpful to use the survey simply as a way to get in touch with their own feelings about another.

If the survey *is* being used as a feedback tool, remind them to be especially conscientious, as they will be sharing their answers with the persons they rated. Remind them that the purpose of the instrument is not only to help them learn about trust and its component parts but to provide feedback to their colleagues in order to improve their working relationships.

Distribute copies of the survey. Instruct participants to think of only one colleague and to use the full range of responses from 1 to 7 when answering each of the questions about that particular colleague. (It is possible to use this survey in a team-building workshop, in which case a small work group fills out surveys on each of their co-workers and their manager and then spends time sharing with one another one-to-one and in a facilitated group discussion.)

After respondents have finished filling out the survey, but prior to scoring it, give a brief explanation about the importance of interpersonal trust in the workplace. Explain the three components of trust that have been identified in the research and distribute a copy of the Cornerstones Trust Survey Handout to each respondent.

Explain that it is important for colleagues to build trust in order to work together effectively and to maximize job satisfaction and organizational commitment. Show the participants the key components of trust, as seen on the diagram on the handout; then read through the handout with them. *Competence* refers to the ability of the individual in question to perform the task or activity on which the assessment of trust is being based. For example, if a person is thinking about allowing a doctor to perform heart surgery on him or her, the person must trust in the doctor's skill as a cardiac surgeon. In the same way, an employee must trust his or her co-worker or manager to carry out assigned duties in a highly effective way. *Credibility* is defined as a measure of the individual's consistency across situations. For example, one person's trust in another is strongly influenced by the degree to which that person's word matches his or her deeds, as well as by the predictability of the person's behaviors based on previous behaviors or statements. Finally, the construct of *care* provides an assessment of how much the individual in question has demonstrated a willingness to value the needs and concerns of the person who is thinking about trusting him or her. People are more likely to trust others if they have evidence to suggest that the others will consider their interests when taking actions that may affect them, especially important in employer/employee relationships.

Scoring the Survey

Hand out copies of the Cornerstones Trust Survey Self-Scoring Sheet. Instruct respondents to transfer their answers to the scoring sheet and to follow the instructions for calculating their scores. Offer assistance to any participants who may need help.

Once respondents have scored their surveys, have them plot their scores to create a visual representation of the levels of trust experienced on the three dimensions using the diagram on the second page of the scoring sheet. The center of the triangle represents 0 and each point of the triangle represents a score of 35 on that dimension. After participants have plotted their scores, tell them to connect the three points to create a "trust triangle" that can be used as a basis for discussion, if desired. If the survey is being used as the focus of a team-building session, repeat the process for each member of the team before continuing.

The Pfeiffer Book of Successful Conflict Management Tools © 2003 John Wiley & Sons, Inc.

INTERPRETING THE RESULTS

Next, help the respondents interpret their results. Draw a sample triangle on a piece of flip-chart paper with scores of 10, 23, and 15 on care, competence, and credibility, respectively. Note how, in this case, the respondent feels that the person is skilled, but the respondent is not confident that the individual being rated cares about him or her personally or would be truthful under all circumstances. On the other hand, if the scores were high on care, high on credibility, and low on competence, the interpretation might be that the respondent thinks the person is open, honest, and can be trusted, but that he or she needs to improve his or her overall competence in doing the work. Finally, tell respondents that the overall size of the triangle can be interpreted as a measure of general trust, with a small but balanced triangle suggesting that improving trust on all three dimensions might be useful. Suggest that examining individual items to detect particular areas of strength or weakness in their level of trust for the other person can also be beneficial. They should mark items that they want to discuss one-on-one.

USING THE RESULTS

Following are a number of ways that the Cornerstones Trust Survey can be used.

1. The survey can be included as an activity in a workshop module on trust, leadership, or team building. The focus would be on understanding the components of trust and on learning more about the implications of levels of trust in work relationships. Additional discussion topics might include ways of building trust in work relationships.

2. The survey can provide a basis for intervention in dyads offering one another one-on-one feedback. Participants can provide feedback to one another in pairs, using their survey results. In some cases, it may be useful for this discussion to be facilitated by a skilled consultant. In preparation for giving one another feedback, the participants may want to review specific items with particularly high or low scores. As with any form of feedback, remind participants to provide examples and to focus on actual behavior rather than on personal characteristics or on supposition about another's motives.

3. The survey can be employed in 360-degree feedback sessions by aggregating a number of respondents' scores for one individual and providing the scores to that person with accompanying qualitative feedback.

4. The survey may be adopted on a team or organization-wide basis to assess general levels of trust within the organization by compiling a number of individual results.

   In all of these cases, an action plan should be created to assist the individual(s) to apply what each has learned. Generally speaking, an action plan would include goals, specific action steps leading to the achievement of the goals, and a time frame for accomplishing each step.

PSYCHOMETRIC PROPERTIES OF THE INSTRUMENT

Demographics of the Sample

In order to test reliability of the instrument, 118 employees from a variety of organizations completed the Cornerstones Trust Survey. Of those completing the survey, 69.8 percent were female and 30.2 percent were male. The large majority of the respondents were working adults, 88.7 percent of whom were twenty-six or older (61.7 percent were thirty-six or older). Racial breakdowns were as follows: 82.8 percent Caucasian, 9.5 percent African-American, 3.4 percent Asian-American, 3.4 percent Latino, and .9 percent "other."

Reliability

Internal consistency for the overall scale and each of the three subscales was calculated using Cronbach's alpha for the full sample of 118 participants. The internal consistency score for the overall scale of fifteen items was very high, with an alpha of .96. Alpha coefficients for the subscales of competence, caring, and credibility were .95, .92, and .92, respectively.

Validity

Validity of the instrument as a measure of trust in a work relationship was assessed by examining the relationship between scores on the scales and a separate item about trust. The item was "This is a person I trust." Correlations between the item and the scales are noted in Table 1. All correlations were significant at the p<.01 level.

Table 1. Correlations for General Item

	General Trust Item
Competence Score	.617
Care Score	.860
Credibility Score	.853

References

Mayer, R.C., Davis, J.H., & Schoorman, F.D. (1995). An integrative model of organizational trust. *Academy of Management Review, 20*(3), 709–734.

McAllister, D.J. (1995). Affect- and cognition-based trust as foundations for interpersonal cooperation in organization. *Academy of Management Journal, 38*(1), 24–59.

Mishra, J., & Morrisey, M.A. (1990). Trust in employee/employer relationships: A survey of West Michigan managers. *Public Personnel Management, 19*(4), 443–486.

Posner, B., & Kouzes, J. (1988). Relating leadership and credibility. *Psychological Reports, 63*(2), 527–530.

Originally published in The 2002 Annual, Vol. 2, Consulting.

CORNERSTONES TRUST SURVEY

Amy M. Birtel, Valerie C. Nellen, and Susan B. Wilkes

Instructions: Think of the individual for whom you are filling out this survey and, using the seven-point scale below, respond to the following with only that person in mind. Circle the numbers that correspond to your level of agreement. If you will be sharing your feedback with this person, write his or her name at the top of the page.

1 = Very strongly disagree	2 = Strongly disagree	3 = Disagree	4 = Neutral	5 = Agree	6 = Strongly agree	7 = Very strongly agree

This is a person . . .

1. who effectively completes the tasks on which he or she works.	1	2	3	4	5	6	7
2. who tells me the truth.	1	2	3	4	5	6	7
3. who considers my needs and interests when making decisions that impact me.	1	2	3	4	5	6	7
4. to whom I would delegate important tasks, if I had the opportunity.	1	2	3	4	5	6	7
5. who keeps confidential any information that he or she has promised not to share.	1	2	3	4	5	6	7
6. who does things to help me out when I need help.	1	2	3	4	5	6	7
7. who demonstrates an appropriate level of skill in completing tasks.	1	2	3	4	5	6	7
8. who honors his or her commitments.	1	2	3	4	5	6	7
9. who demonstrates concern for my well-being.	1	2	3	4	5	6	7
10. who produces work that is useful to others.	1	2	3	4	5	6	7

1 = Very strongly disagree	2 = Strongly disagree	3 = Disagree	4 = Neutral	5 = Agree	6 = Strongly agree	7 = Very strongly agree

11. who is honest about his or her own
ability to get things done.   1   2   3   4   5   6   7

12. who has expectations of me that
challenge me, but who provides
the support I need to live up to
those expectations.   1   2   3   4   5   6   7

13. who demonstrates competence in
his or her work.   1   2   3   4   5   6   7

14. who makes statements that are
credible.   1   2   3   4   5   6   7

15. who knows some personal details
of my life outside of work because
I've felt comfortable sharing that
information.   1   2   3   4   5   6   7

Cornerstones Trust Survey Self-Scoring Sheet

Instructions: Transfer your responses for each question to this page. Add the numbers in each column to obtain a total score for each dimension of trust.

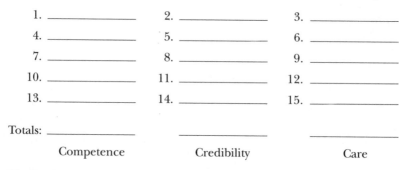

1. _____	2. _____	3. _____
4. _____	5. _____	6. _____
7. _____	8. _____	9. _____
10. _____	11. _____	12. _____
13. _____	14. _____	15. _____

Totals: _____   _____   _____

Competence   Credibility   Care

What Your Scores Mean

29 through 35: You have a great deal of trust in this individual on this dimension.

20 through 28: You have a reasonable amount of trust in this individual on this dimension, but would like to feel more comfortable trusting the individual.

11 through 19: You are somewhat wary of this individual on this dimension, and your relationship would likely benefit from increased trust.

5 through 10: You have very little trust in this individual on this dimension, and it is imperative that this be improved in order for you to work well together.

Now, plot your scores on the following diagram, with the middle of the triangle representing a score of 0 and each end point representing a score of 35 on the dimension identified. Finally, connect the plotted points to create a "trust triangle" representing your overall level of trust in the identified individual.

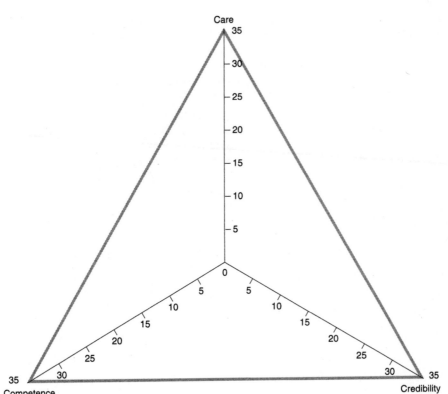

Cornerstones Trust Survey Handout

Competence refers to the ability of the individual in question to perform the task or activity on which the assessment of trust is being based. For example, if a person is thinking about allowing a doctor to perform heart surgery on him or her, the person must trust in the doctor's skill as a cardiac surgeon. In the same way, an employee must trust his or her co-worker or manager to carry out assigned duties in a highly effective way.

Credibility is defined as a measure of the individual's consistency across situations. For example, one person's trust in another is strongly influenced by the degree to which that person's word matches his or her deeds, as well as by the predictability of the person's behaviors based on previous behaviors or statements.

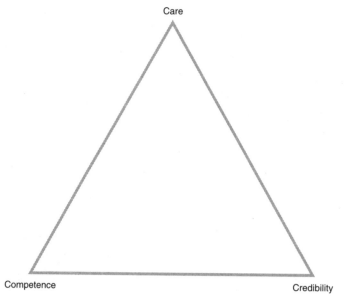

Finally, the construct of *care* provides an assessment of how much the individual in question has demonstrated a willingness to value the needs and concerns of the person who is thinking about trusting him or her. People are more likely to trust others if they have evidence to suggest that the other will consider their interests when taking actions that may affect them, especially important in employer/employee relationships.

The Pfeiffer Book of Successful Conflict Management Tools © 2003 John Wiley & Sons, Inc.

3

The Team Effectiveness Critique

Mark Alexander

Most groups exist and persist because (a) the purpose of the group cannot be accomplished by individuals working on their own, and (b) certain needs of individual members can be satisfied by belonging to the group. Of course, the mere existence of a group does not ensure that it will operate effectively; a group is effective only to the degree to which it is able to use its individual and collective resources. The measure of the group's effectiveness is its ability to achieve its objectives and satisfy the needs of the individuals in the group.

An organization is a collection of groups. The success of an organization depends on the ability of the groups within it to work together to attain commonly held objectives. Because organizations are becoming increasingly more complex, their leaders must be concerned with developing more cohesive and cooperative relationships between individuals and groups. Similarly, the development of effective groups or teams within the organization will determine, to a large extent, the ability of the organization to attain its goals.

FACTORS CONTRIBUTING TO TEAM DEVELOPMENT AND EFFECTIVENESS

Team development is based on the assumption that any group is able to work more effectively if its members are prepared to confront questions such as: How can this collection of individuals work together more effectively as a team? How can we better use the resources we represent? How can we communicate with one another more effectively to make better decisions? What is impeding our performance?

The answers to these questions may be found by examining the factors that lead to team development and effectiveness. These factors can be measured, or inventoried, by team members with the use of the Team Effectiveness Critique. Before the critique form is administered, however, all team members should understand the terminology used to describe the nine factors. The following descriptions can be presented in a lecturette format to the team members prior to completion of the critique.

1. Shared Goals and Objectives

In order for a team to operate effectively, it must have stated goals and objectives. These goals are not a simple understanding of the immediate task, but an overall understanding of the role of the group in the total organization, its responsibilities, and the things the team wants to accomplish. In addition, the members of the team must be committed to the goals. Such commitment comes from involving all team members in defining the goals and relating the goals to specific problems that are relevant to team members. The time spent on goal definition in the initial stages of a team's life results in less time needed later to resolve problems and misunderstandings.

2. Utilization of Resources

The ultimate purpose of a team is to do things effectively. In order to accomplish this, the team must use effectively all the resources at its disposal. This means establishing an environment that allows individual resources to be used. Team effectiveness is enhanced when every member has the opportunity to contribute and when all opinions are heard and considered. It is the team's responsibility to create an atmosphere in which individuals can state their opinions without fear of ridicule or reprisal. It is each individual's responsibility to contribute information and ideas and to be prepared to support them with rational arguments. Maximum utilization of team members requires full participation and self-regulation.

3. Trust and Conflict Resolution

In any team situation, disagreement is likely to occur. The ability to openly recognize conflict and seek to resolve it through discussion is critical to the team's success. People do not automatically work well together just because they happen to belong to the same work group or share the same job function. For a team to become effective, it must deal with the emotional problems and needs of its members and the interpersonal problems that arise in order to build working relationships that are characterized by openness and trust. The creation of a feeling of mutual trust, respect, and understanding and the ability of the team to deal with the inevitable conflicts that occur in any group situation are key factors in team development.

4. Shared Leadership

Individuals will not function as a team if they are brought together simply to endorse decisions made by their leader or others not in the group. The development and cohesion of a team occurs only when there is a feeling of shared leadership among all team members. This means that all members accept some responsibility for task functions—those things necessary to do the job— and maintenance functions—those things necessary to keep the group together and interacting effectively. Task functions include: initiating discussions or actions, clarifying issues and goals, summarizing points, testing for consensus or agreement, and seeking or giving information. Task leadership helps the group to establish its direction and assists the group in moving toward its goals. Maintenance functions include encouraging involvement and participation, sensing and expressing group feelings, harmonizing and facilitating reconciliation of disagreements, setting standards for the group, and "gatekeeping" or bringing people into discussions. No one person can be expected to perform all these required leadership functions effectively all the time. Groups perform better when all members perform both task and maintenance functions.

5. Control and Procedures

A group needs to establish procedures that can be used to guide or regulate its activities. For example, a meeting agenda serves to guide group activities during a meeting. Schedules of when specific actions will be taken also regulate team activities. Team development and team-member commitment is facilitated through maximum involvement in the establishment of agendas, schedules, and other procedures. Of course, the team should determine how it wishes to maintain control. In meeting situations, control most often is achieved through the appointment of a chairperson whose responsibility is to facilitate the procedure established by the team. Some teams find that they do not need a formal leader; each member regulates his or her own contributions and behavior as well as those of others.

6. Effective Interpersonal Communications

Effective team development depends on the ability of team members to communicate with one another in an open and honest manner. Effective interpersonal communications are apparent when team members listen to one another and attempt to build on one another's contributions. Effective interpersonal communications are achieved through self-regulation by team members, so that everyone in the group has an equal opportunity to participate in discussions.

7. Approach to Problem Solving and Decision Making

Solving problems and making decisions are two critical team functions. If a group is going to improve its ability to function as a team, recognized methods for solving problems and making decisions should be studied and adopted. The lack of agreed-on approaches to problem solving and decision making can result in wasted time, misunderstandings, frustration, and—more importantly—"bad" decisions.

A generally accepted, step-by-step procedure for problem solving and decision making is as follows:

1. Identify the problem (being careful to differentiate between the real problem and symptoms of the problem).
2. Develop criteria (or goals).
3. Gather relevant data.
4. Identify all feasible, alternative solutions or courses of action.
5. Evaluate the alternatives in light of the data and the objectives of the team.
6. Reach a decision.
7. Implement the decision.

Needless to say, there are variations of this procedure. However, whatever method is used, an effective team will have an agreed-on approach to problem solving and decision making that is shared and supported by all members.

8. Experimentation/Creativity

Just as it is important for a team to have certain structured procedures, it also is important that the team be prepared occasionally to move beyond the boundaries of established procedures and processes in order to experiment with new ways of doing things. Techniques such as "brainstorming" as a means of increasing creativity should be tried periodically to generate new ways to increase the team's effectiveness. An experimental attitude should be adopted in order to allow the team greater flexibility in dealing with problems and decision-making situations.

9. Evaluation

The team periodically should examine its group processes from both task and maintenance aspects. This examination or "critique" requires the team to stop and look at how well it is doing and what, if anything, may be hindering its operation. Problems may result from procedures or methods, or may be caused by individual team members. Such problems should be resolved through discussion before the team attempts further task accomplishment. Effective self-evaluation is probably one of the most critical factors leading to team development.

Ultimately, the strength and degree of a team's development will be measured in two ways: first, in its ability to get things done_its effectiveness—and second, in terms of its cohesiveness—the sense of belonging that individual members have and the degree of their commitment to one another and the goals of the team.

USE OF THE TEAM EFFECTIVENESS CRITIQUE

The periodic review of a team's operating practices in light of the factors leading to team development is a simple and useful method for improving a team's effectiveness. The Team Effectiveness Critique can be used as an observational tool by an independent observer or as an intervention device for the entire team. In this case, the critique should be completed by each individual team member, who will then share his or her assessment with the entire team. This sharing can be expanded to a consensus activity by asking team members to reach a common assessment for each of the nine factors. (This use of the critique would be most appropriate with ongoing organizational teams.) Agreement about areas in which improvements could be made would then lead to team action planning.

The critique also can be used as an experiential training device. Participants would be asked to complete a group task on a simulation basis and would then assess their teamwork using the critique form. Again, the group members would discuss their assessments with one another, focusing on generally recognized weaknesses.

The Team Effectiveness Critique is intended to be used as a training and team-development tool; it is not intended to be used for statistical or research purposes. Therefore, the face validity of the form and its usefulness in team work speak for themselves. No statistical validity has been established.

Originally published in The 1985 Annual: Developing Human Resources.

THE TEAM EFFECTIVENESS CRITIQUE

Mark Alexander

Instructions: Indicate on the scales that follow your assessment of your team and the way it functions by circling the number on each scale that you feel is most descriptive of your team.

1. Goals and Objectives

   There is a lack of commonly understood goals and objectives.　　　Team members understand and agree on goals and objectives.

   ```
   1        2        3        4        5        6        7
   ```

2. Utilization of Resources

   All member resources are not recognized and/or utilized.　　　Member resources are fully recognized and utilized.

   ```
   1        2        3        4        5        6        7
   ```

3. Trust and Conflict

   There is little trust among members, and conflict is evident.　　　There is high degree of trust among members, and conflict is dealt with openly and worked through.

   ```
   1        2        3        4        5        6        7
   ```

4. Leadership

   One person dominates, and leadership roles are not carried out or shared.　　　There is full participation in leadership; leadership roles are shared by members.

   ```
   1        2        3        4        5        6        7
   ```

5. Control and Procedures

   There is little control, and there is a lack of procedures to guide team functioning.　　　There are effective procedures to guide team functioning; team members support these procedures and regulate themselves.

1	2	3	4	5	6	7

6. Interpersonal Communications

Communications between members are closed and guarded.

Communications between members are open and participative.

1	2	3	4	5	6	7

7. Problem Solving/Decision Making

The team has no agreed-on approaches to problem solving and decision making.

The team has well-established and agreed-on approaches to problem solving and decision making.

1	2	3	4	5	6	7

8. Experimentation/Creativity

The team is rigid and does not experiment with how things are done.

The team experiments with different ways of doing things and is creative in this approach.

1	2	3	4	5	6	7

9. Evaluation

The group never evaluates its functioning and process.

The group often evaluates its functioning or process.

1	2	3	4	5	6	7

4

Trust-Orientation Profile

Myron R. Chartier

BACKGROUND

Trust is the basis of human relationships; it grounds much of intellectual and scientific research; and it supports the ethical norms of human behavior. Indeed, trust is fundamental to much human experience. Yet, if one looks at the history of human thinking, from the radical doubt of Descartes to the nihilism of modern philosophy, one discovers that this fundamental human attitude is a rare commodity. Gibb (1978, p. 13) writes: " . . .our present national culture—social, economic, even artistic, as well as political—is inhospitable to trust." Global and cultural realities do not reinforce efforts to build trust. Terrorist activities around the world and the displacement of people from their homes and their countries quickly provide a picture of mistrust and fear. Trust does not come naturally; people must want it and work for it.

Trust is difficult to achieve. People must engage in consistent hard work to obtain it, for trust grows slowly. The task is more difficult because human beings are finite in nature; they are limited by space, time, and energy. These constraints impose limitations on the building of trust. Because of the complex dynamics surrounding trust, it cannot be built in a short period of time and have lasting value. It takes time, physical presence, and human energy.

However, as trust between people grows, behaviors change and interpersonal dynamics are transformed. Diverse skills and abilities become recognized and appreciated as strengths. People begin to accept one another's attitudes and feelings; they learn to be themselves instead of playing roles. As trust grows, the barriers that prevent candor and openness lessen. People become more expressive, impulsive, frank, and spontaneous. Their communication is efficient and clear. They risk conflict and confrontation, opening the doors to deeper communication, involvement, and commitment. Congestion and blocking lessen. The flow of data is open and uninhibited; indeed, information that is "negative" is highly valued. Hiding negative information and not being willing to listen to negative data can ruin a relationship. When trust is present, people gather data quickly and make decisions effectively. These principles are as true in work teams as they are in other interpersonal relationships.

CREATING AND MAINTAINING TRUST

The creation of trust calls for a collage of personal characteristics and attitudes. Figure 1 presents various personal characteristics, attitudes, and behaviors that contribute to a climate of trust and those that contribute to a climate of mistrust.

These items demonstrate the complexity of trust. All of these positive characteristics, attitudes, and behaviors do not have to be present for a trustworthy climate to exist. However, the trust level depends on the degree to which some or all are present. Mistrust will be present to the degree that the negative characteristics, attitudes, and behaviors are present. Each of the pairs of characteristics is described more fully in the Trust-Orientation Profile Interpretation Sheet.

THE INSTRUMENT

The Trust-Orientation Profile is useful in a number of ways: (1) as a survey of the trust climate in interpersonal relationships; (2) as a survey of the trust climate within a team or an organization; and (3) as a tool for team-building and team-development sessions with coworkers. The potential value of this instrument is higher in the context of interpersonal and team relationships than it is when used by individuals.

Trust-Building Characteristics and Attitudes	Mistrust-Building Characteristics and Attitudes
Open	Closed
Supportive	Controlling
Willing to Risk	Unwilling to Risk
Respectful	Disrespectful
Genuine	Hypocritical
Cooperative	Competitive
Mutual	Superior
Problem Centered	Solution Minded
Accepting and Warm	Rejecting and Cold
Dependable	Capricious
Expert	Inept
Accountable	Unaccountable

Figure 1. Contributors to Trusting Versus Mistrusting

Format

The Trust-Orientation Profile contains twenty-four items, each consisting of two statements. Respondents distribute five points between the two alternatives (A and B) based on how they actually behave or feel or how they actually perceive the situation.

Scoring

Respondents transfer their point scores to the scoring matrix and compute totals. Two items (four statements) are associated with each of twelve dimensions of trust. Respondents calculate trust/mistrust ratios for themselves on each of the twelve dimensions and for trust as a whole.

Validity and Reliability

No reliability or validity data are available on the instrument, but it does have face validity. It can be used for the stated objectives and for planning action steps for turning desired qualities into reality.

Interpretation

After respondents have completed the instrument, they should be given the theory associated with the Trust-Orientation Profile, including an explanation of the twelve dimensions of trust orientation. Respondents then should be asked to predict their own scores. After the scoring process, the theory sheets should be distributed and the facilitator should be available to help with interpreting scores. Scores can be posted, and the respondents should be asked to discuss both the process and the results.

Conclusion

Even when trust has been built, it can be demolished quickly and easily. One misguided action can erase trust that has taken months or years to build. When trust is betrayed, hurt, anger, fear, and defensiveness arise and people take on self-protecting roles. Once a trusting relationship is violated, a predictable pattern of diminishing confidence takes place. If a person lies to another person, trust collapses instantly. Suspicion is aroused, causing one to question whether the relationship had ever been honest. People may try to rebuild a relationship after a breach, but they can rarely restore it to its prior state. If that same person lies a second time, the relationship stands little chance of survival. At best, it becomes filled with doubt, suspicion, and mistrust, becoming barely functional.

Trust must be nurtured and maintained if people are to enjoy their interpersonal relationships and attain their objectives. Trust building takes hard work, time, and energy; it also involves risk. The challenge is to become trustworthy persons to one another, constantly investing the time and energy it takes and being willing to take the necessary risks. For trust to grow and deepen, each person needs to be a person worthy of trust and must continue to earn the right to be trusted.

Contemporary organizations are presented with complex problems that require multiple perspectives to understand and to resolve. In such settings, teamwork becomes more and more important. Solutions increasingly will come as a result of collaborative action by groups of individuals who have multiple motives, objectives, and energies but who can focus on a single objective. Effective teams are those whose members work well together, and the ability to work well together flourishes in an atmosphere of trust. Team development through trust building thus seems to be a major agenda item for organizations today. The Trust-Orientation Profile is useful not only as a climate survey of trust but also as a tool for team-building and team-development sessions.

References and Bibliography

Bennis, W., & Nanus, B. (1985). *Leaders: The strategies for taking charge.* New York: Harper & Row.

Gibb, J.R. (1978). Trust: *A new view of personal and organizational development.* Los Angeles: Guild of Tutors Press.

Giffin, K., & Barnes, R.E. (1976). *Trusting me, trusting you.* Westerville, OH: Charles E. Merrill.

Gratton, C. (1982). *Trusting: Theory and practice.* New York: Crossroad.

Johnson, D.W. (1986). *Reaching out: Interpersonal effectiveness and self-actualization* (3rd ed.). Englewood Cliffs, NJ: Prentice-Hall.

Larson, C.E., & LaFasto, F.M.J. (1989). *Teamwork: What must go right/what can go wrong.* Beverly Hills, CA: Sage.

McGregor, D. (1967). *The professional manager.* New York: McGraw-Hill.

Originally published in The 1991 Annual: Developing Human Resources.

TRUST-ORIENTATION PROFILE

Myron R. Chartier

Instructions: For each of the situations described below, you are to distribute five points between two alternatives (A and B). Base your answers on how you actually behave or feel or how you actually perceive the situation, not on how you think you should respond. Although some sets of alternatives might seem to be equally true, assign more points to the alternative that is more representative of your personal experience.

1. If A is completely characteristic of you or your views and B is completely uncharacteristic, write 5 under A and 0 under B.

2. If A is considerably characteristic of you and B is somewhat characteristic, write 4 under A and 1 under B.

3. If A is only slightly more characteristic of you than B, write 3 under A and 2 under B.

4. Each of the above three combinations may be reversed. If you feel B is slightly more characteristic of you than A, write 2 under A and 3 under B, and so on for A = 1 and B = 4, or A = 0 and B = 5.

Be sure the numbers you assign to each pair add up to 5.

1. _____ (A) My coworkers have all the knowledge and experience they need to do their jobs effectively.
   _____ (B) My coworkers seem to lack the knowledge and/or experience they need to do their jobs effectively.

2. _____ (A) I cannot predict how my coworkers will respond in a given situation.
   _____ (B) I can predict how my coworkers will respond in a given situation.

3. _____ (A) I share my honest thoughts and feelings with my coworkers.
   _____ (B) I keep my honest thoughts and feelings to myself.

4. _____ (A) I help my coworkers to see what their goals and concerns should be.
   _____ (B) I let my coworkers know that I understand and appreciate their individual goals and concerns.

The Pfeiffer Book of Successful Conflict Management Tools © 2003 John Wiley & Sons, Inc.

5. _____ (A) I trust my coworkers; I believe they won't let me down.
   _____ (B) I "play it safe" and trust only myself; this way no one else can let me down.

6. _____ (A) I am not convinced that each of my coworkers is worthy of my respect.
   _____ (B) I respect my coworkers; each of them has a unique contribution to make.

7. _____ (A) I encourage my coworkers to comment on their thoughts and feelings.
   _____ (B) I would prefer not to hear my coworkers' expressions of their thoughts and feelings.

8. _____ (A) I believe in the old saying "Do as I say, not as I do."
   _____ (B) I say what I mean and mean what I say.

9. _____ (A) When I am in a bind, I know I can depend on my coworkers to help me out.
   _____ (B) When I am in a bind, I have to rely exclusively on myself.

10. _____ (A) My abilities are superior to those of my coworkers.
    _____ (B) My coworkers and I are all at the same level of competence.

11. _____ (A) I let myself be vulnerable with my coworkers.
    _____ (B) I protect myself and try not to be vulnerable with my coworkers.

12. _____ (A) The term "commitment" doesn't seem to mean much to my coworkers.
    _____ (B) I can depend on my coworkers to follow through on their commitments.

13. _____ (A) My coworkers and I cooperate with one another.
    _____ (B) My coworkers and I compete with one another.

14. _____ (A) My coworkers behave as if they think they are better than I am.
    _____ (B) My coworkers treat me as an equal.

15. _____ (A) I can count on my coworkers to meet the deadlines and performance standards defined for their work.
    _____ (B) I cannot count on my coworkers to meet their deadlines and performance standards.

16. _____ (A) When faced with a problem, I figure out the best solution and present my idea to my coworkers.

_____ (B) When faced with a problem, I collaborate with my coworkers to define the problem, explore alternatives, and arrive at a solution.

17. _____ (A) My team is warm, accepting, and free of hostility.

_____ (B) There is hostility in my team.

18. _____ (A) I cannot rely on my coworkers.

_____ (B) I can rely on my coworkers.

19. _____ (A) My coworkers and I are knowledgeable and experienced in our respective skill areas and in our ability to interact with one another.

_____ (B) My coworkers and I lack the knowledge and experience to function as effectively as we might.

20. _____ (A) I wonder if my coworkers appreciate my work; I sometimes think they question the value of my contributions.

_____ (B) I know that my coworkers are concerned about my well-being; they "play fairly" and respect my unique contributions.

21. _____ (A) My coworkers hold themselves accountable for their work.

_____ (B) My coworkers do not hold themselves accountable for their work.

22. _____ (A) I prefer my own solutions to problems.

_____ (B) I am willing to accept solutions proposed by my coworkers.

23. _____ (A) No matter what I share with my team members, they are not judgmental.

_____ (B) I am careful about what I share with my team members because they may judge me harshly.

24. _____ (A) I assume that my coworkers could use my help in doing their jobs.

_____ (B) I assume that my coworkers are capable of doing their jobs.

TRUST-ORIENTATION PROFILE
SCORING SHEET

Characteristic	Trust	Mistrust
Open Versus Closed	3A _____ 7A _____	3B _____ 7B _____
Willing to Risk Versus Unwilling to Risk	5A _____ 11A _____	5B _____ 11B _____
Cooperative Versus Competitive	9A _____ 13A _____	9B _____ 13B _____
Accepting and Warm Versus Rejecting and Cold	17A _____ 23A _____	17B _____ 23B _____
Expert Versus Inept	1A _____ 19A _____	1B _____ 19B _____
Accountable Versus Unaccountable	15A _____ 21A _____	15B _____ 21B _____
Supportive Versus Controlling	4B _____ 24B _____	4A _____ 24A _____

Characteristic	Trust	Mistrust
Respectful Versus Disrespectful	6B _____ 20B _____	6A _____ 20A _____
Genuine Versus Hypocritical	8B _____ 12B _____	8A _____ 12A _____
Mutual Versus Superior	10B _____ 14B _____	10A _____ 14A _____
Open Minded About Problems Versus Fixated on Predeter- mined Solutions	16B _____ 22B _____	16A _____ 22A _____
Dependable Versus Capricious	2B _____ 18B _____	2A _____ 18A _____
TOTALS		

TRUST-ORIENTATION PROFILE INTERPRETATION SHEET

Instructions: Transfer your scores from the scoring sheet to the lines that follow in order to compute your trust-orientation score.

Total Trust Score   _____

Minus   __

Total Mistrust Score   _____

Trust Orientation   ┌──────────────┐
                     │   │
                     └──────────────┘

Plot your trust-orientation score on the continuum that follows.

-60 or more   -50   -40   -30   -20   -10   0   +10   +20   +30   +40   +50   +60 or more
___|_____|____|____|____|____|____|____|____|____|____|____|_____

Mistrust   Trust

TRUST-ORIENTATION PROFILE THEORY SHEET

The following descriptions contrast the characteristics that build trust to those that build mistrust. Read this interpretation sheet in the context of your personal trust and mistrust scores. You may want to pay particular attention to mistrust items to which you assigned four or five points.

Open Versus Closed

Open people share their innermost thoughts and feelings with others and are receptive to data, ideas, perceptions, and feelings. Closed people keep their thoughts and feelings to themselves and project an attitude of being nonreceptive to others' communications. Every person has a right to not share certain thoughts and aspects of his or her life. However, effective interpersonal relationships are impossible when information is deliberately kept from others or is ignored. Shared information contributes to trust between people. In order to create a climate of mutual trust, people must be appropriately open with one another.

Supportive Versus Controlling

The supportive person seeks to be encouraging; reassuring; and understanding of others, their agendas, and their goals. The controlling person tries to bind others to his or her desires and wishes, operating on the assumption that others are inadequate and need to be dominated by someone who "has it together." Supportiveness creates a climate of trust, whereas control engenders a climate of resistance and defensiveness. It is easy to trust supportive persons. A supportive attitude among people contributes to a trustworthy climate in which effective interpersonal relationships are possible.

Willing to Risk Versus Unwilling to Risk

To trust another person is risky; a decision to trust can lead to either good or bad consequences. To entrust one's well-being to another person makes a person vulnerable. Risking is the process of deciding to accept potentially adverse results that may come from trusting another. The greater the risk involved, the more one is required to trust another. Taking such risks with others creates a trusting climate because it communicates trust. Playing it safe communicates one's unwillingness to trust and fails to generate trust among people.

Respectful Versus Disrespectful

Situations in which people are convinced that others respect them for who they are and for what they have to contribute are conducive to trust. Knowing that others are concerned about one's well-being goes a long way in helping a person to believe that the risk of trust is worthwhile. In situations in which verbal or even physical abuse takes place, fear overwhelms the bonds of trust and impedes effective interpersonal relationships. Respectful people look out for one another's welfare and thereby create a climate of trust.

Genuine Versus Hypocritical

A genuine person is a person of integrity. The genuine person's thoughts, feelings, and actions are consistent. It is difficult to trust someone whose words and conduct are inconsistent. If one can never be certain about the meaning of another's words, true intentions, or actions, he or she experiences the other person as hypocritical. Genuine people are honest. Trusting them comes easily because they say what they mean; they clarify their intentions; and they follow through on their promises. Interpersonal relationships are enhanced when people are genuine.

Cooperative Versus Competitive

A cooperative attitude builds trust; when people experience a spirit of cooperation, they share relevant information openly, clearly, and honestly. In a competitive atmosphere, communication is either lacking or misleading. Whereas cooperation requires teamwork to achieve common goals, competition stresses personal objectives at the expense of common objectives. When a competitive spirit pervades the climate, trust may be difficult to achieve; fear and defensiveness are the likely result. On the other hand, the give-and-take of cooperation builds a fellowship of trust among people.

Mutual Versus Superior

When people communicate that they feel superior to others, a climate conducive to mistrust and defensiveness is assured. When people sense a spirit of mutuality, an environment conducive to openness and trustworthiness results.

Mutuality makes it possible for people to resolve issues through problem solving. There is a desire for two-way communication; power is shared; role status is minimized; and appreciation of individuals is maximized. Each person's self-worth is valued. A spirit of mutuality generates a trustworthy climate in which each person's abilities and interests are valued and nurtured.

Problem Centered Versus Solution Minded

People with a problem-centered attitude work collaboratively to define problems, explore alternatives, and arrive at solutions. They have no preplanned solutions and encourage others to set goals, make decisions, and evaluate progress in light of the nature of the problem and the various alternatives open to them. Solution-minded people assume that recognizing a problem is equivalent to understanding it. They are quick to arrive at solutions and fail to explore the nature of the problem. They often have a strong tendency to impose their answers on others. Adopting an immediate-solution approach tends to generate negative feelings, a divisive climate, and an atmosphere of endless argumentation and fruitless debate.

Accepting and Warm Versus Rejecting and Cold

An accepting, warm attitude is a major contributor to trust building. On the other hand, a rejecting, cold attitude creates feelings of rejection, low self-esteem, and hostility, which lead to mistrust and suspicion. Accepting attitudes lead to feelings of psychological safety, which lead people to believe that no matter what they share, others will respond in an accepting, nonjudgmental manner. Warmth in relationships is essential to creating a trustworthy climate for effective teamwork. When an attitude of warmth is communicated, people feel prized for who they are and what they have to contribute.

Dependable Versus Capricious

Probably the most critical characteristic in the creation of trust is dependability. Human beings will trust others more easily and more deeply if they believe they can rely on them. A person's trust will be more widespread if he or she can predict how others will respond, whether the situation is simple or complex. Capricious people cannot be relied on; their behavior is often quite unpredictable, which can lead to deep mistrust. Being dependable is crucial to building trust.

Expert Versus Inept

People trust others who are knowledgeable and experienced in the area in which trust is to be granted (Giffin & Barnes, 1976). People do not trust those who have little or no knowledge in a given area. There is a high trust level in relationships in which people possess and exercise what Giffin and Barnes (1976) label "relevant wisdom." When people are inept with respect to the substantive knowledge, interpersonal qualities, skills, and abilities needed to work collaboratively, they often blame others for their ineffectiveness. When people lack expert technical and relational competencies, the results are poor communication dynamics and a hostile, defensive environment. Such an untrustworthy climate undercuts effective interpersonal relationships.

Accountable Versus Unaccountable

Trust is enhanced when people are willing to be accountable to one another. Eventually, any interpersonal relationship is based on the assumption of personal responsibilities and accountability. Without accountability, all efforts become random, haphazard, even chaotic. This result leads to an undependable climate in which people do not know whether or not they can count on others to do what they have said they would do. Accountable relationships create and maintain a trustworthy climate.

Conclusion

The preceding principles of trust-building and mistrust-building attitudes hold true in relationships between two people and among members of a group. If you decide to foster more trust-building attitudes, you can take certain actions. The following interpersonal behaviors can help to build trust:

- Initiating communication or action with others;
- Establishing eye contact;
- Communicating clearly;
- Giving and receiving feedback;
- Listening empathically;
- Expressing personal feelings;
- Accepting the feelings of others;

- Using "I" messages;
- Affirming the self-images of others;
- Being present and involved;
- Acting consistently; and
- Appreciating the trust of others.

Reference

Giffin, K, & Barnes, R.E. (1976). *Trusting me, trusting you.* Westerville, OH: Charles E. Merrill.

5

Conflict-Management Style Survey

Marc Robert

Because people's rational responses are usually short-circuited by the stress of the moment, behavior in complex interpersonal and intergroup confrontations is difficult—if not impossible—to predict. Self-help formulas that promise to make people more assertive or effective in dealing with conflict in their lives will not work if they do not fit the "style" of the person using them. Accepting suggestions for handling conflict before increasing personal awareness and self-knowledge is like buying mail-order clothes. The more one learns about how he or she might react, the greater chance of selecting an appropriate course of action.

Each person must know his or her own strengths, weaknesses, natural inclinations, and preferences, because in conflict these positions tend to become even more rigid and fixed and to inhibit a satisfactory resolution. Unfortunately, such self-knowledge does not come easily. True self-knowledge can only be gained by actively seeking out information about oneself and then acting on it in the next situation, asking for feedback, and then trying again. Self-awareness can be achieved through one or more of the following methods:

Intrapersonal Awareness. Listening to our internal dialogue, being aware of our true feelings, and checking out our physical reactions at the time of conflict can be eye opening.

Observation of Others' Reactions. Being aware of subtle verbal and physical cues that others give in reaction to our behavior can lead to new insights.

Direct Feedback from Others. Asking others for their reactions to what we say or do is the most psychologically threatening route to self-knowledge, but it may be worth the pain to discover areas that need work.

Behavioral Science Measurement. Taking self-rating questionnaires is a less demanding way to learn personal behavioral characteristics.

The *Conflict-Management Style Survey* was designed to help people assess their responses to everyday situations that involve conflict.[1] The respondent's frame of reference must be clear and answers must be consistent with the type of conflict situations he or she wishes to work on.

The real value of taking this instrument is in the interpretation and discussion of results. The survey is meant to heighten awareness and to provide an incentive to change unproductive behavior. Participants can compare scores and discuss differences, similarities, and possible trouble spots in relating to one another. The instrument also can be given to friends or coworkers to be completed as the person thinks the participants would complete it. This yields insight for the participant about how he or she is seen to handle conflict.

References

Porter, E.H. (1973). *Strength Deployment Inventory.* Pacific Palisades, CA: Personal Strengths Assessment Service.

Robert, M. (1982). *Managing conflict from the inside out.* San Francisco, CA: Jossey-Bass/Pfeiffer.

Thomas, K.W., & Kilmann, R.H. (1974). *Thomas-Kilmann Conflict Mode Instrument.* Sterling Forest, Tuxedo, NY: Xicom.

Originally published in The 1982 Annual Handbook for Facilitators, Trainers, and Consultants.

---

[1]Some other helpful instruments for measuring style of managing conflict include the Strength Deployment Inventory (Porter, 1973) and the Conflict Mode Instrument (Thomas & Kilmann, 1974).

CONFLICT-MANAGEMENT STYLE SURVEY

Marc Robert

Name _____

Date _____

Instructions: Choose a single frame of reference for answering all fifteen items (e.g., work-related conflicts, family conflicts, or social conflicts) and keep that frame of reference in mind when answering the items.

   Allocate ten points among the four possible answers given for each of the fifteen items below.

   Example: When the people I supervise become involved in a personal conflict, I usually:

Intervene to settle the dispute.	Call a meeting to talk over the problem.	Offer to help if I can.	Ignore the problem.
3	6	1	0

Be certain that your answers add up to 10.

1. When someone *I care about* is actively hostile toward me, i.e., yelling, threatening, abusive, etc., I tend to:

Respond in a hostile manner.	Try to persuade the person to give up his/her actively hostile behavior.	Stay and listen as long as possible.	Walk away.
_____	_____	_____	_____

2. When someone *who is relatively unimportant to me* is actively hostile toward me, i.e., yelling, threatening, abusive, etc., I tend to:

Respond in a hostile manner.	Try to persuade the person to give up his/her actively hostile behavior.	Stay and listen as long as possible.	Walk away.
_____	_____	_____	_____

3. When I observe people in conflicts in which anger, threats, hostility, and strong opinions are present, I tend to:

Become involved and take a position.	Attempt to mediate.	Observe to see what happens.	Leave as quickly as possible.
_____	_____	_____	_____

4. When I perceive another person as meeting his/her needs at my expense, I am apt to:

Work to do anything I can to change that person.	Rely on persuasion and "facts" when attempting to have that person change.	Work hard at changing how I relate to that person.	Accept the situation as it is.
_____	_____	_____	_____

5. When involved in an interpersonal dispute, my general pattern is to:

Draw the other person into seeing the problem as I do.	Examine the issues between us as logically as possible.	Look hard for a workable compromise.	Let time take its course and let the problem work itself out.
_____	_____	_____	_____

6. The quality that I value the most in dealing with conflict would be:

Emotional strength and security.	Intelligence.	Love and openness.	Patience.
_____	_____	_____	_____

7. Following a serious altercation with someone I care for deeply, I:

Strongly desire to go back and settle things my way.	Want to go back and work it out— whatever give-and-take is necessary.	Worry about it a lot but not plan to initiate further contact.	Let it lie and not plan to initiate further contact.
_____	_____	_____	_____

8. When I see a serious conflict developing between two people _I care about,_ I tend to:

Express my disappointment that this had to happen.	Attempt to persuade them to resolve their differences.	Watch to see what develops.	Leave the scene.
_____	_____	_____	_____

9. When I see a serious conflict developing between two people who are _relatively unimportant to me,_ I tend to:

Express my disappointment that this had to to happen.	Attempt to persuade them to resolve their differences.	Watch to see what develops.	Leave the scene.
_____	_____	_____	_____

10.The feedback that I receive from most people about how I behave when faced with conflict and opposition indicates that I:

Try hard to get my way.	Try to work out differences cooperatively.	Am easygoing and take a soft or conciliatory position.	Usually avoid the conflict.
_____	_____	_____	_____

11.When communicating with someone with whom I am having a serious conflict, I:

Try to overpower the other person with my speech.	Talk a little bit more than I listen.	Am an active listener (feeding back words and feelings).	Am a passive listener (agreeing and apologizing).
_____	_____	_____	_____

12. When involved in an unpleasant conflict, I:

Use humor with the other party.	Make an occasional quip or joke about the situation or the relationship.	Relate humor only to myself.	Suppress all attempts at humor.
_____	_____	_____	_____

13. When someone does something that irritates me (e.g., smokes in a non-smoking area or crowds in line in front of me), my tendency in communicating with the offending person is to:

Insist that the person look me in the eye.	Look the person directly in the eye and maintain eye contact.	Maintain intermittent eye contact.	Avoid looking directly at the person.
_____	_____	_____	_____

The Pfeiffer Book of Successful Conflict Management Tools © 2003 John Wiley & Sons, Inc.

14. When I am involved in a conflict with another person, I:

Stand close and make physical contact.	Use my hands and body to illustrate my points.	Stand close to the person without touching himor her.	Stand back and keep my hands to myself.
_____	_____	_____	_____

15. When I have a conflict with someone else who is becoming "physical," I:

Use strong direct language and tell the person to stop.	Try to persuade the person to stop.	Talk gently and tell the person what my feelings are.	Say and do nothing.
_____	_____	_____	_____

CONFLICT-MANAGEMENT STYLE SURVEY
SCORING AND INTERPRETATION SHEET

Instructions: When you have completed all fifteen items, add your scores vertically, resulting in four column totals. Put these in the blanks below.

Totals: _____ _____ _____ _____

        Column 1   Column 2   Column 3   Column 4

Using your total scores in each column, fill in the bar graph below.

Total Points	1	2	3	4
150				
125				
100				
75				
50				
25				
0				

Column 1. Aggressive/Confrontive. High scores indicate a tendency toward "taking the bull by the horns" and a strong need to control situations and/or people. Those who use this style are often directive and judgmental.

Column 2. Assertive/Persuasive. High scores indicate a tendency to stand up for oneself without being pushy, a proactive approach to conflict, and a willingness to collaborate. People who use this style depend heavily on their verbal skills.

Column 3. Observant/Introspective. High scores indicate a tendency to observe others and examine oneself analytically in response to conflict situations as well as a need to adopt counseling and listening modes of behavior. Those who use this style are likely to be cooperative, even conciliatory.

Column 4. Avoiding/Reactive. High scores indicate a tendency toward passivity or withdrawal in conflict situations and a need to avoid confrontation. Those who use this style are usually accepting and patient, often suppressing their strong feelings.

Now total your scores for Columns 1 and 2 and Columns 3 and 4.

	Score		Score
Column 1 + Column 2 = _____	A	Column 3 + Column 4 = _____	B

If Score A is significantly higher than Score B (25 points or more), it may indicate a tendency toward aggressive/assertive conflict management. A significantly higher B score signals a more conciliatory approach.

6

Communication Audit: A Pairs Analysis

Scott B. Parry

Abstract: If we consider all the skills needed to succeed in our work and to enjoy life to the fullest, the ability to communicate effectively probably leads the list. Our desire to understand others and to be understood is one of humankind's most basic needs. *Effective* communication requires much more than grammar and vocabulary. Words such as trust, openness, respect, and empathy come to mind as qualities that must accompany the written or spoken message if it is to achieve its intended results. This audit enables respondents to assess their ability to communicate both within the workplace and within more intimate groups.

INTRODUCTION

Communication is the cement that holds an organization together; lack of communication can cause it to fall apart. This is true whether the organization referred to is a society, an organization, a department, a work group, a marriage, a family, a club, or a social group.

This Communication Audit enables respondents to identify the strengths and weaknesses that are characteristic of the communications in which they engage. Part One is an assessment of one's workplace and the "state of health" of the communication that comes from three sources within it: senior management, the respondent's immediate supervisor, and him- or herself. Part Two is an assessment of the quality of the interpersonal communications that regularly take place between the respondent and those closest to him or her—family, friends, or immediate work group members.

Three major benefits can be expected from taking the Communication Audit. The first is that respondents will take stock of their strengths and weaknesses of communication on two levels: organizational and interpersonal. The Audit can be thought of as a needs analysis in which respondents can pinpoint those attributes of their communication that are healthy and those that require work.

The second benefit is that the Audit will equip respondents with a set of criteria and a common vocabulary for describing interpersonal communications. This allows them to gain a better understanding of and ability to discuss the process with one another.

A third benefit comes from respondents' discussion of their perceptions with others who also fill out the Audit (for Part One, their supervisors; for Part Two, others with whom they communicate on a regular basis). Within the workshop setting, you can help manager and employee or two co-workers to develop action plans to improve the quality of their communications.

ADMINISTRATION OF THE AUDIT

Instructions for completing the Communication Audit are given at the beginning of each part. Hand copies out to participants and ask them to read the instructions and begin. If the workshop is focused only on communication between manager and employee, ask that they fill in only Part One. If they will also have a chance to discuss their communication style with co-workers, ask them to also complete Part Two, but assign pairs before beginning. You may also wish to make extra copies of the Audit for those who would like to use it at home or in a nonwork setting at a later date.

Part One

Tell everyone that the Audit they will complete focuses on communication between them and their managers and upper management at work. Explain that they will not be able to fill in the totals until after you've provided scoring instructions, which you will do later.

The Pfeiffer Book of Successful Conflict Management Tools © 2003 John Wiley & Sons, Inc.

After everyone has completed the Audit, give respondents the appropriate Instructions for Scoring and Interpreting the results. Guidelines for analyzing scores are provided, along with some interpretation implications and suggestions for taking appropriate actions.

Part Two

In this next section of the Audit, respondents will examine their interpersonal communications with those with whom they work. Explain that there are fourteen sets of adjectives and they are to decide where along a continuum they would rate the other person's and their own communication behavior. Tell them that you will give them copies of the instrument (two per communication partner) if they want to use it at home or in another setting to focus on their interpersonal communications.

Hand out the second part of the audit and ask everyone to complete it according to the instructions. Remind them to be honest in assessing their own behavior.

SCORING AND INTERPRETING THE RESULTS

Tell participants that they are now ready to score their responses, interpret the results, share their insights, and decide what actions are appropriate for improving the quality of their interactions. Say that you first want to discuss briefly the importance of interpersonal communication. The following text can be used to provide a basis for the discussion.

"If we consider all the skills needed to succeed in our work and to enjoy life to the fullest, we will probably conclude that the ability to communicate effectively is the most important set of skills we will ever develop. Indeed, many of the other skills in our jobs depend heavily on the quality of our communication—time management and prioritizing, negotiating, persuading others, evaluating alternatives, and so on.

"In short, the quality of our relations with others at work, at home, and at play depend on our ability to communicate effectively. Our ability to solve problems, make decisions, set realistic goals and a timetable for accomplishing them, assess people and situations, and perform the hundreds of activities that fill our daily work depends on the ability to communicate. It's what makes marriage or a relationship with a lifetime partner a success. It's what keeps us together—as a family, a team, a club, a class, a social group. It's what occupies us during most of the work day. And our time spent communicating at work typically divides as follows:"

List the following categories on a flip chart:

	Giving Information	**Receiving Information**
Spoken	Speaking 30%	Listening 45%
Written	Writing 9%	Reading 16%

"Given the critical importance of speaking and listening, which together make up three-quarters of our communications, anything we can do to improve the quality of our interactions will be time well-invested. And there should be add-on benefits through our improvement in many of the other skills that depend so heavily on interpersonal communications."

Now distribute copies of the Scoring and Interpreting sheets and direct the participants to score Part One of the Audit. Then ask participants to get together with their pre-assigned partners and to compare their ratings of themselves with the ratings of them by the other person. Rarely do managers see themselves as their subordinates see them, and nowhere is this more true than in their communication effectiveness. Partners should then be given time to complete the interpretation for Part Two of the Audit.

After the participants have completed the Scoring and Interpreting sheets, say to them:

"Organizations differ greatly with regard to their style of communication. I want you to explore this topic by discussing the following questions in your pre-assigned pairs:

- If you were to describe this style of your organization to an outsider, what adjectives would you use?
- What analogies would you make?
- What characteristics of the organization are illustrated by the style of communication that's prevalent here?
- On which items do you and your supervisor differ most?"

Post these questions and allow the pairs ten or fifteen minutes to discuss them.

MAKING ACTION PLANS

After paired discussions between supervisor and employee and between co-workers, hand out copies of the Communication Audit Action Planning Samples and discuss how to write an action plan. Have partners write similar plans for enhancing their own communications with one another.

Originally published in The 2001 Annual, Vol. 2, Consulting.

COMMUNICATION AUDIT

Scott B. Parry

Part One: Communication with Supervisors

Instructions: Listed below are a number of phrases describing how *senior management* in your organization, your *supervisor,* and *you* behave while communicating with one another. Evaluate each of the others and yourself by circling the letter for each relationship that indicates whether this is a behavior the person does "always," "usually," "sometimes," "rarely," or "never."

If you wish, you may go through the twenty items three separate times, or answer the question for all three communication relationships as you go.

A = Always   U = Usually   S = Sometimes   R = Rarely   N = Never

	Senior Management	Your Supervisor	Yourself
1. Listens closely to find out others' facts and feelings before reacting.	A U S R N	A U S R N	A U S R N
2. Plays games with others and manipulates their responses.	A U S R N	A U S R N	A U S R N
3. Asks good questions and is effective in drawing others out.	A U S R N	A U S R N	A U S R N
4. Is defensive and displays an element of distrust.	A U S R N	A U S R N	A U S R N
5. Summarizes and restates to increase mutual understanding.	A U S R N	A U S R N	A U S R N
6. Fills the "parent" role and puts others in the "child" role.	A U S R N	A U S R N	A U S R N
7. Sticks to the subject and the aim of the communication.	A U S R N	A U S R N	A U S R N
8. Is unable to establish an open climate of trust and candor.	A U S R N	A U S R N	A U S R N

A = Always   U = Usually   S = Sometimes   R = Rarely   N = Never

	Senior Management	Your Supervisor	Yourself
9. Gives good feedback to show understanding of what the other person has said.	A U S R N	A U S R N	A U S R N
10. Uses time asked for by others to meet personal agendas.	A U S R N	A U S R N	A U S R N
11. Remains neutral (low bias) to elicit the feelings of others.	A U S R N	A U S R N	A U S R N
12. Has difficulty expressing ideas clearly and concisely.	A U S R N	A U S R N	A U S R N
13. Uses analogies, examples, etc., to bring a message to life.	A U S R N	A U S R N	A U S R N
14. Interrupts, making it hard for others to express themselves.	A U S R N	A U S R N	A U S R N
15. Is persuasive; others go along because they are convinced.	A U S R N	A U S R N	A U S R N
16. High bias leads others to say what is expedient and expected.	A U S R N	A U S R N	A U S R N
17. Maintains favorable climate, reflecting mutual respect and benefit.	A U S R N	A U S R N	A U S R N
18. Pulls rank and tends to dominate when with subordinates.	A U S R N	A U S R N	A U S R N
19. Uses probes well to draw out the feelings of others.	A U S R N	A U S R N	A U S R N
20. Fails to follow up to see whether message was acted on.	A U S R N	A U S R N	A U S R N
Totals:			

Part Two: Interpersonal Communication

Instructions: Listed below are fourteen pairs of adjectives. They describe the major attributes of most interpersonal communications. A seven-point rating scale separates each pair, with the range extending from + + + (extremely high on the adjective at the left) to − − − (extremely high on the adjective at the right). Circle the rating for each pair of adjectives that best describes your interactions with *the person with whom you are completing this Audit.*

Remember that your rating does not necessarily indicate praise or censure of the other person. Rather, it describes the nature of the interpersonal communication that regularly takes place between you. *Both of you* are responsible for the quality of this communication. When you are finished, you will discuss what each of you has said.

goal-directed	+ + +	+ +	+	0	−	− −	− − −	unclear, unfocused
constructive	+ + +	+ +	+	0	−	− −	− − −	destructive
unhurried	+ + +	+ +	+	0	−	− −	− − −	rushed
useful	+ + +	+ +	+	0	−	− −	− − −	waste of time
complete	+ + +	+ +	+	0	−	− −	− − −	fragmented
supportive	+ + +	+ +	+	0	−	− −	− − −	defensive
candid	+ + +	+ +	+	0	−	− −	− − −	hidden agenda
accepting	+ + +	+ +	+	0	−	− −	− − −	fault-finding
open	+ + +	+ +	+	0	−	− −	− − −	guarded
adult-adult	+ + +	+ +	+	0	−	− −	− − −	parent-child
informal, relaxed	+ + +	+ +	+	0	−	− −	− − −	formal, rigid
unbiased	+ + +	+ +	+	0	−	− −	− − −	biased
trusting	+ + +	+ +	+	0	−	− −	− − −	distrusting
"win-win"	+ + +	+ +	+	0	−	− −	− − −	"win-lose," manipulative

Now multiply the numbers below by the number of times you circled the response in the column above it. Write the totals in the blanks provided.

Point value of each column x number of items in column

+++	++	+	0	−	− −	− − −
7 ×	6 ×	5 ×	4 ×	3 ×	2 ×	1 ×
_____	_____	_____	_____	_____	_____	_____

Now add all your points together and write your total score below.

Total Score: _____

Guidelines for Scoring and Interpreting Part One

Instructions: The paragraphs that follow contain guidelines for scoring your responses and questions to help you interpret the results and take appropriate actions.

As you may have noticed, every odd-numbered statement on the audit describes a *desirable* trait. On these items an "always" response is worth 5 points, a "usually" is worth 4 points, a "sometimes" rates 3 points, a "seldom" gets 2 points, and a "never" is worth 1 point. In other words, on the odd-numbered items, the scores descend from left to right—from 5 to 1.

Look back at your answers on the odd-numbered items only (1, 3, 5, 7, 9, 11, 13, 15, 17, 19). Place a number beside each letter that you circled to indicate its point value—from 5 to 1.

Now look at the even-numbered statements, which describe undesirable traits. On these items an "always" is worth 1 point, a "usually" is worth 2 points, a "sometimes" rates 3 points, a "seldom" gets 4 points, and a "never" is worth the full 5 points. Use this reverse scale to mark your score on the even-numbered items (2, 4, 6, 8, 10, 12, 14, 16, 18, 20).

You are now ready to determine the total score you have given senior management at your organization, your direct supervisor, and yourself. Add all numbers in the five senior management columns and enter the numbers at the bottom of the senior management columns. Then add these numbers together to obtain the score you have given to senior management. Then follow the same procedure to determine the score you have given your supervisor and yourself.

There are twenty items, each worth up to five points, so a perfect score is 100 points. A score of 85 or better indicates that communications are quite healthy. Scores that are significantly below this level indicate a need to work on weak areas—those behaviors that received ratings of only 1 or 2 points each.

The Pfeiffer Book of Successful Conflict Management Tools © 2003 John Wiley & Sons, Inc.

GUIDELINES FOR INTERPRETING PART TWO

Instructions: After you have completed this audit and discussed your results with your partner, it's time to draw some conclusions about your own communication style. This will be especially instructive for you if you have completed the Audit and discussed the results with several different partners.

Fill out the answers to the questions below:

1. Of the fourteen adjective pairs (qualities) listed, which ones seemed to be the strongest aspects of your interpersonal communications? What qualities were consistently rated very high, regardless of who your partner was?

2. As you evaluate your results, were there any adjective pairs (qualities) that were rated low, regardless of the person with whom you were communicating? Are these qualities that you may be lacking?

3. There are fourteen qualities and a maximum of seven points for each. Thus, a "perfect" score is ninety-eight points. How big was the gap between your total score and your partner's total score? (Do this for each partner.) What does the size of the gap tell you? Discuss this with your partner(s).

4. Was there a tendency for you to rank your interactions more favorably or less favorably than your partner(s) did? Or did the ratings tend to balance out? How do you interpret this?

5. Which of the fourteen qualities are ones that you and your partner(s) see a need to improve? What made you pick these?

6. Can the qualities that you listed above be improved through individual work? Are they closely tied to personality and so deeply rooted that they are not likely to change much over time?

7. What actions do you each plan to take to improve the quality of your interpersonal communications on those attributes you've selected?

COMMUNICATION AUDIT ACTION PLANNING SAMPLES

The following samples are provided so that you can write your own plan for change.

- "I've identified four areas in the interactions with my supervisor that need improvement. I plan to sit down with her to discuss them and, hopefully, to agree on things we can each do to improve these areas (Numbers 5, 9, 10, 14)."

- "The members of my special project team don't always understand me. I often find out too late that they're doing things differently from what I said (or thought I said). So I'm going to focus on improving in three of the areas listed: Numbers 3, 5, and 13. I'll remember three key words—*ask* (Number 3), *summarize* (Number 5), and *illustrate* (Number 13)—as my constant reminder whenever I'm talking to someone, to make sure I do these things until they become natural for me."

- "Two other people with whom I work closely took Part Two. Although I met with each separately to discuss our scores, the ratings of each were very similar. And we were all in agreement on the qualities that were weak in all of us. So the three of us got together and agreed to concentrate on changing from 'unfocused, rushed, and fragmented' interactions to taking more time to clue the others in, so that we all have the same picture in our heads. Often it's a case of our assuming that the others know the background and understand what we're talking about."

- "My wife and I went through Part Two. We both agreed that our interactions were becoming 'destructive, fault-finding, parent-child, win-lose, and manipulative.' We couldn't agree on why this was happening and lapsed into fault-finding when we tried to! However, we did agree that when either of us felt that the other was doing it, we would call 'time out' before continuing. This should increase our awareness and sensitivity, and thus reduce our destructive comments."

- "Six people work with me in our section. I'm the group leader. I plan to make extra copies of the Communication Audit so that we can each go through it as individuals. Then we'll get together and compare answers. In the middle column of Part One they will be evaluating me, so we can make this part confidential or discuss it openly, whichever they prefer. Either way, I'm sure we can identify the things that they and I need to work on to improve our communications."

7

Inventory of
Anger Communication (IAC)

Millard J. Bienvenu, Sr.

One of the major components of healthy interpersonal communication is the individual's ability to deal with his or her own angry feelings and those of others. Some people, through the mechanism of denial, are not aware of their angry feelings and repress them rather deeply. Others, although aware of these feelings, suppress the expression of them, fearing angry responses from others. Many individuals become upset when they simply disagree with others or when others disagree with them. Finally, those individuals who do express angry feelings often do so in destructive ways, e.g., with physical violence, insults, and shouting.

The development of the Inventory of Anger Communication (IAC) was an outgrowth of the author's earlier communication scales, the results of which indicated that anger was an inherent yet troublesome aspect of the communication process among individuals. In studying marital communication, the author found that a couple's difficulty in handling their differences and in expressing their anger disrupted their communication process. Some persons avoid venting marital grievances because they have great difficulty handling and tolerating another person's anger. In studying hundreds of premarital couples, the author also found that couples, when angry, either avoided dealing with negative feelings or—the other extreme—withdrew or lost control of their feelings. In other studies of the general population, effective communicators were distinguished from poor communicators by the way they handled their angry feelings.

The IAC has been used as a diagnostic tool in initial interviews, as an aid in ongoing counseling, and as a teaching device in communication classes. It also lends itself to human relations training and to research as a measurement technique.

A thirty-item scale, the IAC is intended to identify the subjective and interactional aspects of anger as manifested by the individual. In the *subjective* category, awareness of the expression of anger, intensity of anger, attitudes toward the expression of anger, and the reaction of the individual to his or her own anger are explored. Items relating to the *interactional* aspects of anger focus on the verbal and physical manner of expressing anger and the manner in which the individual handles it with himself or herself and with others. Subjects respond to the self-inventory by checking one of three possible responses: "Usually," "Sometimes," or "Seldom." The responses to the items are scored from 0 to 3, with a favorable response given the higher score.

Originally, forty-five items were formulated from a review of the literature and from the author's communication scales and clinical experiences. To test the validity of the items, they were presented to several psychologists, psychiatrists, and psychiatric social workers. Based on their feedback and on follow-up studies, fifteen items were eventually discarded, resulting in the current thirty-item version of the inventory.

The IAC is probably best suited for individuals of high school age and older with sufficient mental maturity to attempt to be frank and objective in responding to the items. It can be adapted to either sex and to any marital status.

References

Bienvenu, M.J., Sr. (1969). Measurement of parent-adolescent communication. *The Family Coordinator, 18*, 117–121.

Bienvenu, M.J., Sr. (1970). Measurement of marital communication. *The Family Coordinator, 19*, 26–31.

Bienvenu, M.J., Sr. (1971). An interpersonal communication inventory. *The Journal of Communication, 21*(4), 381–388.

Bienvenu, M.J., Sr. (1975). A measurement of premarital communication. *The Family Coordinator, 24*, 65–68.

Originally published in The 1981 Annual Handbook for Group Facilitators.

INVENTORY OF ANGER COMMUNICATION (IAC)[1]

Millard J. Bienvenu, Sr.

Anger is a very basic human emotion that plays an important role in the way we communicate with others. This inventory offers you an opportunity to make an objective self-study of how anger affects you and how you deal with it in your daily contacts with others. This increased awareness on your part may provide insights and clues for feeling more comfortable with yourself and improving your relationships with others. Please do not place your name on this form; if any of the questions are offensive to you, feel free not to answer them.

Instructions:

- Please answer each question as quickly as you can according to the way you feel at the moment (not the way you usually feel or felt last week).

- Please do not consult with anyone while completing this inventory. You may discuss it with someone after you have completed it. Remember that the value of this form will be lost if you change any answer during or after the discussion.

- Honest answers are necessary. Please be as frank as possible, since your answers are confidential.

- Use the following examples for practice. Put a check (✓) in *one* of the three blanks on the right to show how the question applies to your situation.

	Yes (usually)	**No** (seldom)	**Sometimes**
Do you have a tendency to take digs at others?	————	————	————
Do you get very upset when someone disagrees with you?	————	————	————

- The Yes column is to be used when the question can be answered as happening *most of the time or usually*. The No column is to be used when the question can be answered as *seldom or never*.

- The Sometimes column should be marked when you cannot definitely answer Yes or No. *Use this column as little as possible.*

- Read each question carefully. If you cannot give the exact answer to a question, answer the best you can but be sure to answer each one. There are no right or wrong answers. Answer according to the way *you* feel *at the present time.*

	Yes (usually)	**No** (seldom)	**Sometimes**
1. Do you admit that you are angry when asked by someone else?	_____	_____	_____
2. Do you have a tendency to take your anger out on someone other than the person you are angry with?	_____	_____	_____
3. When you are angry with someone, do you discuss it with that person?	_____	_____	_____
4. Do you keep things in until you finally explode with anger?	_____	_____	_____
5. Do you pout or sulk for a long time (a couple of days or so) when someone hurts your feelings?	_____	_____	_____
6. Do you disagree with others even though you feel they might get angry?	_____	_____	_____
7. Do you hit others when you get angry?	_____	_____	_____
8. Does it upset you *a great deal* when someone disagrees with you?	_____	_____	_____
9. Do you express your ideas when they differ from those of others?	_____	_____	_____

	Yes (usually)	No (seldom)	Sometimes
10. Do you have a tendency to be very critical of others?	———	———	———
11. Are you satisfied with the way in which you settle your differences with others?	———	———	———
12. Is it very difficult for you to say nice things to other people?	———	———	———
13. Do you have good control of your temper?	———	———	———
14. Do you become depressed very easily?	———	———	———
15. When a problem arises between you and another person, do you discuss it without losing control of your emotions?	———	———	———

Please go back and circle any questions that were not clear to you.

	Yes (usually)	No (seldom)	Sometimes
16. Do you have a tendency to criticize or put down other people?	———	———	———
17. When someone has hurt your feelings, do you discuss the matter with that person?	———	———	———
18. Do you have frequent arguments with others?	———	———	———
19. Do you often *feel* like hitting someone else?	———	———	———
20. Do you, at times, feel some anger toward someone you love?	———	———	———
21. Do you have a strong urge to do something harmful?	———	———	———

	Yes (usually)	No (seldom)	**Sometimes**
22. Do you keep your cool (control) when you are angry with someone?	_____	_____	_____
23. Do you tend to feel very bad or very guilty after getting angry at someone?	_____	_____	_____
24. When you become angry, do you pull away or withdraw from people?	_____	_____	_____
25. When someone is angry with you, do you automatically or quickly strike back with your own feelings of anger?	_____	_____	_____
26. Are you aware of when you are angry?	_____	_____	_____
27. Provided the timing is appropriate, do you express your angry feelings without exploding?	_____	_____	_____
28. Do you tend to make cutting remarks to others?	_____	_____	_____
29. Do you control yourself when things do not go your way?	_____	_____	_____
30. Do you feel that anger is a normal emotion?	_____	_____	_____

Please go back and circle any questions that were not clear to you.

The Pfeiffer Book of Successful Conflict Management Tools © 2003 John Wiley & Sons, Inc.

CHECK YOURSELF

Instructions: Please write down the first thing that comes to your mind when you read the following words or phrases. Be honest with yourself in order to gain the most from this exercise.

1. When people get mad they should _____

_____

2. Feeling angry is _____

_____

3. People who get angry are _____

_____

4. When I get angry I _____

_____

5. I get angry when _____

_____

6. People make me angry when _____

_____

7. When my father got angry he _____

_____

8. When my mother got angry she _____

_____

9. The best way to describe myself is _____

_____

General Information

My age _____ Sex: ☐ Male   ☐ Female   Education _____

Occupation _____

My marital status: ☐ Single   ☐ Married   ☐ Divorced

☐ Separated   ☐ Widowed

In my family, I am (was) the: ☐ Oldest Child   ☐ Middle Child

☐ Youngest Child   ☐ Only Child

While I was growing up, my parents were:

☐ Married and living together   ☐ Separated/divorced

☐ One or more deceased

INVENTORY OF ANGER COMMUNICATION SCORING KEY

Instructions: Look at how you responded to each item in the IAC. In front of the item write the appropriate weight from the table on this page. For example, if you answered "Yes" to item 1, you would find below that you get three points; write the number 3 in front of item 1 in the inventory and proceed to score item 2. When you have finished scoring each of the thirty items, add up your total score.

Scoring Interpretation

Generally, the higher the sum of scores, the more effectively you are handling your angry feelings. Review your answers to each item to see if a pattern of anger expression can be discerned. Attend carefully to the items you marked "sometimes"; they may indicate areas for explanation and work. Discuss your inventory with someone who knows you well for a perception check.

	Yes	No	Sometimes		Yes	No	Sometimes
1.	3	0	2	16.	0	3	1
2.	0	3	1	17.	3	0	2
3.	3	0	2	18.	0	3	1
4.	0	3	1	19.	0	3	1
5.	0	3	1	20.	3	0	2
6.	3	0	2	21.	0	3	1
7.	0	3	1	22.	3	0	2
8.	0	3	1	23.	0	3	1
9.	3	0	2	24.	0	3	1
10.	0	3	1	25.	0	3	1
11.	3	0	2	26.	3	0	2
12.	0	3	1	27.	3	0	2
13.	3	0	2	28.	0	3	1
14.	0	3	1	29.	3	0	2
15.	3	0	2	30.	3	0	2

8

The Defensiveness Inventory

Beverly Byrum-Robinson and B.J. Hennig

Abstract: Defensiveness affects a host of communication functions in organizations as well as individual understanding and perceptions, interpersonal effectiveness, work effectiveness, and organizational effectiveness. This article presents a new model of the defensiveness. The Defensiveness Inventory assesses four dimensions of defensive reactions: feelings of fear and sadness, feeling attacked, consequent behaviors, and sensitivity to flaw. Respondents rate twenty-eight items in respect to a critical incident in which they felt defensive. The inventory can be used for self-discovery and growth, team building, coaching in interpersonal relationships, process consulting, performance-appraisal training, and other applications.

Defensiveness—the act of protecting one's self—often is viewed as a serious threat to communication and the subsequent success of organizations (Argyris, 1986; Baker, 1980; Giacalone, 1987; Peterson, 1977; Sussman, 1991). Paradoxically, organizational change efforts breed defensiveness, which occurs when clear communication is most needed.

Baker (1980) cites communication as the most influential variable in organizational effectiveness. Clear communication leads to accurate perceptions and the efficient exchange of information between and among individuals.

Messages can be analyzed objectively, which helps in making timely, high-quality, and accepted decisions, which leads to individual and organizational effectiveness. On the other hand, defensive communication can lead to inaccurate perceptions, misinformation, and ineffective decisions.

This article provides a framework for conceptualizing defensiveness and presents a Defensiveness Inventory for use by the HRD practitioner. The inventory can be used in both individual and group interventions.

THE IMPORTANCE OF DEFENSIVENESS

Defensiveness affects employee self-understanding, interpersonal effectiveness, and work effectiveness.

Self-Understanding

Self-understanding is an important prerequisite to understanding and relating with others. Self-understanding is enhanced when one can identify the reasons one becomes defensive and the behaviors one exhibits when defensive. If someone tells a trainer in a training session that he or she does not live in the "real world," so the skills he or she teaches won't work, the trainer feels defensive. The reasons may be:

- The trainer's credibility is being attacked, so he or she feels attacked.
- The trainer feels threatened (someone may think he or she is incompetent).
- The trainer feels angry because he or she thinks the skills being taught are very practical.

Because of these feelings, the trainer switches to a self-protective mode, which results in defensive behaviors. These may include:

- Responding with a sarcastic comment.
- Overexplaining and justifying.
- Asserting his or her status as an expert.

Unfortunately, behaviors such as these are unlikely to change the other person's mind or help the trainer to feel better.

Individuals need to know what they respond to defensively and how they respond defensively. The focus needs to be on their own behaviors (which are under their control), not on the correctness or fairness of the other person's behavior. In the example above, if the trainer were more aware of the triggering behaviors, he or she could handle the situation better and contribute to a productive outcome.

Interpersonal Effectiveness

Interpersonal effectiveness is the ability to communicate effectively and to resolve problems with others. Controlling defensiveness enhances interpersonal effectiveness. Continuing with the example, if the trainer responds with a sarcastic answer to the person who tells him or her that he or she doesn't live in the "real world," the trainee may not participate for the rest of the session. If the trainer simply reasserts his or her explanation and justification, the trainee may not feel listened to. If the trainer reasserts his or her status as an expert, the trainee will feel discounted.

Thus, defensiveness results in deterioration of communication, which may lead to withdrawal, win/lose arguments, and/or standoffs. None of these situations allow relationships to be built or problems to be solved.

Work Effectiveness

Because defensiveness prevents individuals from establishing trusting relationships, issues cannot be openly discussed; valuable opinions are not offered; and information may be withheld. Problem solving then cannot address all necessary facts. Consequently, defensive behavior polarizes individuals and eliminates the possibility of arriving at creative and collaborative alternatives.

Organizational Effectiveness

To the extent that members of an organization are defensive, organizational productivity suffers. Intra- and interdepartmental communication may be distorted or nonexistent. When the corporate culture is one of protection, the ability to respond to change is reduced.

A Model for Defensiveness

The model used for the original defensiveness inventory was based on Ellis' (1974) rational emotive therapy, in which an activating event stimulates certain beliefs about the event, which lead to certain reactions. This model demonstrates that the event does not cause the consequence; what goes on in the mind does. For example, if the activating event is "these ideas won't work in the real world," and the consequence is anger, then the interceding belief may be that "these skills are great and anyone who disagrees is stupid." Ellis also includes a "D" for disputation of irrational beliefs, e.g., "maybe these skills are great in my perception; that doesn't mean that everyone is going to see the benefit in them; I can just try my best to present them as practical tools, and if someone doesn't agree, that's ok." The purpose of this approach is to teach people to control their thinking, so that their reactions and behaviors are more rational (i.e., less defensive).

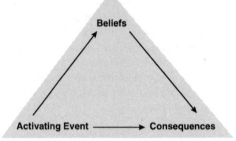

The model was further extended to include the following:

- activating event
- thoughts
- feelings
- physical reactions
- behaviors
- consequences

A situation stimulates defensive thoughts or interpretations, which stimulate emotions and physical reactions. The thoughts and feelings can intensify one another, resulting in behaviors that lead to consequences. For example, the event is an announcement of company downsizing. The thought is "I'm going to lose my job." The feelings are fear and anger. The physical reactions are tension and insomnia. The behavior is inability to concentrate and procrastination. The consequences are poor performance.

The Pfeiffer Book of Successful Conflict Management Tools © 2003 John Wiley & Sons, Inc.

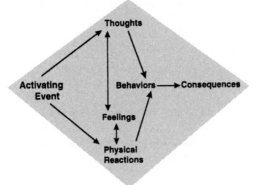

Based on this model, a survey was developed, with items divided into six sections, each section corresponding to an element of the model. Some examples for each follow.

Activating Event:

- I had a personality conflict.
- I thought someone had power over me.
- The other person verbally attacked me.

Thoughts:

- I thought I was incompetent.
- I thought everyone was out to get me.
- I wanted to "get even."

Feelings:

- I felt ignored.
- I felt hurt.
- I felt scared.

Physical Reactions:

- I cried.
- My heart raced.
- I experienced a surge of energy.

Behaviors:

- I blamed someone else.
- I tried to justify my behavior.
- I lectured the other person.

Consequences:

- I could not perform my job.
- My relationship with the other person improved.
- I detached myself from others.

Development and Testing of the Instrument

The instrument was administered to undergraduates at a large Midwestern university. Part 1 of the instrument consisted of a brief description of defensive behavior. Following this description, respondents were asked to recall and describe an incident in which they became defensive. (In its current form, respondents are asked to respond to a work situation in which they became defensive.) In this methodology, the feelings associated with defensiveness are recalled before the respondent reacts to the items. If a situation could not be recalled, subjects were provided with an incident.

The first step in the data analysis was a factor analysis of the items. A principal-components analysis of the items was conducted using an equamax rotation. An eigenvalue of greater than 4.0 was used to determine the optimal number of factors. The factor analysis yielded a 4 factor solution accounting for 40 percent of the variance in scores.

The first factor appears to cluster around items intended to measure the subjects' emotional reaction to the defensive situation. To a certain extent, the items intended to measure physical symptoms loaded on the same factor.

This may indicate a lack of independence between the physical symptoms and emotional reactions surrounding defensive behavior. This is not surprising, as these two aspects of interaction are highly intertwined and dependent on each other. The highest correlation, however, was among the emotional-reaction statements. Factor one accounted for almost 20 percent of the variance in responses. These items have been retained as a single scale.

Factor two clustered around statements that dealt with emotional feelings of injustice, being attacked, and holding a flawed viewpoint. These items reflect the view of defensive communication that holds that the element of perceived attack in the others' behavior is an antecedent to defensive behavior. Conflict, injustice, and discontent may reflect inner feelings, which give way to defensive behavior as a coping and/or defense mechanism. This scale would be supported in research on defense mechanisms and defensive communication. Factor two accounted for almost 10 percent of the variance in scores.

The third factor clustered around items dealing with both immediate and long-term consequences of defensive behavior. The element of aggression and emotional reaction remains salient in these items. This factor accounted for 8 percent of the total variance in scores.

The final factor clustered around items that tap into the individual's sensitivity to a flaw. In the literature on defensive communication, defensiveness is often instigated by an other's identification of a flaw in the self. The defensive situation may result only when that flaw is one to which the individual is indeed sensitive. This factor accounted for 2 percent of the variance in scores.

Items with common factor loadings were retained for use in the final version of the instrument. Statements loading on more than one factor were discarded. The following are the remaining statements, grouped according to the four factors described earlier.

Factor 1: Feelings, Fear, Sadness

I felt depressed.

I felt scared

I felt alone.

I felt uncertain.

I felt ashamed.

I felt hurt.

I felt deflated.

I felt flushed.

My voice became "shaky."

Table 1. Summary of Factor Analysis Factor Loadings

Items	Factor 1 Feelings, Fear, Sadness	Factor 2 Feeling Attacked	Factor 3 Consequent Behaviors	Factor 4 Sensitivity to Flaw
I felt depressed	.7371	.1003	.1078	.0780
I felt scared	.6932	.1614	.0421	.1513
I felt alone	.6747	.0989	.0688	.0338
I felt uncertain	.6669	.0209	.2937	.2307
I thought I was not a good person	.6301	.2413	.0848	.3583
I felt guilty	.6108	.3082	.1242	.1459
I felt ashamed	.6016	.3520	.1809	.2327
I began to tremble	.5986	.3081	.0134	.1763
I felt sad	.5978	.0524	.4027	.1190
I felt hurt	.5953	.2842	.1279	.0115
I felt deflated	.5920	.0648	.0293	.0390
I felt flushed	.5909	.0804	.0957	.1396
I felt uninvolved	.5901	.1408	.2008	.1167
My voice became "shaky"	.5884	.3320	.0818	.2695
I felt inadequate	.5879	.1793	.1831	.1640
I felt disappointed	.5624	.2345	.0271	.0939
I had been wrongly attacked	.2371	.4770	.0258	.0800
I felt a sense of injustice	.0578	.4345	.0920	.0126
I had a "personality conflict" with someone	.1409	.4247	.3419	.1343
I felt discounted	.0787	.4225	.0571	.1773
I realized there was a flaw in my viewpoint	.3217	.4221	.0061	.0299

Table 1. Summary of Factor Analysis Factor Loadings, *continued*

Items	Factor 1 Feelings, Fear, Sadness	Factor 2 Feeling Attacked	Factor 3 Consequent Behaviors	Factor 4 Sensitivity to Flaw
I wanted to hurt the person(s) who made me defensive	.3898	.0223	.6065	.1465
I wanted to damage something	.3889	.0319	.5745	.2313
I lectured the person	.1251	.1852	.5068	.4806
I wanted to get even	.3988	.1465	.2709	.0702
I became defensive toward person(s) similar to those involved in this situation	.3280	.0432	.4380	.0200
I screamed	.3010	.1152	.1107	.4723
I did not let the other person talk	.2359	.2913	.2136	.4055
I thought that I was different/did not belong	.2703	.1350	.0553	.4051
I cried	.2923	.1154	.1106	.4011
I thought my values/beliefs were attacked/challenged	.1231	.0024	.1310	.3209
I felt uncomfortable with my surroundings	.1904	.0302	.2206	.3050
I was emotional about the topic	.2756	.2718	.0617	.3032

I felt inadequate.

I felt disappointed.

Factor 2: Feeling Attacked

I had been wrongly attacked.

I felt a sense of injustice.

I had a "personality conflict" with someone.

I felt discounted.

I realized there was a flaw in my viewpoint.

Factor 3: Consequent Behaviors

I wanted to hurt the person(s) who made me defensive.

I wanted to damage something.

I lectured the person.

I wanted to get even.

I became defensive toward person(s) similar to those involved in this situation.

Factor 4: Sensitivity to Flaw

I screamed.

I did not let the other person talk.

I thought that I was different/did not belong.

I cried.

I thought my values/beliefs were attacked/challenged.

I felt uncomfortable with my surroundings.

I was emotional about the topic.

Based on the findings, an adjusted model of defensiveness was adopted, as follows:

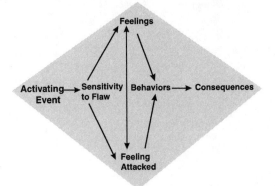

Gender Differences

The following are the gender differences from the original inventory, administered to 136 students in a university communications course (fifty-five males, eighty-one females). Differences in percentages by gender are rounded to the nearest whole number.

Agree	**Disagree**
Male %	**%**
Female %	**%**

1. I thought my values/beliefs were attacked/challenged

   M 31   10

   F 46   14

2. I felt uncertain

   M 21   19

   F 33   27

3. I had been wrongly attacked

   M 33   7

   F 48   11

Agree	Disagree
Male %	**%**
Female %	**%**

4. I wanted to damage something

M 17	24
F 27	33

5. I realized there was flaw in my viewpoint

M 15	26
F 20	40

6. I felt deflated

M 27	14
F 38	22

7. I felt uncomfortable with my surroundings

M 19	21
F 32	28

8. I felt scared

M 14	26
F 25	35

9. I felt a sense of injustice

M 29	11
F 50	10

10. I wanted to hurt the person(s) who made me defensive

M 19	22
F 28	32

11. I felt emotional about the topic

M 34	7
F 50	10

12. I felt disappointed

M 28	13
F 47	13

	Agree Male % Female %	Disagree % %

13. I felt discounted

    M 25   10

    F 54   11

14. I felt depressed

    M 19   21

    F 36   24

15. I lectured the person

    M 22   19

    F 32   28

16. I screamed

    M 13   27

    F 27   33

17. I felt inadequate

    M 14   26

    F 32   28

18. I cried

    M 7   33

    F 20   40

19. I wanted to get even

    M 19   22

    F 28   32

20. My voice became shaky

    M 18   22

    F 28   32

21. I did not let the other person talk

    M 17   23

    F 28   33

	Agree	**Disagree**
	Male %	**%**
	Female %	**%**

22. I felt alone

    M 22   19

    F 30   30

23. I had a "personality conflict" with someone

    M 23   17

    F 35   25

24. I felt hurt

    M 26   14

    F 46   14

25. I felt flushed

    M 20   20

    F 36   23

26. I thought that I was different/did not belong

    M 16   24

    F 20   39

27. I felt ashamed

    M 14   25

    F 20   41

28. I became defensive toward persons similar to those involved in the situation

    M 18   24

    F 37   21

The Pfeiffer Book of Successful Conflict Management Tools © 2003 John Wiley & Sons, Inc.

INSTRUMENT ITEMS AND SCALING

The final version of the Defensiveness Inventory consists of twenty-eight items. The items ask participants to respond to each statement in terms of how often this statement applied to them in the critical incidents they are remembering. As an option, a critical incident can be given to participants so that they all have the same point of reference for responding. A six-point Likert scale ranging from (1) "never applied to me" to (6) "always applied to me" is used. Individual scores are then calculated for each of the four dimensions described previously.

The six-point scale is utilized because it has been shown that an even number of response options forces people to take a stand, as opposed to an odd number of responses, which encourages a tendency toward the mean. This information is not of the same value when attempting to compare responses to the mean (Paul & Bracken, 1995).

POTENTIAL USES OF THE INSTRUMENT

In addition to being used as a self-discovery tool, the Defensiveness Inventory has the following uses:

- The inventory can be completed by peers and used in a feedback session. This would work particularly well in a team-building session focusing on interpersonal feedback.

- The inventory can be used as a coaching tool for an employee who wishes to improve interpersonal relationships. The coach may complete the form and/or have others complete the form for the person being coached before discussing results.

- The inventory can be followed by an experiential activity such as a role play. If the participants thought of their own critical incidents, various critical incidents can be role-played and processed. If a critical incident is given with the inventory, that also can be role-played. Additionally, the critical incidents could be reenacted to have more productive outcomes after the discussion of theory.

- The inventory can be used in process consulting. Behavioral parts of the inventory could be used by an observer, or the entire inventory could be administered during process-consultation interviews. The results could be fed back to the team to increase knowledge of the incidents that stimulate defensiveness.

- The inventory can be used in performance-appraisal training to demonstrate how people become defensive in that type of evaluative situation.

- If the critical incidents are supplied, participants can rewrite them to show how the situation could have been avoided or how they could reduce defensiveness.

ADMINISTRATION OF THE DEFENSIVENESS INVENTORY

The Defensiveness Inventory should be administered before any lecturette on the topic of defensiveness is offered. Having participants complete the instrument before discussing the topic will lessen their tendency to react to the items in socially desirable ways.

To begin, provide each participant a copy of the Defensiveness Inventory and read the instructions aloud, telling the participants that they have ten minutes in which to complete the inventory, if given an incident, and fifteen minutes, if they are remembering and recording their own.[1]

Make certain that the participants understand that they are to respond to the items in terms of their feelings and behaviors that occurred during their personal incidents. If the critical incident is provided to the participants, instruct them to respond as if they were in that situation.

Scoring

After participants have completed the inventory, ask them to transfer the number they assigned to each item to the appropriate column on the Defensiveness Inventory Scoring Sheet and to total each of the four columns. After they have completed the totals, instruct them to plot their results on the Defensiveness Inventory Profile.

---

[1]Some general critical incidents are supplied following this article for the facilitator's use. If training a homogeneous group, one can create critical incidents based on the group's work.

The Pfeiffer Book of Successful Conflict Management Tools © 2003 John Wiley & Sons, Inc.

Interpretation and Presentation of Theory

A discussion on the interpretation of participants' scores may begin with the definition of defensiveness provided on the inventory. The facilitator may ask the participants how the definition fits for them. The facilitator may also ask how the incident(s) they used influenced their answers.

After the discussion, the model for defensiveness should be provided, accompanied by an explanation of each of the four dimensions of defensiveness. As an explanation of the model and its four elements is presented, the facilitator may ask the participants how they scored on each element. According to the results on their profiles, they will be more or less likely to exhibit the behaviors, feelings, or thoughts associated with each factor. The higher the score on each factor, the more likely the respondent is to display behaviors described by that factor. The percentages along each factor line indicate the total percentage of people, in a sample of 120, who were as likely as the respondent to display behaviors described by that factor.

The processing questions that follow will help lead participants to applications of the learnings from the instrument.

Processing Questions

To improve application, participants can partner with one another before the total-group processing session to discuss their highest and lowest scores and their reactions. The following questions can be asked of participants after they complete the inventory, score it, and hear the theory and interpretation presentations. Scores also can be posted to exhibit any intergroup differences (i.e., between genders, between personal/business situations, between real and provided critical incidents). Normative data follows this discussion.

- What was your highest score? Your lowest? What does that mean to you?
- How does your score fit with the norms? What does that mean to you? How do you feel about that?
- Did anyone notice any gender differences? How does that fit for you?
- How do you think your inventory would have been different if you had thought of a personal, rather than a professional, situation? What does that tell you?
- What have you learned about yourself and defensiveness?
- What have you learned about defensiveness in general?

- What is your hypothesis about how defensiveness affects work relationships? How does it affect the organization?

- What do you want to try to do differently in the future? What reactions or behaviors would you like to change on the job? At home?

- What have you learned about sending messages that engender defensiveness? How might you change your own messages to decrease the likelihood of defensive reactions from others?

REFERENCES

Argyris, C. (1986). Reinforcing organizational defensive routines: An unintended human resource activity. *Human Resource Managment, 25*(4), 541–555.

Baker, W.H. (1980). Defensiveness in communication: Its causes, effects, and cures. *Journal of Business Communication, 17*(3), 33–43.

Ellis, A. (1974). *A guide to rational living.* Englewood Cliffs, NJ: Prentice Hall.

Giacalone, R.A. (1987). Reducing the need for defensive communication. *Management Solutions, 37*(9), 70–75.

Paul, K.B., & Bracken, P.D.W. (1995, January). Everything you wanted to know about employee surveys. *Training & Development,* p. 2.

Peterson, R. (1977). Are "self-defenses" keeping you from being a better manager? *Supervisory Management, 22*(9), 71–74.

Sussman, L. (1991). Managers on the defensive. *Business Horizons, 34*(1), 81–87.

Originally published in The 1997 Annual, Vol. I, Training.

Defensiveness Inventory Sample Critical Incidents

1. Chris enters Casey's office and puts a report on the desk saying, "I need to talk to you about this. There are a number of holes in the recommendations. If the report is presented the way it is now, we'll never gain acceptance. You need to do some more research to substantiate your recommendations. I'm not sure why you didn't do that in the first place."

   If you were Casey, you would:

2. Sue has just presented her proposed advertising plan to the other vice presidents The v.p. of engineering says, "You can't make those kinds of claims. We're nowhere near that target in our development. Where did you get your information? That'll play havoc with the company image."

   If you were Sue, you would:

3. Dale is conducting a performance appraisal for Jo. Dale says, "It seems that you have completed only half of your objectives for the year. What is your explanation for that?"

   If you were Jo, you would:

4. Tim and Tom are working together to assemble manuals in a last-minute rush for a course the next day. Tom says to Tim, "Can you speed it up? We'll never get out of here. Why was this left until the last minute, anyway?"

   If you were Tim, you would:

DEFENSIVENESS INVENTORY

Beverly Byrum-Robinson and B.J. Hennig

Introduction: Defensiveness is a feeling that almost everyone has experienced. It is human nature to defend ourselves against various types of psychological attacks, dangers, or injuries. Degrees of defensiveness may vary, as may the types of responses. In addition, we may feel more defensive on some days than on others. The purpose of this self-discovery inventory is to explore some of the characteristics of defensiveness so that you may better understand your communication behavior during situations of this kind. The inventory will take approximately ten minutes to complete.

Instructions: Think of an incident at work in which you became extremely defensive. What triggered it? Who was involved? How did you feel? What did you say and do? What was the outcome? Based on the experience, rate the extent to which the items presented below describe your reactions in the situation. Please read each statement carefully and respond by circling the appropriate number for each item. Your first response is usually the most honest.

Key to Ratings

Strongly Agree 1	Agree 2	Slightly Agree 3	Slightly Disagree 4	Disagree 5	Strongly Disagree 6

1. I thought my values/beliefs were attacked/challenged	1	2	3	4	5	6
2. I felt uncertain	1	2	3	4	5	6
3. I had been wrongly attacked	1	2	3	4	5	6
4. I wanted to damage something	1	2	3	4	5	6
5. I realized there was a flaw in my viewpoint	1	2	3	4	5	6
6. I felt deflated	1	2	3	4	5	6
7. I felt uncomfortable with my surroundings	1	2	3	4	5	6

Strongly Agree 1	Agree 2	Slightly Agree 3	Slightly Disagree 4	Disagree 5	Strongly Disagree 6

8. I felt scared	1	2	3	4	5	6
9. I felt a sense of injustice	1	2	3	4	5	6
10. I wanted to hurt the person(s) who made me defensive	1	2	3	4	5	6
11. I felt emotional about the topic	1	2	3	4	5	6
12. I felt disappointed	1	2	3	4	5	6
13. I felt discounted	1	2	3	4	5	6
14. I felt depressed	1	2	3	4	5	6
15. I lectured the person	1	2	3	4	5	6
16. I screamed	1	2	3	4	5	6
17. I felt inadequate	1	2	3	4	5	6
18. I cried	1	2	3	4	5	6
19. I wanted to get even	1	2	3	4	5	6
20. My voice became "shaky"	1	2	3	4	5	6
21. I did not let the other person talk	1	2	3	4	5	6
22. I felt alone	1	2	3	4	5	6
23. I had a "personality conflict" with someone	1	2	3	4	5	6
24. I felt hurt	1	2	3	4	5	6
25. I felt flushed	1	2	3	4	5	6
26. I thought that I was different/ did not belong	1	2	3	4	5	6
27. I felt ashamed	1	2	3	4	5	6
28. I became defensive toward persons similar to those involved in the situation	1	2	3	4	5	6

DEFENSIVENESS INVENTORY SCORING SHEET

Instructions: From your completed Defensiveness Inventory, transfer your responses to the appropriate squares below. For example, if you have circled a 2 on item 13, write 2 in the square numbered 13.

Once you have transferred your scores, calculate a total for each column on the line provided. These are your factor scores, to be transferred to your Defensiveness Inventory Profile Sheet.

F1	F2	F3	F4
Scoring Box			
#2 _____	#3 _____	#4 _____	#1 _____
#6 _____	#5 _____	#10 _____	#7 _____
#8 _____	#9 _____	#15 _____	#11 _____
#12 _____	#13 _____	#19 _____	#16 _____
#14 _____	#23 _____	#28 _____	#18 _____
#17 _____			#21 _____
#20 _____			#26 _____
#22 _____			
#24 _____			
#25 _____			
#27 _____			
Factor Scores F1 = _____	F2 = _____	F3 = _____	F4 = _____

Defensiveness Inventory Profile Sheet

Instructions: Transfer your factor scores from the Scoring Sheet to the boxes below. Once you have done this, plot each score at the appropriate point along the Factor Line. The lower your score (vertically), the more likely you are to display behaviors described by the factor.

The percentages along each Factor Line indicate the total percentage of people in a sample of 120 who were as likely as you to display the behaviors described by each factor.

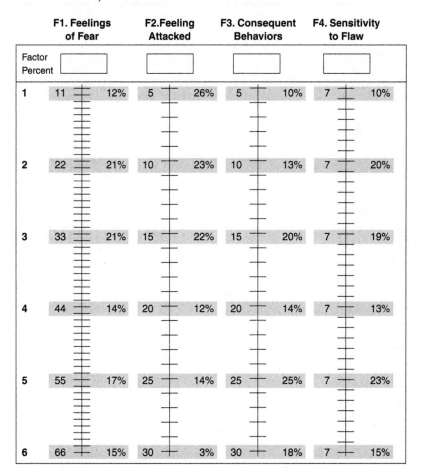

	F1. Feelings of Fear		F2. Feeling Attacked		F3. Consequent Behaviors		F4. Sensitivity to Flaw	
Factor Percent								
1	11	12%	5	26%	5	10%	7	10%
2	22	21%	10	23%	10	13%	7	20%
3	33	21%	15	22%	15	20%	7	19%
4	44	14%	20	12%	20	14%	7	13%
5	55	17%	25	14%	25	25%	7	23%
6	66	15%	30	3%	30	18%	7	15%

Defensiveness Inventory Interpretation Sheet

Factor One

Scoring above the mean on factor one, feelings of fear and sadness, indicates that in a defensive situation, you experience the more "passive" emotions of anxiety and hurt. You may feel inadequate to deal with the situation and may find it difficult to argue for your point of view.

Scoring below the mean on factor one may indicate confidence in your viewpoint, regardless of disconfirming messages. You may also have the ability to avoid taking things personally.

Factor Two

Scoring above the mean on factor two, feeling attacked, indicates that in a defensive situation, you experience more "active" emotions of anger and conflict. You may tend to believe that the situation is being handled unfairly or addressed inappropriately. These feelings may lead you to defend your point of view.

Scoring below the mean on factor two may indicate the ability to see both sides of an issue without feeling threatened.

Factor Three

Scoring above the mean on factor three, consequent behaviors, indicates that, in a defensive situation, you want to take strong action toward the situation or person. You may tend to hold on to defensive feelings until your desired resolution is attained.

Scoring below the mean on factor three may indicate an ability to control aggressive emotional reactions.

Factor Four

Scoring above the mean on factor four, sensitivity to flaw, may indicate a variety of strong feelings and responses to the situation. The behaviors and feelings in this factor are emotionally extreme, from feeling different to emotional outbursts of crying and screaming. These extreme reactions may stem from a general oversensitivity when you are challenged.

The Pfeiffer Book of Successful Conflict Management Tools © 2003 John Wiley & Sons, Inc.

Scoring below the mean on factor four may indicate a general self-confidence and ability to handle challenges with extreme reactions.

Scoring high on factors one and two and low on factors three and four may indicate that you hold your emotions of defensiveness inside, rather than acting them out or expressing them. Conversely, scoring high on factors three and four may indicate a tendency to act at the time on your emotional state.

Suggestions for Improvement

Defensiveness may be reduced by learning any of the following skills:

- Self-talk: to view the other person's comments as information about his or her viewpoint rather than as information about you
- Perception checking: to determine if what you are perceiving the situation to be is correct
- Paraphrasing: to understand the other person's point of view
- Calling time out and setting an appointment to talk at a future time
- Using "I" messages to express to the other person how his or her messages affected you
- Requesting that the person word his or her concern in a way that is easier for you to hear it
- Asking open-ended questions to elicit the other person's real concerns, i.e., what the person wants/needs
- Asking for specifics, examples, or preferences
- Using conflict-management skills to move toward resolution of the issue, as opposed to focusing on the problem